DATE DUE

DEMCO 38-296

Out of Egypt

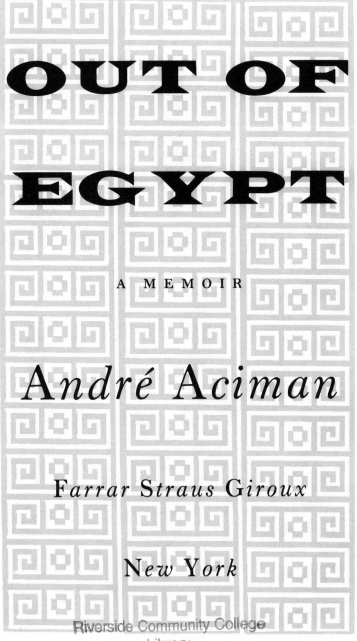

OUT OF EGYPT

A MEMOIR

André Aciman

Farrar Straus Giroux

New York

I wish to thank Neal Kozodoy, whose help, devotion, and time were invaluable;
Sara Bershtel, to whom I owe this book; and my wife, Susan, to whom I owe
everything.

For Alexander, Michael, and Philip,

Henri and Régine,

Alain and Carole,

and Piera

Contents

I

Soldier, Salesman,

Swindler, Spy

"So, are we or aren't we, *siamo o non siamo*," boasted my Great-uncle Vili when the two of us finally sat down late that summer afternoon in a garden overlooking his sprawling estate in Surrey.

"Just look at this," he pointed to a vast expanse of green. "Isn't it splendid?" he asked, as if he had invented the very notion of an afternoon stroll in the English countryside. "Just before sundown and minutes after tea, it always comes: a sense of plenitude, of bliss almost. You know—everything I wanted, I got. Not bad for a man in his nineties." Arrogant self-satisfaction beamed on his features.

I tried to speak to him of Alexandria, of time lost and lost worlds, of the end when the end came, of Monsieur Costa and Montefeltro and Aldo Kohn, of Lotte and Aunt Flora and lives so faraway now. He cut me short and made a disparaging motion with his hand, as if to dismiss a bad odor. "That was rubbish. I live in the present," he said almost vexed by my nostalgia. *"Siamo o non siamo?"* he asked, standing up to stretch his muscles, then pointing to the first owl of the evening.

It was never exactly clear *what* one was or wasn't, but to everyone in the family, including those who don't speak a word of Italian today, this elliptical phrase still captures the strutting, daredevil, cocksure, soldier-braggart who had pulled himself out of an Italian trench during the Great War and then, hidden between rows of trees with his rifle held tightly in both hands, would have mowed down the entire Austro-Hungarian Empire had he not run out of bullets. The phrase expressed the hectoring self-confidence of a drill sergeant surrounded by sissies in need of daily jostling. "Are we man enough or aren't we?" he seemed to say. "Are we going ahead with it or aren't we?" "Are we worth our salt or what?" It was his way of whistling in the dark, of shrugging off defeat, of picking up the pieces and calling it a victory. This, after all, was how he barged in on the affairs of fate and held out for more, taking credit for everything, down to the unforeseen brilliance of his most hapless schemes. He mistook overdrawn luck for foresight, just as he misread courage for what was little more than the gumption of a street urchin. He had pluck. He knew it, and he flaunted it.

Impervious to the humiliating Italian defeat at the Battle of Caporetto in 1917, Uncle Vili remained forever proud of his service to the Italian army, flaunting that as well, with the spirited Florentine lilt he had picked up in Italian Jesuit schools in Constantinople. Like most young Jewish men born in Turkey toward the end of the century, Vili disparaged anything having to do with Ottoman culture and thirsted for the West, finally becoming "Italian" the way most Jews in Turkey did: by claiming ancestral ties with Leghorn, a port city near Pisa where escaped Jews from Spain had settled in the sixteenth century. A very distant Italian relative bearing the Spanish name of Pardo-Roques was conveniently dug up in Leghorn —Vili was half Pardo-Roques himself—whereupon all living "cousins" in Turkey immediately became Italian. They were all, of course, staunch nationalists, monarchists.

When told the Italian army had never been valiant, Uncle Vili had immediately challenged an Alexandrian Greek to a duel, especially after the latter had reminded him that all those Italian medals and trinkets hardly altered the fact that Vili was still a Turkish rascal, and a Jewish one to boot. This infuriated Uncle Vili, not because someone had impugned his Jewishness—he would have been the first to do so—but because he hated to be reminded that many Jews had become Italian through shady means. The weapons their seconds had chosen for the occasion were so obsolete that neither of the two duelists knew how to wield them. No one was hurt, apologies were made, one of them even giggled, and, to foster a spirit of fellowship, Vili suggested a quiet restaurant overlooking the sea, where on this clear Alexandrian day in June everyone ate his heartiest luncheon in years. When it came time for the bill, both the Greek and the Italian insisted on paying, and the tug-of-war would have gone on forever, each alleging his honor and his pleasure, had not Uncle Vili, like a conjurer finally compelled to use magic when all else failed, pulled out his choicest little phrase, in this case meaning, "Now am I or aren't I a man of honor?" The Greek, who was the more gracious of the two, conceded.

Uncle Vili knew how to convey that intangible though unmistakable feeling that he had lineage—a provenance so ancient and so distinguished that it transcended such petty distinctions as birthplace, nationality, or religion. And with the suggestion of lineage came the suggestion of wealth—if always with the vague hint that this wealth was inconveniently tied up elsewhere, in land, for example, foreign land, something no one in the family ever had much of except when it came in clay flowerpots. But lineage earned him credit. And this is what mattered to him most, for this was how he and all the men in the family made, borrowed, lost, and married into fortunes: on credit.

Lineage came naturally to Vili, not because he had it, nor because he mimicked it, nor even because he aspired to it with the leisured polish of lapsed aristocrats. In his case, it was simply the conviction that he was born *better*. He had the imposing bearing of the wealthy, the reluctant smile that immediately sweetens in the company of equals. He was patrician in thrift, politics, and debauchery, intolerant of poor posture more than of bad taste, of bad taste more than of cruelty, and of bad table manners more than of bad eating habits. Above all, he detested what he called the "atavisms" by which Jews gave themselves away, especially when impersonating *goyim*. He derided all in-laws and acquaintances who looked typically Jewish, not because he did not look so himself, or because he hated Jews, but because he knew how much others did. *It's because of Jews like them that they hate Jews like us.* When snubbed by an observant Jew proud of his heritage, Vili's answer trickled down his tongue like a pit he had been twiddling about his mouth for forty years: "Proud of what? Are we or aren't we all peddlers in the end?"

And peddle is what he knew and did best. He even peddled fascism to the British in Egypt and, later, on behalf of the Italians, in Europe as well. He was as devoted to Il Duce as he was to the Pope. His annual addresses to the Hitler Youth in Germany were highly applauded and became a notorious source of strife within the family. "Don't meddle, I know what I'm doing," he would say. Years later, when the British began threatening to round up all adult Italian males living in Alexandria, Uncle Vili suddenly rummaged through his closets and began hawking old certificates from the rabbinate of Constantinople to remind his friends at the British Consulate that, as an Italian Jew, he couldn't possibly be considered a threat to British interests. Would they like him to spy on the Italians? The British could not have asked for better.

He performed so brilliantly that after the war he was rewarded with a Georgian estate in Surrey, where he lived in lordly penury for the remainder of his days under the assumed name of Dr. H. M. Spingarn. Herbert Michael Spingarn was an Englishman whom Vili had met as a child in Constantinople and who had stirred in him two lifelong passions: the Levantine desire to emulate anything British, and the Ottoman contempt for British anything. Uncle Vili, who had given up his distinctly Jewish name for an Anglo-Saxon one, cringed with half-concealed embarrassment when I told him that this fellow Spingarn had himself been a Jew. "Yes, I recall something like that," he said vaguely. "We're everywhere, then, aren't we? Scratch the surface and you'll find everyone's a Jew," jeered the octogenarian Turco-Italian-Anglophile-gentrified-Fascist Jew who had started his professional life peddling Turkish fezzes in Vienna and Berlin and was to end it as the sole auctioneer of deposed King Farouk's property. "The Sotheby's of Egypt; but a peddler nonetheless," he added, reclining in his chair as we both watched a flight of birds descend upon the murky, stagnant waters of what must have once been a splendid pond. "Still, a great people, these Jews," he would say in broken English, affecting a tone of detached condescension so purposefully shallow and so clearly aware of its own fatuousness as to suggest that, when it came to his coreligionists, he always meant the opposite of what he said. Following praise, he would always vilify these admirable yet "scoundrel Jews," only then to change his tune once more. "After all, Einstein, Schnabel, Freud, Disraeli," he would declaim with a glint in his eyes and a half-suppressed smile. "Were they or weren't they?"

■

He had left Egypt—to which the family had moved from Constantinople in 1905—a would-be cadet with fire in his gut and quicksilver in his eyes. He had studied in Germany, served in the Prussian army, changed sides when the Italians joined the war in 1915, and after Caporetto sat out the rest of the war in Cyprus as an interpreter, returning to Egypt four years after his discharge, a polished rake in his late twenties whose insolent good looks betrayed a history of shady deals and ruthless sieges in the battle of the sexes. Impressed by his conquests, his sisters judged him decidedly masculine, what with the roguish tilt of his fedora, the impatient *Come, come now* in his voice, and that patronizing swagger with which he would come up and grab a bottle of champagne you were trying to uncork and say, *Let me*—never overbearing, but just enough to signal there was more, much more. He had fought in all sorts of battles, on all sorts of sides, with all sorts of weapons. He was a consummate marksman, a remarkable athlete, a shrewd businessman, a relentless womanizer—and yes, decidedly masculine.

"Are we or aren't we," he would brag after a conquest, or a killing in the stock market, or on suddenly recovering from a hopeless bout of malaria, or when he saw through a shrewd woman, or knocked down a street ruffian, or when he simply wanted to show the world that he was not easily hoodwinked. It meant: Did I show them or didn't I? He would use this phrase after negotiating a difficult transaction: Didn't I promise they'd come begging for my price? Or when he had a blackmailer thrown in jail: Didn't I warn him not to take me for a pushover? Or when his beloved sister, Aunt Marta, came crying to him hysterically after she had been jilted by yet another fiancé, in which case his phrase meant: Any man worthy of the name could have seen it coming! Didn't I warn you? And then, to remind her she was made of stronger stuff than tears, he would sit her on his lap and, holding both her hands in his, rock her ever so gently, swearing she'd get over her sorrow sooner than she thought, for such was the way with lovesickness, and besides, was she or wasn't she?

Later, he would buy her roses and placate her for a few hours, maybe a few days. But she was not always easily swayed and, sometimes, scarcely would he have let go of her and gone to his study than he would suddenly hear her shrieking hysterically at the other end of the apartment: "But who'll marry me, who?" she kept asking her sisters as she sobbed and blew her nose on the first rag that fell her way.

"Who'll marry me at my age, tell me, who, who?" she would ask, shrieking her way back into his study.

"Someone will, you mark my words," he would say.

"No one will," she insisted. "Can't you see why? Can't you see I'm ugly? Even I know it!"

"Ugly you're not!"

"Just say the truth: ugly!"

"You may not be the most beautiful—"

"But no one in the street will ever turn around to look at me."

"You should be thinking of a home, Marta, not the street."

"You just don't understand, do you? All you do is twist my words and make me sound stupid!" She began raising her voice.

"Look, if you want me to say you're ugly, then all right, you're ugly."

"No one understands, no one."

And she would drift away again like an ailing specter come to seek comfort among the living only to be shooed away.

Aunt Marta's *crises de mariage*, as they were called, were

known to last for hours. Afterward she had such pounding headaches that she would put herself to sleep early in the afternoon and not dare show her face until the next morning, and even then, the storm was not necessarily quelled, for as soon as she got out of bed she would ask whoever crossed her path to look at her eyes. "They are puffy," she would say, "aren't they? Look at them. Just look at this," she would insist, nearly poking her eyes out. "No, they're fine," someone would respond. "You're lying. I can even feel how puffy they are. Now everyone will know I cried over him. They'll tell him, I know they will. I'm so humiliated, so humiliated." Her voice quavered until it broke into a sob, and down came the tears again.

For the rest of the day, her mother, her three sisters, five brothers, and sisters- and brothers-in-law would take turns peeking in her door, carrying pieces of ice in a small bowl for her eyes while she lay in the dark with a compress of her own devising. "I'm suffering. If only you knew how I'm suffering," she would groan, in exactly the same words I heard her whisper more than fifty years later in a hospital room in Paris as she lay dying of cancer. Outside, sitting with his other siblings in the crowded living room, Uncle Vili could no longer control himself. "Enough is enough! What Marta really needs—we all know what it is." "Don't be vulgar now," his sister Clara interrupted, unable to stifle a giggle as she stood at her easel, painting yet another version of Tolstoy's grizzled features. "See?" Uncle Vili retaliated. "You may not like the truth, but everyone agrees with me," he continued with increased exasperation in his voice. "All these years, and the poor girl still doesn't know a man's fore from his aft." Their older brother Isaac burst out laughing. "Can you really imagine her with anyone?" "Enough is enough," snapped their mother, a matriarch nearing her seventies. "We must find her a good Jewish man. Rich, poor, doesn't matter." "But who, who, who, tell me who?" Aunt Marta interrupted, overhearing the tail end of their conversation on her way to the bathroom. "It's hopeless. Hopeless. Why did you make me come to Egypt, why?" she said, turning to her elder sister Esther. "It's hot and muggy, I'm always sweating, and the men are so dreadful."

Uncle Vili stood up, curled his hand around her hip, and said, "Calm yourself, Marta, and don't worry. We'll find you someone. I promise. Leave it to me."

"But you always say that, always, and you don't ever mean it. And besides, who do we know here?"

This was Vili's long-awaited cue. And he rose to the occasion with the studied nonchalance of a man driven to use exactly the words he has been dying to say. In this instance, they meant: Can anyone really doubt that we are well connected?

This was an oblique reference to Uncle Isaac, who, while studying at the University of Turin, had managed to become a very close friend of a fellow student named Fouad, the future king of Egypt. Both men spoke Turkish, Italian, German, some Albanian, and, between them, had concocted a pidgin tongue, rich in obscenities and double entendres, that they called Turkitalbanisch and which they continued to speak into their old age. It was because Uncle Isaac staked all of his hopes on this undying friendship that he had eventually persuaded his parents and siblings to sell everything in Constantinople and move to Alexandria.

Uncle Vili was fond of boasting that his brother—and, by implication, himself as well—"owned" the king. "He has the king in his breast pocket," he would say, pointing to his own breast pocket, in which a silver cigarette case bearing the king's seal was permanently lodged. In the end, it was the king who introduced Isaac to the man who was to play such a significant role in his sister's life.

Aunt Marta, who was nearing forty at the time, was eventually married to this man, a rich Swabian Jew whom everyone in the family called "the Schwab"—his real name was Aldo Kohn—and who did little else but play golf all day, bridge at night, and in between smoked Turkish cigarettes on which his name and family crest had been meticulously inscribed in gold filigree. He was a balding, corpulent man whom Marta had turned down ten years earlier but who was determined to pursue her again and, better yet, without demanding a dowry, which suited everyone. At one of the family gatherings, it was arranged to leave the would-be's alone for a while, and before Marta knew what the Schwab was about, or even had time to turn around and pull herself away, he had grabbed hold of her wrist and fastened around it a lavish bracelet on the back of which his jeweler had inscribed *M'appari*, after the famous aria from von Flotow's *Martha*. Aunt Marta was so flustered she did not realize she had broken into tears, which so moved the poor Schwab that he too started to weep, begging as he sobbed, "Don't say no, don't say no." Arrangements were made, and soon enough everyone noticed an unusually serene and restful glow settle upon Aunt Marta's rosy features. "She'll kill him at this rate," her brothers snickered.

The Schwab was a very dapper but quiet man who had once studied the classics and whose diffident manner made him the butt of household ridicule. He seemed spoiled and stupid, a sure sap, and probably *that way* as well. The brothers had their eyes on him. But the Schwab was no fool. Although he had never worked a day in his life, it was soon discovered that in the space of two years he had trebled his family's fortune on the sugar exchange. When Uncle Vili realized that this incompetent, sniveling, beer keg of a brother-in-law was a "player," he immediately drew up a list of no-risk ventures for him. But the Schwab, who attributed his financial wizardry to luck more than to skill, was reluctant to invest in stocks because he didn't understand a thing about the market. All he understood was sugar, and maybe horses. "Understand?" responded Uncle Vili. "Why should you understand the stock market? I'm here to do it for you." After all, were they or weren't they all related to each other now?

For weeks the Schwab tolerated his brother-in-law's inducements until, one day, he finally exploded. And he did so in style: he borrowed Vili's cherished little phrase, spun it about him awhile like a bodkin to let Vili know that he, the Schwab, known to the rest of the world as Aldo Kohn, and more specifically as Kohn Pasha, was no pushover either. Uncle Vili was totally trumped. Not only was he *pained*—that was his word for it—by his brother-in-law's mistrust, but there was something unbearably vexing in having been flayed with his own knife. It was a low, unsportsmanlike thing to do; it was just another instance of Ashkenazi duplicity. Uncle Vili rarely spoke to him again.

An exception occurred in 1930, when it became obvious that the family had been cheated of the prosperous twenties. It was at about this time that Uncle Vili suggested the family emigrate elsewhere. America? Too many Jews already. England? Too rigid. Australia? Too underdeveloped. Canada? Too cold. South Africa? Too far. It was finally decided that Japan offered ideal prospects for men whose claim to fortune was their exalted, millennial role as itinerant peddlers and master mountebanks.

The Japanese had three advantages: they were hardworking, they were eager to learn and compete, and they had probably never seen Jews before. The brothers picked a city they had never heard of but whose name sounded distantly, and reassuringly, Italian: Nagasaki. "Are you going to peddle baubles and mirrors too?" asked the Schwab. "No. Cars. Luxury cars."

"Which cars?" he asked. "Isotta-Fraschini." "Have you ever sold cars before?" He enjoyed ribbing the clannish brothers whenever he could. "No. Not cars. But we've sold everything else. Rugs. Stocks. Antiques. Gold. Not to mention hope to investors, sand to the Arabs. You name it. And besides, what difference does it make?" asked an exasperated Vili. "Carpets, cars, gold, silver, sisters, it's all the same thing. I can sell anything," he bragged.

The Isotta-Fraschini affair started with everyone in the family rushing to invest in the Middle Eastern and Japanese distributorship for the cars. A Japanese tutor was hired, and on Monday and Thursday afternoons, all five brothers—from Nessim, the oldest, who was over fifty and not entirely convinced about the venture, to Vili, twenty years younger and the demonic propounder of the scheme—would sit in the dining room, their notebooks filled with what looked like the most slovenly ink stains. "Poor boys," Aunt Marta would whisper to her sister Esther whenever she peeped into the dark, wood-paneled room where tea was being served to the classroom. "They haven't even mastered Arabic yet, and now these confounded sounds." Everyone was terror-struck. "Raw fish and all that rice every day! Death by constipation it's going to be. What must we endure next?" was Aunt Clara's only comment. There would be no more time for painting, she was warned. She would have to help in the family business. "Besides, all you've ever painted are portraits of Tolstoy. It's time to change," commented Uncle Isaac.

Their mother was also worried. "We build on bad soil. Always have, always will. God keep us."

Out of spite, no one in the family had ever asked the Schwab to invest a penny in the venture. His punishment would be to witness the clan grow tremendously rich, and finally realize, once and for all, who was and who wasn't.

Two years later, however, he was approached by his wife and asked to contribute something toward the immediate expenses of the firm. The Schwab, who, aside from gambling, hated to invest in intangibles, agreed to help by buying one of these expensive cars at a discount. It soon emerged that, aside from giving each of the five brothers a car, the newly established Isotta-Fraschini Asia-Africa Corporation had sold only two cars. Three years later, after the business collapsed and the demos were returned to Italy, only two persons in Egypt could be seen riding Isotta-Fraschinis: the Schwab and King Fouad.

The Isotta-Fraschini debacle set the family back by a decade. The clan continued to keep up appearances, and its members were often seen Sundaying in the king's gardens or arriving in chauffeured cars at the exclusive Sporting Club, but they were flat broke. Too vain to admit defeat, and too prudent to start baiting their creditors, they began tapping second-tier friends and relatives who could be relied on to keep their secret. Albert, their other brother-in-law, a once-prosperous cigarette manufacturer who had abandoned everything he owned in Turkey to move to Egypt, was asked to contribute something toward family finances. He did so reluctantly and after terrible rows with Esther, his wife, who, like her sister Marta, never doubted that blood was thicker than marriage vows.

Albert had ample reason for neither trusting nor wanting to help them. It was upon the clan's assurances that in 1932 he had finally and recklessly liquidated his cigarette business in Turkey and moved with his family to Egypt, hoping both to invest in his in-laws' firm and to spare his eighteen-year-old son, Henri, the horrors of Turkish barracks life. As soon as he arrived in Alexandria, however, the clan made it quite clear they were not about to let him into their Isotta-Fraschini schemes. Crestfallen, and not knowing what else to do in Alexandria, the erstwhile nicotine merchant took the life savings he had smuggled out of Turkey and became the proprietor of a small pool hall called La Petite Corniche, which faced the six-mile coast road known to all Alexandrians as the Corniche.

He never forgave them this trick. "Come, we'll help you," he would remind his wife, mimicking her brothers' repeated appeals to him. "We'll give you this, we'll give you that. Nothing! My ancestors were important enough to be assassinated by generations of sultans—now, billiards," he would mutter as he stood outside the kitchen door each morning, waiting for the assortment of cheese and spinach pastries that his wife baked at dawn. They sold well and were much liked by the pool players, who enjoyed eating something while drinking anisette.

Not only had his own circumstances been drastically reduced, but Albert was still expected to help out his wife's family. And so Vili's driver, thoroughly convinced that he was picking up money owed to his employer, would stop the car outside La Petite Corniche, walk in, receive a wad of bills, and "remind" Albert that he would be back in a few weeks.

After about the fifth loan, the humble proprietor of the pool hall walked outside with his cue in hand and shattered one of the car windows, informing his brother-in-law, who was skulking in the backseat while the chauffeur ran his errands, that since he was on such good terms with royalty, he should also tap His Majesty for "something to tide him over"—Vili's euphemism for desperate loans.

Esther was horrified when she heard of the confrontation between her husband and her brother. "But he's never done anything like this before," she protested to Vili, "he's not violent at all."

"He's a Turk, through and through."

"And what are you then, Italian by any chance?"

"Italian or not Italian, I know better than to break someone's car window."

"I'll speak to him," she said.

"No, I don't ever want to see him again. He's a terribly ungrateful man. If he weren't your husband, Esther, if he weren't your husband—" started Vili.

"If he weren't my husband, he wouldn't have lent you a penny. And if you weren't my brother, we wouldn't be in the mess we are in now."

■

Vili's given name was Aaron. When he returned to Alexandria in 1922, four years after the signing of the armistice, he had to make up for lost time. With the help of his four brothers, he became a rice expert in one week. Then a sugar-cane examiner. In the space of three months he learned how to cure any conceivable disease afflicting cotton, Egypt's prized export. In half a year's time, he had not only toured all corners of Egypt but had also visited every magnate's home rumored to hold the promise of a young Jewish wife. He married one a little less than a year after returning from Europe.

Having become a respectable citizen now, he reverted to what he liked best of all: married women. It is said that some of his mistresses were so distraught when he was done with them that they would show up on his wife's doorstep, pleading with her to intercede on their behalf, which poor Aunt Lola, whose heart was the biggest organ in her body, would sometimes do.

Seven years after the war, a woman named Lotte appeared at the family's residence with the picture of a man to whom she claimed she had been engaged in Berlin. When a consensus was finally reached on the man's identity, and the woman had put away her handkerchief, she was invited to stay for lunch with the family, most of whose members were due to arrive toward one o'clock. Vili was the last to arrive, but as soon as he walked in, she recognized his footsteps in the vestibule, stood up, put down her glass of sherry, and ran out screaming, "Willy! Willy!" at the top of her lungs.

No one had any idea what the demented woman meant by calling their Aaron by that strange name, but during lunch, when everyone had more or less regained composure, she explained that in 1914 in his new Prussian uniform he had looked so much like Kaiser Wilhelm that she could not resist nicknaming him Willy. His wife found something so endearingly right about "Willy," so stout yet so diminutive, that she too began to call him "Vili," first with reproof, then with raillery, and finally by force of habit, until everyone, including his mother, called him Vili, which eventually acquired its diminutive Greco-Judeo-Spanish form: Vilico.

"Vilico traitor," his mother said some time afterward.

He protested. "I was really in love with her at the time. And besides, it happened long before I'd met Lola."

"I wasn't talking about women. Judas you are, Judas you'll always be."

No one had the heart to ship the resurrected Lotte back to Belgium. So Lotte became Uncle Nessim's secretary, served as a temporary model in Aunt Clara's art class, then as a sales assistant for Uncle Cosimo, who eventually palmed her off on Uncle Isaac, who finally married her. In the family picture taken at their wedding in 1926 in the matriarch's sumptuous apartment in Grand Sporting overlooking the sunny Mediterranean, Tante Lotte is standing next to Uncle Isaac on the veranda, her right hand resting on Uncle Vili's shoulder. Are we, squints Uncle Vili, or aren't we men who share, men who exact the highest sacrifices, men whom women worship.

In the picture, Isaac is already a haggard fifty-year-old trying to cover up a bald spot, and Nessim, then close to retirement, looks older than his mother, whose forced good cheer on the day of her son's nuptials failed to conceal her worries.

"He's a prince, and she's a peasant," she said. "Look how she walks. You can still hear the clatter of Batavian clogs in her steps."

"And on his head you can still see traces of an invisible skullcap. So they're even. Leave them alone," her daughter Esther chided. "All his life with mistresses, and never a wife. It's about time he married."

"Yes, but not a Christian."

"Christian, Jewish, Belgium, Egypt, these are modern times," said Vili, "the twentieth century."

But his mother was not convinced. And in the picture she wears the distrustful gaze of a Hecuba welcoming Helen into her fold.

In back of the assemblage, peeping ever so furtively from behind the veranda's French windows, are the faces of three Egyptians. The maid, Zeinab, no older than twenty and already in the family for a decade, is smiling mischievously. Ahmed, the cook, who is from Khartoum, bashfully attempts to avert his eyes from the photographer, covering his face with his right palm. His younger sister Latifa, a mere child of ten, stares with impish dark eyes into the lens.

■

While the family tried to recover from the Isotta-Fraschini debacle, Uncle Vili was busily pursuing an altogether different career: that of a Fascist. He had become such an ardent supporter of Il Duce that he insisted everyone in the family wear a black shirt and follow the Fascist health regimen by exercising daily. A punctilious observer of all changes inflicted on the Italian language by the Fascists, he tried to purge acquired

Anglicisms from his speech, tastes, and clothing; when Italy went to war against Ethiopia, he asked the family to surrender its gold jewelry to the Italian government to help finance Il Duce's dream of an empire.

The irony behind Uncle Vili's patriotic histrionics is that, all the while proclaiming his undying allegiance to the *fascio*, he had already become an agent of British intelligence. His induction as a spy provided him with the only career for which he was truly suited from birth. It also encouraged everyone else in the family to remain in Egypt, especially now that they were plugged into the affairs of not one but two empires.

Vili's induction into His Majesty's Secret Service in 1936 coincided with another piece of good fortune for the family: his brother Isaac's flourishing friendship with the new King Farouk, Fouad's son. It is not clear how Isaac obtained his appointment as a director at the Ministry of Finance, but shortly after his wedding, he also found himself sitting on the boards of most of the major corporations in Egypt. "Fraterism," which gives to brothers what nepotism gives to nephews and grandchildren, took care of the rest, so that all of my other uncles—Nessim, Cosimo, and Lorenzo—were offered lucrative positions at several banks in Egypt. Vili's auction business was thriving; his mother's apartment overlooking that dazzling expanse of beachfront was given a much-needed sprucing up; Arnaut was born to the Schwab and Marta; and Vili finally made up with his brother-in-law Albert.

At first, Uncle Vili tried to conceal the nature of his new career. Only Aunt Lola and Uncle Isaac knew of it. But secrets of this kind he could never resist divulging, particularly since they stirred everyone's envy and admiration. It was the closest thing to being a soldier again. He carried a pistol wherever he went and, before sitting down to lunch with the rest of the family, he could often be seen fiddling with and loosening his holster. "What is he," asked the Schwab, "a gangster now?" "Shush," Aunt Marta would hiss, "no one is supposed to know." "But he's so obvious about it that he must be a decoy. The British couldn't possibly be that stupid."

But then, wars are won not because one party is the more resourceful, but because the other is a touch more incompetent. The Italians never suspected that Vili had thrown in his lot with the British and continued to use his services in Egypt and elsewhere. Vili was very often absent from Alexandria, either in Ethiopia with the Italian army, or in Italy, or serving in various Italian delegations to Germany. To become still more vital to Italian interests, he made a name for himself as a transportation expert and as a specialist in fuel distribution for desert convoys. How and where he acquired even a nodding acquaintance with these disciplines is beyond conjecture, but the Italians needed anyone they could get. They took advantage of his flourishing auction house as a cover for his frequent comings and goings between Rome and Alexandria. To allay possible British scrutiny, they encouraged him to import antique furniture, and thus, with the help of the Fascists, he managed to purchase rare antiques at a fraction of their cost in Italy only to sell them to Egyptian pashas for a fortune.

He became very wealthy. With time, not only did there accrue to him the many privileges of an English gentleman spy, but his double life allowed him to enact all those elaborate rituals—from breakfast to nightcap—he had always secretly envied the English, while gratifying his undying Italian patriotism whenever he heard the Fascist anthem, or when the Italians—not without German help—finally scored a victory against the Greeks. "We've taken Greece," he suddenly shouted one day, hanging up the telephone with what must also have been Turkish glee in his voice. "We're finally in Athens"—whereupon everyone at home jumped up and down,

stirring up the Egyptian servants and maids, who would ulu-
late at the slightest pretext for celebration, until someone inevitably sobered up the festivities by voicing concern for Greek
Jewry.

Vili's voice had quivered with excitement at the news, as it
did when a group of Italian frogmen stole into the harbor of
Alexandria, causing serious damage to two British battleships.
Vili was thrilled by the valiant frogmen, but totally disheartened when reminded that he had to condemn their mission.
"Gone are the old days," he would say, meaning the days when
you always knew who you were and whose side you were on.

Then something happened. Even he could not quite understand it. "Things aren't going well," Vili said. When
pressed to explain, he would simply say, "Things." Unnerved
by his answers, his sister Esther would try coaxing him: "Is
it that you don't want to say or that you don't know?" "No, I
do know." "Then tell us." "It's about Germany." "Anyone
could have said it was about Germany. What about Germany?"
"They've been nosing around Libya too much. It just doesn't
bode well."

A few months later, my Great-aunt Elsa arrived with her
German husband from Marseilles. "Very bad. Terrible," she
said. They would not give her an exit visa. Isaac, who had
used his connections with French diplomats once to become
a French citizen, had to use them again now to arrange for his
sister's immediate safe conduct. Given her complicated status
as an Italian married to a German Jew in France, additional
measures were needed, and Isaac obtained for her and her
husband diplomatic passports bearing the king of Egypt's seal.
Aunt Elsa complained she had lost her shop of religious ar-
tifacts at Lourdes and had spent two years in extreme poverty.
"That's where I learned to be a miser," she would say, as
though this mitigated what all knew was a case of congenital
avarice.

Hardly a month later, the Schwab's twenty-five-year-old half sister Flora appeared in the family living room. Marta immediately saw the writing on the wall. "If all these Ashkenazi Jews begin swarming in from Germany, it's going to be the end for us. The city will be teeming with tailors, brokers, and more dentists than we know what to do with."

"We couldn't sell anything," said Flora. "They took everything. We left with what we could," she went on. Aunt Flora had come alone with her mother, Frau Kohn, an ailing, aging woman with clear blue eyes and white skin touched with pink, who spoke French poorly and who always seemed to wear a pleading, terrified look on her face. "They slapped her on the streets two months ago," explained her daughter. "Then she was insulted by a local shopkeeper. Now she keeps to herself."

■

For several weeks early that summer, the streets were rife with rumors of an impending, perhaps decisive, battle with the Afrika Korps. Rommel's forces had seized one stronghold after another, working their way along the Libyan coastline. "There's going to be a terrible battle. Then the Germans will invade." The British, Vili said, were totally demoralized, especially after Tobruk. Panic struck everyone. The small resort town of Mersah-Matrouh on the coast near the Libyan border had fallen into German hands. "They hate us Jews more than they despise Arabs," said Aunt Marta, as though this were totally incomprehensible. Uncle Isaac, who had heard a lot about German anti-Semitism, had put together a terrifying account, made up of rumors and haunting reminders of the Armenian massacre of 1895, which he had witnessed. "First they find out who is Jewish, then they send trucks at night and force all the Jewish men into them, and then they take you to distant factories, leaving women and children to starve by themselves."

"All you're doing is scaring everyone, so stop it right now," said Esther, who, like other members of her family, had witnessed at least two Armenian massacres in Turkey.

"Yes, but the Armenians had been spying for the British for far too long," protested Vili, who, in this case, sympathized with the Turks, even though he had fought against them on the British and Italian side during the Great War, while Albert, his brother-in-law, who had fought with the Turks against the British, condemned the massacres as barbarous. "The Turks simply had to put a stop to it in the only way they knew how: with blood and more blood. But what have Jews ever done to the Germans?" asked Uncle Nessim. "The way some Jews behave," Aunt Clara jumped in, "I'd run them out of this world into the next. It's because of Jews like them that they hate Jews like us," she said, eyeing her brother Vili, one of whose favorite maxims she had just quoted. "Then, they're really going to take us away, you think," interrupted Marta, her voice already quaking. "Don't start now with the crying, please! We're in the middle of a war," said an exasperated Esther. "But it's because we're in the middle of a war that I'm crying," Aunt Marta insisted, "don't you see?" "No, I don't see. If they take us away, then they'll take us away, and that'll be the end of that—"

Weeks before the first battle of El Alamein, the matriarch decided to put into effect an old family expedient. She summoned all members of her family to stay in her large apartment for as long as the situation warranted. None declined the offer, and they came, like Noah's beasts, in twos and fours, some from Cairo and Port Said, and some from as far as Khartoum, where they would have been safer than in Alexandria. Mattresses were laid out side by side on the floor, extra leaves were added to the dining room table, and two more cooks were hired, one of whom raised doves and chickens in the event of a food shortage. A sheep and two ewes were secretly brought in under cover of night and tied upstairs on the terrace next to the makeshift coop.

During the day, family members would leave and tend to business. Then all would return for lunch, and during those long summer afternoons, some of the men would sit around the dining room table naming their worst fears while the children napped and the women mended and knitted things in other rooms. Warm clothing was particularly needed; winters in Germany were harsh, they said. At the entrance to the apartment stood a row of very small suitcases neatly stacked in a corner, some dating back to their owners' youth in Turkey and to their school days abroad. Now, blotched and tattered by age, bearing yellowed stickers from Europe's grand hotels, they waited meekly in the vestibule for that day when the Nazis would march into Alexandria and round up all Jewish males above eighteen, allowing each a small suitcase with bare necessaries.

Later in the afternoon some members of the family would go out, and the women might stop at the Sporting Club. But by teatime most were already home. Dinner was usually light and quick, consisting of bread, jam, fruit, cheese, chocolate, and homemade yogurt, reflecting Aunt Elsa's tight management of family finances, Uncle Vili's spartan dietary norms, and my great-grandmother's humble origins. After dinner, coffee would be brought out and everyone would crowd into the living room to listen to the radio. Sometimes they listened to the BBC, other times to the Italian stations; the reports were always confusing.

"All I know is that the Germans need Suez. Therefore, they must attack," Vili maintained.

"Yes, but can we stop them?"

"Only for the short term. Long term, who knows? General

Montgomery may be a genius, but Rommel is Rommel," Uncle Vili decreed.

"Then what shall we do?" asked Aunt Marta, always ready to break into hysterics.

"Do? There is nothing we can do."

"What do you mean there is nothing we can do? We can escape."

"Escape where?" asked Esther turning red.

"Escape. I don't know. Escape!"

"But where?" continued her sister. "To Greece? They've already taken Greece. To Turkey? We've just barely gotten out of there. To Italy? They'd throw us into jail. To Libya? The Germans are there already. Don't you see that once they take Suez, it'll all be finished?"

"What do you mean, 'finished'? So you *do* think that they'll win?"

"Oh, I don't know," Vili sighed.

"Just come out and say it. They'll win and then they'll come and take us all away."

Vili did not answer.

"How about going to Madagascar, then?" offered Aunt Marta.

"Madagascar! Please, Marta, do me a favor!" interjected Uncle Isaac.

"Or South Africa. Or India. What's wrong with just keeping one step ahead of them. Maybe they'll lose."

There was a moment's pause.

"They won't lose," said Aunt Flora finally.

"Since you're so quick to talk, Flora, why haven't you already left, then," asked Marta, almost seething with contempt. "Why are you still here?"

"You forget that I've already left one place."

Aunt Flora drew deeply on her cigarette, thought awhile,

and then exhaled with a dreamy, wistful air, leaning toward the tea table from the corner of the sofa where she was sitting, and stubbed out her cigarette. Everyone had turned to her, the women and the men always wondering why she habitually wore black when green was what matched her eyes best. "I don't know," she added, still gazing at her hand, which continued slow, stubbing motions long after she had put out her cigarette. "I don't know," she hesitated. "There's nowhere to go. I'm tired of running. I'm even more tired of worrying where to run. The world isn't big enough. And there's not enough time. I'm sorry," she said, turning to her brother, "I don't want to go anywhere. I don't even want to travel." Silence filled the living room. "The truth is, if I believed we had a chance, I'd hide in the desert. But I don't believe it."

"Such pessimism, and at so young an age," Vili broke in, assuming the condescending smile of a man who knew all there was to know about frightened women and how to placate them. "It's not written that the Germans have to win, you know. They may lose. Their fuel supplies are terribly low, and they have overextended themselves. Let them attack Egypt, let them venture as deeply into Egypt as they want. Sand always wins in the end—remember that," he continued, advocating the strategic restraint of Hannibal's foe, Quintus Fabius Maximus, known to history as Cunctator, the temporizer.

" 'Sand always wins in the end.' Really, Vili," Aunt Flora said mockingly and walked out to the balcony, where she lit another cigarette. "Whatever does he mean?" she scoffed out loud, turning to Esther's son, who was also smoking on the balcony.

"*Sand always wins*," repeated Vili with surprised emphasis, as if it should have made perfect sense the first time. "Their invasion plans may be flawless, but we are better armed, better supplied, and we have more men. You'll see what damage a few months of desert sand can do to Rommel's armored cars. So, let's not abandon hope. We'll find a way. We've survived worse enemies before, we'll outlive this one too."

"Well said," replied Esther, who, for all her grim realism, loved positive thinking and could never bring herself to believe that disaster was as imminent as all that. "I knew *you* would come up with something in the end," she said, eyeing her silent husband with that scornful, doubtful look that all members of her family reserved for their spouses during family gatherings.

"As long as we have courage and stand together and don't panic and don't listen to idle rumors floating between seamstress this and hairdresser that, *sisters*," he emphasized, "we'll pull through this one as well." He declaimed this exhortation in the only style he knew: by borrowing from Churchill and Mussolini.

"So we wait, in other words," concluded Marta.

"So we wait."

And there it was, poised in midair, hovering in the wings like a pianist cracking his knuckles before making a long-awaited appearance, or like an actor clearing his throat as he walks onto the stage. It was ushered in by the confident glint in his eye, the arching of his back, and that all-too-familiar quiver in his voice as it rose and reached the perfect pitch: "We've waited things out before, we'll wait this one out as well. After all, each of us here is a five-thousand-year-old Jew—*are we or aren't we?*"

The mood in the room livened, and Vili, who had a good touch of demagoguery in him, turned to Flora and asked her to play something by Goldberg or Brandenburg, he couldn't remember which.

"You mean Bach," said Flora, walking up to the piano.

"Bach, Offenbach, *c'est tout la même chose*, it's all the same.

Todos Lechli, all of them Ashkenazi," he muttered. Only Esther heard him say that. She immediately turned and grimaced a severe shush, "She understands!" But Vili was unmoved. "There is only one thing she understands, and all the men in this room know what it is."

The Schwab's half sister did not hear this exchange. She took off her ring, placed it next to the keys, and began playing something by Schubert. Everyone was overjoyed.

And she played till very late that night, till one after the other, everyone had gone to sleep, and she played softly every night, ignoring the men who were growing tired of waiting up for her, deriding Esther's son and his shallow Wertherisms when they ended up alone in the living room one night and she had stopped playing and he had tried to kiss away all that heartless talk of love in the time of war. In the maid Latifa's room, which was Flora's now, she had taken off her ring again and her earrings and, depositing her glass of cognac on a makeshift bedstand, had said, "Now you can kiss me." But she kissed him first. "It means nothing," she added as she looked away and lit the kerosene lamp, bringing down the wick till it glowed less than her cigarette. "As long as we're clear that it means nothing," she said almost enjoying the cruelty with which she foisted despair on everyone.

■

Then came the wonderful news. The British Eighth Army had managed to halt Rommel's advance at El Alamein and, in the fall of 1942, finally mounted a decisive attack upon the Afrika Korps. The battle lasted twelve days. At night, everyone in the family would stand for hours on the balcony, as if waiting for holiday fireworks, straining their eyes west of the city to catch a glimpse of the historic battle that was to decide their fates. Some smoked, others chatted among themselves or with neighbors upstairs or downstairs, likewise perched on their balconies, waving at one another, grimacing hope and resignation, while, from emptied rooms, came an incessant crackle of shortwave bulletins announcing the most recent developments in North Africa. A distant, half-inch halo hovered over the western horizon, swaying in the blackout, suddenly beaming like an approaching vehicle coming uphill, only to fade again, a pale amber moon on a misty night. All they heard was a distant, muffled drone, like the whir of fans on quiet summer evenings or the sound of the large refrigerator humming in the pantry. People went to sleep to the faraway rumble of battle.

"See? All your fears of being taken away have come to nothing. Didn't I tell you?" said Vili to his sister Marta when it became clear that the British had scored a decisive victory.

Everyone was readying to leave the old mother's home. Yet the preparations were slow, uncertain, even dilatory, partly because everyone had grown accustomed to the refugee lifestyle and was reluctant to abandon its solidarity, but also because no one wanted to tempt providence by proclaiming all danger averted. "What's the hurry?" said my great-grandmother. "There are still many pigeons and chickens left. Besides, one never knows with the Germans. They could be back in a matter of weeks." Packing, however, continued.

As a going-away gift, the old mother decided to give each of her sons and daughters a crystal goblet bearing golden fleurs-de-lis. They had been manufactured in their father's glass factory in Turkey.

"This is the last time this apartment will ever house so many," the old woman explained.

"The way the world is going, I wouldn't be so sure," said Esther.

Esther was right. The family would seek refuge in the old

matriarch's home on three subsequent occasions: once during the Suez War, in 1956; then a decade later; and once, earlier, in 1948, after Vili was hunted down by Zionist agents who beat him severely for spying for the British and then threatened to do the same to other men in the family. Two months later Vili got wind they were on his tracks again and that this time they meant to kill him. He took cover in his mother's home. One day, he took out his good-luck pendulum and on the table placed a cyanide pill he had been keeping ever since the days of El Alamein. The pendulum said no.

Vili was spirited away to Italy, then to England, where he changed names, converted to Christianity, and forswore all previous nationalities. But it was only about four years later that he resurfaced in Egypt for what proved to be the most spectacular business deal in his career as spy, soldier, and swindler: the auctioning of the deposed king's property.

∎

"It was the end of the end," he explained many years later in his garden in Surrey. "The end of an era, the end of a world. Everything fell apart after that."

By now he was in his middle eighties, he liked horses, candies, and dirty jokes, using a fist at the end of a stiffened forearm to illustrate the ribald tales which he liked to tell in the old style: with bawdy gestures and exaggerated pantomime. Wearing old tweeds, Clark boots, an ascot, and a stained cashmere cardigan, he looked the part he had been rehearsing all his life: a Victorian gentleman who couldn't care less what his inferiors thought of either him or his clothes. What made his aristocratic bearing especially convincing was that, on looking at him, one immediately suspected poverty.

He had shown me his orchard where nothing good ever grew, the huge lake in need of sprucing up—"But who cares"—the stables with more horses than there was room for, and beyond these, the woods where no one dared take a walk, a sort of Jane Austen world gone feral. "I don't know," he answered when I asked what his woods abutted. "I suppose a neighbor. But then, these English lords, whoever really knows them?"

It was not true. He knew them quite well. In fact, he knew everyone. At the local post office, at the bank, and at one of the pubs where he offered me a beer, everyone knew Dr. Spingarn. "Well, hello" and "Cheerio" slipped from his tongue as though he had spoken English from the day he was born. He knew everything there was to know about soccer. When a Mini Morris stopped us on our way to town one morning, I realized how thoroughly grafted he was onto his new homeland. This was Lady Something-or-other on her way to London, wanting to know whether there was anything he needed. "No trouble at all," she said after he finally agreed to let her pick up a case of French wine at some merchant. "*Sans façons,*" she added, pleased to show off her French and promising to have Arthur, the lord himself, deliver it this evening. "*Entendu,*" we heard her say as she rolled up her window and began speeding up the quiet country road, headed toward the highway.

"She's as dry as a pitted prune, that one. Like all Englishwomen."

"I thought she was very nice," I protested, reminding him that the lady had first gone to his home and, on being told he was out for a walk, had driven about looking for him. "Very nice, very nice," he repeated, "all of them are very nice here. You don't understand a thing."

In town, Vili waved at the local antiques dealer and decided to pay him a visit.

"Good morning, Dr. Spingarn," said the dealer.

"Greetings," he replied and introduced me. "Have you found my Turkish coffeepot yet?"

"Still looking, still looking," chanted the dealer, as he continued to dust an old clock.

"It's been nine years," chuckled Vili. "I'm afraid I'll die before you find it."

"No fearing that, Dr. Spingarn. You'll outlive us all, sir."

"They're slower than Arabs and twice as stupid. How on earth did they ever manage to have an empire once?" he said as soon as we stepped outside the shop.

Back at home, his wife, daughter, and married grandson and great-grandchild were waiting for us. "See this table?" He palmed the huge antique oak dining table on which food was being served. "I paid five pounds for it. And see these chairs? There were twelve of them. Seven pounds the lot, with eight more in the attic. And this huge clock here? Guess how much." "One pound," I guessed. "Wrong! I paid nothing at all for it. It came with the chairs." He burst out laughing as he spread a thick piece of butter on a slice of bread.

"You sound like a typical *parvenu juif*," jeered his daughter.

"And what else are we if not *des parvenus juifs*?"

After lunch he insisted we have coffee alone together, "*Lui et moi seuls*," he told the others. "Come," he said, pointing to the kitchen, where he proceeded to brew Turkish coffee. "You see, all you need is a little pot like this, preferably made of brass, but aluminum will do. I had this one made in Manchester. By a Greek. But do you think our antiques dealer is smart enough to figure out that's all he had to do? Never! That's why I go to him every once in a while. As long as he remains stupid and as long as I am lucid enough to know it, then things are well with me. Do you see?" he winked at me, complicity beaming in his eyes. I nodded but missed the point. It occurred to me that I would never have lasted a day in the world of his youth. *"De l'audace, toujours de l'audace,"* he replied. "You see, in life, it's not only knowing what you want that matters. That's easy. It's knowing *how* to want." I was not sure I understood this either, but again I nodded. "But I was lucky. I had a good life," he went on. "Life gives us all a few trump cards when we're born, and then that's it. By the time I was twenty I had already wasted all of mine. Life gave them back to me many times. Not many can claim the same."

When coffee was ready, he took out two demitasses and proceeded to pour, holding the pot precariously high above the cups and aiming the coffee into them, the way good Arab servants did, to allow the brew to cool somewhat as it was being poured. "May God rest his soul, but no one made coffee like your grandfather," he said. "A snake, with a cleft tongue, who bubbled like milk when he lost his temper and then cut you to pieces, but still, the best brewer of coffee in the world. Come." He indicated the drawing room as we passed through a different corridor. The room was filled with antiques and Persian rugs. On the glistening old parquet sat a band of afternoon sunlight in which an overfed cat had fallen asleep, its legs stretched out awkwardly.

"See this smoking jacket?" he said. "Feel it." I leaned over to him and touched the fabric on the shawl collar. "At least forty years old," he said, looking terribly amused. "Guess whose?" "Your father's," I said. "Don't be stupid," he snapped, practically losing his temper. "My father died eons ago." "One of your brothers'?" "No, no, no." "I don't know then." "I'll give you a hint. Guess who made the cloth? Best fabric in the world." It took me a while. "My father?" I asked. "Right. Woven in the basement of his factory in Ibrahimieh during the war. This jacket belonged to your grandfather Albert."

"He gave it to you?"

"In a manner of speaking, yes."

"On what occasion?"

"After he died. It was Esther who gave it to me. Where would you ever find such fine wool nowadays? It's one of the few things I treasure," he joked. "Here, feel again!" he ordered.

Ever the master salesman, I thought. "Let me explain," he said, his face uncomfortably nearing mine. He looked around to see no one was listening.

"Do you remember Flora, *la belle romaine*, as we used to call her?"

It was Flora who had taught me all about the pianist Schnabel, I replied.

"That's right. During the war, in the days of Alamein, we all stayed in your great-grandmother's house. You have no idea how crowded it was. Well, one day, in walks this dark-haired, beautiful, but painfully beautiful woman who plays the piano every evening, who smokes all the time, who looks a trifle worn but sexier for it, and who flirts with all of us, though you'd swear she didn't know it. In short, we were all madly in love with her. Madly."

"What does that have to do with my grandfather?"

"Wait, let me *finish*!" He had almost lost his temper. "Well, the tension was such—you have to realize there were at least seven grown men in the house, not to mention younger men who were just as predatory—that every day we would start quarreling. Over nothing, and over everything. Your grandfather and I quarreled every day. Every day. Then we would make up and play backgammon. And then quarrel again. Do you play backgammon?"

"Poorly."

"I thought so. At any rate, it becomes quite evident that Flora has singled me out. Of course, I make no passes, I have to behave—in my mother's house and all that, and my wife snooping about, you understand. I have to move very slowly.

So I finally say to your grandfather, 'Albert, this woman wants me. What should I do?' He says, 'Do you want her?' And I say, 'Don't you?' He does not reply. So I say to him, 'Albert, you've got to help me.' That cunning wretch of your grandfather smiles awhile and finally says, 'I'll see.' Everyone else knew—Frau Kohn, your grandmother, Isaac. Everyone, except me. I found out about them years later, when Flora came to visit us here and saw me wearing his smoking jacket. She recognized it immediately."

"Yes?" I asked.

"Don't you get it?"

I shook my head.

"She probably had it made for him as a present. I felt like a complete dolt. The only woman I wanted and never slept with. Being jealous like this after forty years, what a dolt!" A moment of silence elapsed. I was tempted to tell him it was not my grandfather but my father who had loved Flora on those summer nights of 1942, and that the jacket was his, not his father's. My grandfather had simply "inherited" it from his son, the way he "inherited" everything my father stopped wearing. But I said nothing, for I wanted my grandfather to win one bout against Vili. "You should have seen us back then, though," he went on, "everyone asking her to play the piano, everyone drinking more cognac than was usual, waiting for all the others to tire and go to sleep. Frankly, staying up so late was never my style."

I watched him relish his revelation as he picked up both our emptied demitasses. "Come," he finally said. And before I knew it, he had taken me to the garden, where his grandson and his wife were reading the local newspaper.

"Have you had your little chat?" asked his wife.

"We have indeed," replied Vili.

A small incident occurred over dinner. A couple of Gypsies

were observed through the dining room window roaming the grounds. Without hesitating, Vili went into the drawing room, got his shotgun, and fired two shots in the air, rousing the dogs and the horses. "Have you gone mad," his daughter shouted, jumping up and trying to grab the gun from his hands. "They could kill you if they wanted to."

"Let them try. Do you think I'm afraid of them? I'd go after every one of them—" And then it came, as a farewell present, as a memento of my visit to England, a final concession on his part to the visitor who had come to hear the words spoken from his own lips. "Me afraid of them? Me frightened? What do you think? Am I or aren't I?"

That night, he came into my room to say farewell to me. "I insist on adieu," he said, "because at my age one never knows." He stared at my things, looked over my books, picked one up with something like mock scorn on his face. "Do people still read this?" "More than ever," I replied. "Another Jew," he said. "No, a half-Jew," I said. "No. When your mother is Jewish you are never half-Jewish."

Perhaps it was the subject, or maybe this was why he had come upstairs to my room, but he asked about his mother. I told him what I could remember. No, there had been no pain. Yes, she was lucid until the very end. Yes, she still laughed and still made those short, lapidary pronouncements that made one squirm like a trampled worm. Yes, she understood she was dying. And so on, until I told him that she couldn't see well because she had developed cataracts, and that a light, yellowish film had veiled her eyes. I had said it in passing, not thinking that cataracts were a particularly serious impairment.

"So she couldn't see then," he said. "She couldn't see," he repeated, as though trying to scan in the words and the syllables themselves some secret meaning, some revealed purpose behind the cruelty of fate and the vulnerability of old age. "So she couldn't see," he said like someone gripped by a sorrow so powerful that all he can do is repeat the words until they finally bring tears to his eyes.

"You won't understand this," he said, "but I think of her sometimes. Old, lonely, everyone gone, and, now that you mention it, blind, dying practically all by herself in Egypt. And I think of how I could have made things better for her had I not misspent my life trying out all these flimsy schemes of mine. But then, that is how life is. Now that I have the house, I haven't got the mother. And yet I wanted this house for her. Sometimes, I think of her simply as mother, the way children do when they need something only mothers have. You would think because I'm old enough to be a great-grandfather that I couldn't possibly think of my mother in those terms. Well, I still do. Strange, isn't it?" He smiled, placed the volume back on my nightstand, and, perhaps meaning to surprise me, began quoting in French the long, sinuous prose of the first few sentences.

"Good night, *Herr Doktor*," he said abruptly.

"Good night, Dr. Spingarn," I replied, resigned never to ask how he had come to know this passage by Proust.

Half an hour later, on my way to the shower, I was stopped by my cousin and his wife. "If you're quiet you won't regret this." They explained that every evening, between ten and eleven o'clock, Vili would listen to the French-language short-wave broadcast from Israel. I expressed surprise. "It's always the last thing he does. Then he turns off the lights and goes to sleep." "So?" I asked. "So, you'll see." For a while we waited outside his door. "It's the same thing every night," she whispered. Were they going to knock and ask to be admitted, or were they simply going to barge in on him? "You'll see." Finally, we heard the Israeli national anthem. It was followed by various signing-off signals. "It's about over now," my cousin warned. Something gave a click in his room. Vili had just turned off his radio. Then we heard the sound of bedsprings yielding under his weight, followed by a rustle of sheets, and suddenly the band of light went out from under the door. All was quiet for a second. And then I thought I heard it, a faint, reedy, muted buzzing, emanating from within the small room like a vapor of sound working its way out the keyhole, under the door, through the cracks in the lintel, filling the dark silence where we three stood now like incense and premonition; an eerie garble of familiar words murmured to a cadence I too had learned long ago, whispered as if in stealth and shame.

"He'll deny it if you ask him," said my cousin.

2

Rue Memphis

To the two ladies who were to become my grandmothers one day and who met for the first time in '44 in a small marketplace in Alexandria eyeing a suspiciously old catch of red mullet, this was indeed a very small, very strange world. Past their first, shy, tentative remarks spoken from behind thick lipstick and respectable hat-veils, something like intense sunshine erupted on their speech and suddenly the two strangers, who had known each other by sight for more than a decade without ever daring to utter a word to the other, began to twitter away with the heady good cheer of old classmates picking up exactly where they left off fifty years earlier. Each was accompanied by a boy servant whom neither trusted or talked to but whose job it was to trail behind his wise old *mazmazelle*—all European ladies of a certain age and station were called *mademoiselle* or *signora* in Egypt—and watch her pick out the good from bad fruit, hear her haggle in the most incomprehensible Arabic, intervene if things got out of hand, and finally ferry the load from one food vendor to the next until he was sent home to start cooking lunch. *Mazmazelles* would not think twice of touching raw liver with their bare hands, or of fingering the gills of red mullet to prove the fish wasn't at all fresh that day; but they never took anything from the loutish food vendor's hand. That was the boy servant's task. *Mazmazelles* were then free to do as they pleased until about one o'clock, when their husbands came home to eat and sleep.

"No mullet then," concluded one to the other. "Such a shame, though. To think that all these years I've been buying bad fish and didn't even know it," she said sadly.

"It's in the gills. Not the eyes. Gills must be bright red. Otherwise, don't buy."

"Such a shame," repeated the meeker of the two as they made their way home. "All these years living exactly across the street from each other, and not so much as a peep for a greeting."

"But why didn't you ever speak to me?" insisted the one who knew everything about fish.

"I used to think you were French," replied her meeker neighbor, implying high-society French.

"French? And whatever made you think *I* was French? *Je suis italienne, madame*," she added, as if that were a far greater distinction.

"As am I!"

"Yes? Are you? But we are from Leghorn."

"But so are we! What a marvelous coincidence." A small world indeed, they said in Ladino (which each insisted on calling Spanish), a language each found out the other spoke because, at the fish vendor's stand, as one tried to explain why the mullet were not good that day, it suddenly occurred to both that of the six to seven languages each spoke fluently neither knew the name for mullet except in Ladino.

When it was time to say goodbye, both agreed to meet and shop together early the next day.

"She is so distinguished," reported the meeker of the two to her husband that day. "Distinguished my eye," he had snickered. "Her husband owns a billiard hall." "Why, is your bicycle shop much better?" she retorted. "A hundred thousand times better." He had even raised his voice.

Heedless of her husband's pronouncements, she was determined to refer to her neighbor as *une vraie princesse*, while the other, who must have had more or less the same conversation with her husband, concluded that although her neighbor may not have been *très high-class*, she was nothing short of *une sainte*.

The Saint was a gentle, melancholy grandmother who sometimes spoke to herself and who often lost and forgot things. She forgot where she hid them or whom she was hiding them from. She lost keys and gloves, forgot names, dates, debts, and quarrels. She would lose the thread of her story and, drawing a blank in her mind, grope about for ideas, stringing idle words together, hoping to convey a semblance of continuity if she spoke fast enough, not realizing that her rapid succession of non sequiturs was precisely what betrayed her lapses most. Sometimes, feeling totally disoriented, she would own defeat. "It's nothing, it happens to everyone," she would say, taking a deep breath, trying to suppress a surge of anxiety. "I'll remember later," she would promise, knowing that, in the Italo-Byzantine world she came from, if a sneeze in mid-sentence confirmed the truth of what one was saying, forgetfulness was a sign of deceit. She tried to allay this suspicion by punctuating those sudden pauses in her speech with little oaths, such as *On my daughter's eyes* or *On my mother's tombstone*, but, by dint of swearing so often, she herself began to doubt her own tales, thinking, as happens so often among the elderly, that perhaps she was exaggerating more than she was forgetting.

When she had trouble remembering your name, she would search for it through an elaborate maze of other names in the family, thus betraying where you ranked in the hierarchy of her heart: first her son, Robert, then his three daughters, me, then her daughter who was deaf, her brothers, neighbors, her husband.

She cried once when I told her I had seen Uncle Robert in a dream. "And what did he say to you?" she fretted. More than a year had elapsed since his expulsion from Egypt after the 1956 war, and by then her life was entirely unsettled. "He said his daughter wanted to bring you a present," I lied, thinking my dream would make her happy. But according to established Levantine custom, dreams always portend the opposite of what they say, which implied that her son in France was desperately in need of funds for his children.

Hence the frantic shopping for clothes, the scrupulous wrapping of parcels, the tireless standing in line at the post office, followed by epic worry sessions in the living room every evening as she, and anyone who happened to be visiting at that time, would sit and stew and fill themselves with as much gall as each could secrete, waiting for confirmation that the package had not fallen into the hands of the police or that some crafty postal clerk had not looted its contents. Wrapped in cobalt-blue paper, durable string, and stained with brittle reddish wax seals so old they bore her maiden name, her parcels were the product of a mind so naïve and so transparent that they might have fooled a master spy but not a child: a pair of home-knit overalls for each of her granddaughters, medicine that was hard to come by in France, a naughty assortment of rock candy carefully wrapped in colored cellophane paper, and, as though stitched by thoughtful celestial hands, a folded hundred-pound note sewn discreetly into the cuff of a child's shirtsleeve. Her husband would find out sooner or later, and there were bound to be scenes. But her grandchildren come first she told the Princess, who, more than ever now, was convinced that this was truly a saint, though she noticed—as those who loved her sometimes did not—that her mind had already started to wander. "She is like a dove," the Princess went on, "totally without bile." "And without brains, either," her husband immediately replied.

A month later word arrived that the candies, overalls, magazines, and the *petite surprise* woven in by the hands of fate had arrived safely. "I knew it, I always knew it," she exclaimed with great glee. "Then why did you worry so much?" asked the Princess, who had spent too many evenings soothing her neighbor's worst fears to see them so readily dispelled now. "Because if I hadn't worried, they might not have gotten there," she replied, as though this were the most evident truth in the world. "I don't understand," added the Princess. "If you don't understand, Madame Esther, then you don't understand," she would retort curtly, meaning she was certainly not about to divulge rituals that were so elaborate and so delicate that merely thinking about them, let alone discussing them with the uninitiated, might strip them of their spell.

"But please explain," the Princess would insist, waiting to see what demented piece of logic might surface in her neighbor's explanation. Like all mystics, however, the Saint refused to be baited.

"Madame Esther, I may not be learned," she would say, "but I'm very sharp, *très lucide*. I sniff things out long before they happen." Whenever she suspected someone was trying to make fun of her or pull the wool over her eyes, she would indicate her nose with an admonitory upraised index finger, as if her nostrils were a passageway to a venerable sixth sense. "And she thinks she's sharp," the Princess's husband would scoff, sometimes even in the Saint's presence. "She's got the brains of a turnip, and the demented goathead goes around claiming she's sharp—please!" Unruffled by the smirks around her, she would raise her inspired index finger, point to her nose a few times, smile her faint sagacious smile, and, whispering in my direction, say, "Let them. They think I don't know, but I know." She would look around sadly and sigh, reminded of yet sadder things in life.

"I'd give everything to see you grow into a young man. But that's for an *otra venida*," she would smile, referring to another lifetime, the one *to come*, that storehouse of might-have-beens and second-time-arounds where all of life's blemishes are polished over and edged in gold and filigree.

That was my cue, for on hearing her speak of *la otra venida*, I would lunge toward her and clasp her tightly, while she struggled with mock annoyed shoves, like a person about to be tickled or embraced in public, feigning to ask how dare I kiss her now after doing what I had done—which was to outlive her and deprive her of me someday. But then, seeing that I refused to release my hold, she would slacken and cease to fight and hug me back, staring into my face as if to make out whether I was indeed worthy of so much love, finally taking a deep, intoxicated breath, filled with longing and premonition and the yearning to inhale my entire being. All I had to do then was squeeze a bit harder, and out would come the sob she had been struggling to contain.

"You love me, I know, but you must love your other grandmother more," she would say.

"Pathologically Sephardi," observed Aunt Flora, who had witnessed the scene and had no patience for these emotional torsions that go by the name of love on the Mediterranean. "Nothing was ever more hostile," she told me years later, "than this gnarled, twisted selflessness that chokes you like a bad debt and always makes you feel slightly unworthy and always unkind in the end."

"But why won't you let him say he loves you more, Madame Adèle?" Aunt Flora would protest half-jokingly on those hot summer afternoons when they drew the shutters to keep the sun out of the Saint's living room while the two women played music for four hands. It was upon the Princess's recommendation during the last days of the war that the Saint had hired Aunt Flora as a piano teacher. Now, a decade later, they had become like mother and daughter.

"Don't you think I want him to love me more?" the Saint would ask.

"But why not let him, then?"

Irked, my grandmother would answer, "If you don't understand, Flora, then I'm really sorry."

On those summer afternoons, it would grow so quiet in the Saint's apartment—and downstairs on Rue Memphis and all over Ibrahimieh—that, while my grandfather Jacques slept in his room, I too would often doze on the sofa, letting the chatter of the two women and of their piano exercises lull me into a long and restful nap. Sometimes, in mid-sleep, I was roused by the stirring of long spoons in tall lemonade glasses, or by the persistent whispers of the two women, or by a fly wandering about my face, it too woven into a dream along with the music of Liszt and the cooing of turtledoves who would come to rest on the windowsill where yesterday's rice had been left for them by the Saint.

"At least I want him to love her the same," my grandmother would insist, as though upholding a stubborn, principled egalitarianism in matters of love.

"But why ask anyone to love anyone *the same*? Besides, did wanting anything ever move the heart?" Flora would ask, adding, as she did so many years later in Venice, when we walked around Campo Morosini one summer afternoon, that "one seldom loves anyone at all, much less loves them well."

"You don't understand, Flora," insisted the Saint, "I want him to love her so she won't be jealous of me. I worry. What kind of grandmother do you think she'll be for him once I'm gone?" "What do you mean, 'gone'?" "Gone. As in gone away, Flora." "What are you saying? You're hardly sixty!" "I meant gone to France, Flora, not gone *like that*! Gone to England. To Constantinople. How do I know. Gone." She paused a moment, probably realizing that the other meaning was not so farfetched either. "And besides, how many more do you think I've got left?" she asked, meaning years.

Fearing the Princess's resentment, the Saint resolved to conceal all of my visits from her neighbor across the street. Whenever she met the Princess, she never failed to ask after me, to let it seem she seldom saw me—all of it exquisitely Byzantine but quite pointless, as it would never have occurred to the Princess that she was not the more favored of the two.

Since the Princess was so punctilious in her daily schedule, it was never too difficult to hide my visits from her. At two in the afternoon, having had her lunch and being fully bedecked for a summer afternoon, the Princess would shut the door behind her and leave her house, slamming the green shutters tight one after the other from the outside. She would walk to the tramway station and there either hire a carriage or take the tram two stations up to Sporting where her mother lived and where the entire family was about to have coffee, before setting out for the Sporting Club.

These were the choicest hours of her life and she never let anything interfere with them—not her health, when it failed her, nor anyone else's. It was then, just after lunch, that my mother would take me to her mother's.

Often, a neighbor, friends, Aunt Flora, or others would sit

on the balcony outside of the Saint's dining room, and everyone would talk quietly under the delicate shade of a striped awning, hardly a breeze fluttering, with sunlight shifting so slowly that it could be hours before everyone would pick up their chairs and move to an adjacent balcony to resume conversations filled invariably with gossip, tears, venom, and self-pity. When one of the women was moved to cry, she would do so softly, quietly, her face folded into her chest, holding a crumpled handkerchief against her mouth, not because she was ashamed of crying in front of the others, but so as not to wake up Monsieur Jacques, who did not like having his naps interrupted by women whom he lumped together dismissively in the category of *sales co-médiennes*, sobbing or no sobbing.

Thus the summer hours would linger, and the Sudanese boy servant, who had taken forever to bring out the rainbow assortment of sherbets, seemed to take yet another eternity to come back to clear the sticky dishes from the balcony. And even then, there were still so many more of these afternoon hours before dusk set in that, in Aunt Flora's words, Egypt had the longest hours in the world.

"How time passes," my grandmother would say in one of her unworried moments, thinking that this is how she wanted to end her days, with her friends, her family, her home, her piano, whiling away the hours in the peaceful glow of the noonday sun. This is what she meant by preparing herself for a sound old age, *une bonne vieillesse*. In her case, *une bonne vieillesse* did not just mean healthy, vigorous old age, free of ailments and worldly cares, with plenty of time to put her *things* in order and never ask *anyone for anything*; it had also come to mean the sort of old age that allows one to be taken by a friendly hand and, preferably in mid-sleep, ferried across to the *other side*, having been spared both the shame and in-dignity of dying.

■

"There she is," one of the four or five women on the balcony would finally interrupt as soon as they noticed the Princess turning the corner of Rue Memphis and heading home. "Already six o'clock!" someone would exclaim. Instinctively, the Saint would tell me to go inside. "How are you today, madame?" she would shout, her voice flying from her balcony, eager as she always was to be the first to greet anyone—a habit that invariably left you feeling remiss by comparison. For couched in the joy that lit up her face whenever she saw you on the street was the mild, unspoken reproof that your tardiness in seeing her either betrayed a desire to avoid speaking to her or that, if she always noticed you first, it was only because she thought of you more often than you did of her.

This time she greeted her neighbor with exceptional zeal, precisely because, with me in the house, she had every reason to avoid greeting her. She had stood up too swiftly, her flustered expression belying her nonchalant pose against the banister. "Ah, I didn't see you, Madame Adèle," said the Princess, stopping exactly under the balcony. From within the living room, through the space between the open French window frame and the door jamb, I spied her familiar handbag and folded fan, watched her raise an awkward hand to block out the sun from her face. "And what are you doing later?" asked the Princess. "Me? Nothing. I was thinking of buying some cloth—my tailor is coming in a few days—but with this heat, I doubt I'll ever go now." "If you wish, I can walk with you." "I don't know, perhaps another time." They said goodbye.

"She always fights with her husband," whispered the Saint to one of her guests. "You should hear the horrible things they say to each other at night."

Then she would change her mind, and still confused and

dazed in her thinking, would shout out to the Princess, "*At-tendez*, wait," from the top of her balcony after the other had already crossed the street and was about to open the wrought-iron gate to her garden. "Maybe I will buy cloth after all. There are so many receptions this fall, and my clothes are so old, Madame Esther," she would lament, hinting for the nth time that she had not yet been invited to the Princess's mother's centennial ball that was to take place early that autumn.

"Do you want me to come upstairs, then?"

"No, no, I'll be down in a jiffy." Then, turning to my mother, she would say, "Wait until we're gone before leaving."

Five minutes later, the two *mazmazelles* could be seen hobbling down the street toward the Camp de César station, one with an unusually wide-rimmed hat, the other carrying a folded fan in one hand, her handbag and a white glove in the other, chattering away in the language that had brought them together and which, despite their repeated reminders to themselves and everyone else in the world that they had absolutely nothing else in common, despite their rivalry, their barbs, their petty distrust of one another, would always rescue a friendship that remained close until the very, very end.

■

The Saint's conversation was mostly plaintive, with a repertory of unflagging complaints: her health, her son, those daily reminders of unrest and turmoil in Egypt, the servants, who robbed her down to the last tablespoon of sugar, and her daughter, my mother, whose deafness had robbed her of the best years of her life. Since she was always scattered and vague in her speech, once the mood for complaining had set in, she would digress from one woe to another, weaving a never-ending yarn filled with subplots in which the principal villains were her ailments, heartaches, and humiliations, with herself cast in the role of the hapless victim fending off adversities as best she could, a medieval martyr tied to a post surrounded by advancing dragons—all of it leading up to the gallstones that would drive her out of bed at night with never a soul to complain to except the wind on her balcony, which was where she sat all night, staring at an emptied Rue Memphis, heeding the tick of the pendulum in the hallway with its occasional, subdued gong announcing, as she always feared it might, that it was still very early, and that the hours would crawl into dawn before she heard the quiet, welcome steps of Mohammed coming in through the service door. For now, there was just the stillness and the tireless caterwauling, rising and subsiding in waves, as glinting cats' eyes flitted about in the dark, crossing Rue Memphis, turning toward her balcony with defiance and suspicion, followed by a limping *chienne* whom everyone feared. "My nights," she called them.

"I know," said the Princess, who would try to steer her neighbor clear of unhappy thoughts, which wasn't so difficult, for just as the Saint was known to drift from one shoal to the other, with some steering she could be made to sway into the opposite direction and seek out cheerful islands in the sun— as though what ultimately mattered to her when she spoke was not so much her inventory of woes and heartaches as the right to digress, to lose her thread, to say what came to mind, which is exactly what everyone, particularly her husband, never allowed her.

■

Sometimes, in the middle of the night, while she sat alone on her balcony, nursing the gallbladder pain in her side—years before they met over red mullet—the Saint would watch the lights suddenly go on in the veranda across the street, and out would come the Princess wearing a bathrobe, carrying a large cup in one hand, with something like a flat hot-water bottle in the other, followed by my grandfather, his hair undone, staggering about the porch till his unsteady hand grasped the banister and he dropped into an armchair.

Facing one another across Rue Memphis, my grandparents-to-be would sometimes wonder what secret ailment kept the other awake, for neither dared speak, much less inquire into the other's health by way of neighborly conversation during the day.

"It would have been so indiscreet," said the Saint when asked by the Princess's husband why she had never even waved at night.

"I'm a refined woman," she added with mild apology in her voice.

"*I'm a refined woman,*" he mimicked and right away would slip in a word or two in Ladino. "Sit here and don't move," he said, himself seized by the intimacy that had sprung up between the two women. "You are one of the very few people here who speak Ladino well. The others belong to my wife's family, and they're too stuffy to speak *real* Ladino. Do you think I'll let you go now that I've found someone to speak with?"

Phrases like "sit here and don't move" set the tone for a friendship that was to last until the day my grandfather died —he always pretending to want to shock her, she pretending to tolerate someone who was too much of a scalawag to be taken seriously, and the Princess, always fast to find fault with her husband's manners, forever eager to shield Madame her neighbor from her husband's wanton humor. It was an easy familiarity that came as much from the city and the world where they were born as from the language they spoke in it. To the three who had discovered one another, Ladino spoke of their homesickness for Constantinople. To them, it was a language of loosened neckties, unbuttoned shirts, and overused slippers, a language as intimate, as natural, and as necessary as the odor of one's sheets, of one's closets, of one's cooking. They returned to it after speaking French, with the gratified relief of left-handed people who, once in private, are no longer forced to do things with their right.

All had studied and knew French exceedingly well, the way Lysias knew Greek—that is, better than the Athenians—gliding through the imperfect subjunctive with the unruffled ease of those who never err when it comes to grammar because, despite all of their efforts, they will never be native speakers. But French was a foreign, stuffy idiom and, as the Princess herself would tell me many years later, after speaking French for more than two hours, she would begin to salivate. "Spanish, on the other hand, *réveille l'âme*, lifts up the soul." And she would always slip in a proverb to prove her point.

The Saint and the Princess met at least twice a day, once in the morning on their way to the market, and once after the Princess had come back from her sisters. Since her husband was rarely in his billiard hall after six, all three would regularly have tea in the Princess's garden, under an old linden tree whose perfume filled the late afternoon air until it was time to move indoors, where more tea was served.

The Saint's husband, a Jew born in Aleppo who spoke no Ladino, would often return from work and peek through the wrought-iron fence into the arbor. Sometimes, having opened the gate to the Princess's garden and made his way past the guava trees, Monsieur Jacques would look through the living room window and knock at the glass door with something of a grudge. "It is time to go home," he would tell his wife after perfunctory pleasantries with the owner of the pool hall. "Just when we were beginning to enjoy ourselves," someone would say. "Spanish, Spanish," the Aleppid would mutter as he and his wife crossed Rue Memphis on their way home, "always your damned Spanish," while she apologized for not being home yet, trying to explain to a man whose native tongue was Arabic why she had tarried past her usual hour.

"But it's only a quarter to seven."

"I don't care. By eight o'clock I want to have supper."

"But Mohammed is cooking it at this very moment," she protested. "What's the matter with you?"

"What's the matter? I'll tell you *what's the matter*. I don't like having to come looking for my wife in another man's house, that's what." He was working himself into a temper, and the more he felt his anger rise, the more he was convinced he was right.

Monsieur Jacques was the type of husband who was jealous of his authority, not of his wife, just as he loved his comforts, not those who provided them. He despised Ladino because everything about it conspired to exclude him from a world whose culture was foreign to him, as much by its customs and sounds as by its insidious niceties and clannish etiquette. The more his wife delighted in speaking it, the more repulsive it became, and the more it pleased her to remind him—as her father had reminded her to remind him—that Arabic may have been Arabic, but Spanish was always going to remain Spanish!

To him Ladino was a form of cackling, and he called his neighbors' home a chicken coop, a *poulailler*, referring to them as the "owners" of the "henhouse," not knowing that they had come to regard his inability to enter into their world with the stately arrogance of erstwhile Ottoman masters. "Syrian hypocrite" and "dirty Turk" were bandied about behind everyone's back, all of which inevitably devolved late one Sunday afternoon, as both men were returning from their respective cafés, into a face-to-face confrontation in which the degenerate *turc barbare* called the *juif arabe* a "dirty, scoundrel Jew." Stunned, the bicycle shop owner, who was quite devout, said thank you, thank you, which was how the insulted taught the insultor a lesson in good manners, reminding the pool hall owner that he was truly tempted to insult him back but had decided otherwise, seeing that the Turk's own wife, as the entire neighborhood could hear clearly enough when the Princess lost her temper, did so better than anyone else in the world.

Everyone was sufficiently hurt and shamed, including the Princess, who found herself implicated in a quarrel that should have stayed strictly between the men. Monsieur Jacques vowed never to set foot *chez les barbares*, Monsieur Albert thanked him for staying out of people's homes, and both resolved never to say *bonjour* whenever they happened to meet on Rue Memphis. Only the Saint was left untouched, though she was the most perturbed of the four, and would continue to do everything to bring about a reconciliation between both families. "You may say whatever crosses your mind when you're angry, Monsieur Albert," she chided, a few days after the incident, "but that—never! Never!" she repeated, her nether lip quivering, her eyes welling up. Her simple, stainless soul had peered into an ugly, scurrilous world from which her strict upbringing had always protected her.

"But he didn't mean anything by it," the Princess said to Monsieur Jacques, trying as well to repair the damage. "Do you think the kettle means anything when it goes about calling other kettles black? How could it if it's a kettle itself?"

"*How could it*, madame? Easily. First, by forgetting it's black. Then by forgetting it's a kettle in the first place—which it should be proud of being, considering such kettles don't survive five thousand years unless there's a good God watching over them. And let me tell you something else, Madame Esther: any kettle that slanders its own kind is no kettle worthy of my home, and certainly not of God's kitchen!"

"Monsieur Jacques, don't get carried away now. I was only

speaking about a sixty-year-old man who is very sick and to whom life has been good in such small doses you'd think God's kindness was squeezed out of an eye dropper. He is a very unhappy and bitter man. His is an old kettle with hardly a whistle left to it."

"The whistle is quite intact, thank you very much," said the infidel Turk when the Saint reported this conversation to him and, as usual, was lured into playing cards with him. "My wife should be the last to judge such things, seeing she is the most unmusical woman in the world."

"But she loves to hear me play the piano," the Saint responded.

"I wasn't talking about piano music."

The Saint paused.

"Oh, I see," she said.

"No, you don't," he was about to reply but caught himself and said, "You see through everything, don't you, down into the most hidden recesses of the heart. And yet you never let on that you do. Meanwhile you've figured us all out, you with that dangerous *flair* of yours." To which she replied with her favorite little apothegm. "I may not be learned, Monsieur Albert, but I am sharp, sharp enough to see that you are poking fun at me right now." She sorted out cards and produced a winning combination. "Thank God I can win at cards, for otherwise you would think me a real dolt."

"Madame Adèle, where were you when I was a young man?"

"Monsieur Albert, don't speak like that. God gave each of us the life we deserve. You yours, and me mine."

"*You yours, and me mine,*" he mimicked as he shuffled the cards. "Do you think we can persuade Him to reserve a berth for you in my cabin when it's time to take the long journey?"

"When the time comes for that, I want to return to my parents."

"Not to Monsieur Jacques?"

"Monsieur Jacques has given me his life. His afterlife he can give someone else."

She pondered her cards a moment. "Will your wife be joining you in the afterlife?" she said with a lambent tremor on her lips, averting her eyes.

"Jealous as she is—"

"Who, your wife? How little you know women, Monsieur Albert."

"And how little you know my wife! She is so spiteful that if she were to die before me, she would immediately send for me so as never to allow me to forget I was ever married to her."

Indeed, the Princess's jealousy had nothing to do with love. The more she disliked her husband, and the more he fled from her, the more she was afraid of losing him. She was a model of dutiful solicitude because she wished him dead in small doses every day—which is how he loathed her, with the scrupulous devotion of weak, unfaithful husbands. She was attentive to his minutest needs: his specially brewed coffee in the morning, his ration of spinach pastries at noon, her special consommés for his special rice, the dried fruit sauce for his lean meats, his lightly starched shirts and neatly pressed handkerchiefs whose creases she was forever smoothing; down to the way she would decorate his plate with assorted cheeses, dips, and olives when it was time for his raki at night—in all this, she was the most punctilious of wives, begrudging him nothing, yet with every gesture reminding him that she had brought nothing into his life save those things he had never asked for. Ironically, he had far greater need of her love—of which she had some—than she had of his—of which there was none.

"You should never say such things about her," said the Saint, who was always eager to come to anyone's defense, partly because she was kind and didn't like to encourage slander, but also because her little rebukes always seemed to force people to intensify their original indictments of others.

"She's been the perfect wife for you: your cook, your maid, your nurse, your seamstress, your barber, your mother even. How many times has she saved you from certain ruin? She's the most intelligent woman on Rue Memphis."

"I know," he said turning to the Saint with doleful sarcasm in his eyes. "I know. God gave her the biggest brain in the world. But he gave her nothing else. In her company even an iceberg would catch cold."

At that moment the Princess returned from her daily visit with her siblings. "How could you two be playing cards in the dark like this?"

"Romance," explained the husband without looking up.

"But didn't you hear the news?"

"What news?"

"The war is over."

■

To celebrate the armistice, the Princess, who had just walked in with Madame Dalmedigo, decided to improvise *a real tea*, with meringue, fig and date jams, petits fours, and homemade biscuits, which she kept under lock and key in one of the many cupboards in the pantry. Another neighbor, Arlette Joanides, who was walking past their veranda with her daughter Micheline, was stopped, told of the news, and summarily invited for tea. Half an hour later, Aunt Flora, her mother, Marie Cantacouzenos, and Fortunée Lombroso, still later joined by Maurice Franco and Liliane Arditi, had come also —so that, when Monsieur Jacques arrived home from work, he was informed by his daughter that her mother was still visiting across the street. "Then go fetch her and tell her, once and for all, that her place is here"—indicating their dark and empty living room—"and not there," pointing to the henhouse. The families were back on speaking terms, but there always remained a certain *froid* between the men. The eighteen-year-old daughter, who had been reading a novel, slipped a cardigan over her shoulders, rushed downstairs, and in a second was ringing at their neighbor's door. "I've come to tell my mother that my father wants her to come home now."

"Come in and don't be silly. Where are we, in the Middle Ages?" cried the Princess, who by now had learned to understand the deaf girl's speech. "We're having tea and playing cards, come in."

The young girl came in but continued to linger near the doorway.

"Your father wants me to be home, doesn't he?" asked the Saint as soon as she caught sight of her daughter standing awkwardly outside the living room.

The girl nodded. The Princess thrust a cup and saucer in the girl's hands, which she accepted absentmindedly.

"A real tyrant, that's what he is," said the Princess's husband.

"You men are all tyrants," rejoined Arlette Joanides.

"And what are women, then?" he asked, turning to Monsieur Franco.

"To marry men like you one has to be a fool," said one of the women.

"Anyone who marries is a fool," said the Princess's husband. "But those who stay married after realizing their mistake are criminally stupid."

"Stop these roguish airs and play," snapped the Princess to her husband.

"Is what I say false?" he asked the young girl who was now sitting next to her mother.

She made no response.

"How like a woman. Doesn't answer when it's not convenient."

"All this banter about women!" said one of the women, "but when you need us to hem a sleeve so you can go out and impress your twopenny waitresses, you come crawling to us. Marriage!"

"Marriage, indeed!" the Princess's husband jumped in. "Even life sentences are commuted. But marriage, you have to die first before they loosen that noose."

"Oh, stop all this nonsense and play your hand," said the Princess.

At that moment the doorbell rang.

"Will someone open the door?" asked the Princess. The Saint glanced at her daughter and signaled to her to open the door. The girl did as asked and found a man standing there, staring at her.

"Yes?" she asked.

For a moment he started to smile. Then he asked if Madame Something-or-other was in.

He didn't make out what she said, but she motioned him to wait on the landing. Then, before he knew it, she shut the door in his face and rushed to tell the Princess there was a man asking to see someone.

"A man?" she started.

When the Princess finally stood up and opened the door she burst out laughing. "But it's my son," she shouted. "Your daughter wouldn't let him in," she said, turning to the Saint. Everyone laughed.

The girl blushed repeatedly.

"I'm sorry," she said.

"But don't worry, dear, he tricked you, that's all," said the Saint to her daughter.

The Princess apologized again for her son's behavior, while

the girl, probably to make up for her gaffe, silently offered to take his raincoat. Then the girl realized she did not know where to hang it and gave it back to him, smiling apologetically without saying a word. Unlike her father, he did not remove his jacket together with his raincoat so as to hang both on the same hanger. He kept his jacket on, checking his watch twice in the space of five minutes, tucking it back into his vest pocket, looking very pleased with himself.

"Who's winning?" he asked.

"Me, of course," replied Madame Lombroso.

The servant brought the young man tea, and he took it, turning to the newspaper that was hanging on the arm of the sofa.

"You heard?" asked his mother.

"Yes, I heard. It means the British army won't be buying from us any longer. Not exactly thrilling news."

"Always looking at the darker side of things," said Arlette Joanides.

"It's a sign of intelligence, madame," said the Saint, coming to his defense.

The girl sat quietly next to the Saint, looking over her mother's shoulder while the mother fanned out her cards. Once in a while the young girl would remind her that her father had sent for her. "I know, I know," her mother would answer, as though trying to stave off an unpleasant thought.

"See what happens when you marry?" said the Princess's husband, all the while staring at his new hand. "You can't even play cards." Then, as an afterthought, he added, "Or maybe all you can do is play cards."

"Play," came his wife's rebuke.

"No, no, let him be as bitter as he wants, that won't change the fact that he's losing," Aunt Flora taunted.

"Losing to you never makes one bitter," he replied without

lifting his head. "But losing to her," he indicated the Saint, "is a devastating affair."

"Because he thinks I'm stupid," said the Saint. "Let him think whatever he pleases. I may not be learned, but I'm very sharp, and I'll show him who's stupid tonight."

"With your luck tonight, it's no great feat to appear a genius," he added.

"Luck and a few other things as well." The Saint indicated her nose.

"Ah, yes, the nose. The nose, ladies and gentlemen!"

"Let him rant all he wants—but am I listening to him? No."

"I would come to my mother's defense if I were you," said the Princess's son to the Saint's daughter.

The girl lifted up her face, smiled politely, and shook her puzzled head as if to say it was not her place to speak on such matters.

"Such discretion," commented the son after all the guests had left that evening. "Never a misplaced syllable, always sweet, and so very gentle. Where have they been keeping her all these years?"

"Don't you know Syrian Jews?" his father asked, helping his wife clear the cards off the table. "Stealthy to the bone, every one of them, including her, don't you worry."

"She's serene and priceless, she is," added the Princess. "And rich too. Her father's in bicycles."

"She's stunning," continued her son.

"Stunning or not, it still wasn't kind of you to play that nasty trick on her at the door. You should have apologized."

"But I did apologize. So I played a little trick on her—"

"It *would* be just like you not to have noticed," she said.

"Noticed what?" he asked.

"Noticed that she's deaf."

"But I spoke to her—"

"Deaf all the same. That loud voice you hear from across the street is hers."

The son looked totally bewildered. His mother watched him and, reading his mind, hastily added, "Stay away. She's a good girl."

Soon someone rang at the door; it was the friend her son had been expecting for more than an hour.

"They're celebrating at the French Consulate tonight. I've been invited."

"But I haven't."

"It's all right, I'm inviting you now. Hurry. Everyone is celebrating."

"Won't it be too crowded, though?"

"Of course it will be too crowded, come on."

■

When he returned late that night, my father wrote in his diary that he had *finally* met *her.* He did not portray her as the woman of his dreams, nor as the most beautiful, nor did he describe any of her features. Superstitious as ever, he even avoided mentioning her name. She was simply and so clearly *her* that the need to capture her on paper or to probe the more elusive aspects of her personality proved too elaborate a task for the man who had merely written: *I want to think of her.* He did not write what he felt upon first setting eyes on her or what he thought of each time he caught his mind drifting toward her. He merely described her gray skirt and maroon cardigan and the way she crossed her legs when she sat behind her mother, the skin of her knee pressed against the edge of the card table as she kept her eyes glued to her mother's cards. At one point she had smiled when she caught him looking at her, a kind, indulgent smile filled with languor and mild apology.

She tapped him on the shoulder later that evening on the crowded patio of the French Consulate. People brimmed over into the garden and onto the street, where the city's French, Greek, Jewish, and Italian youth were gathered about in a chaos of standing bicycles and car horns, singing. Everyone had come to celebrate. The same, it appeared, was happening farther off at the Italian and British consulates.

"You're not dancing?" she asked, when he turned around. He couldn't understand a word she said.

"Isn't it too crowded?" he said, thinking she had asked him to dance. Do the deaf dance? he thought, conjuring a grotesque picture of a waltz danced like a tango.

"It's such a wonderful evening," she said. She was wearing a sleeveless white cotton dress, a thin necklace, and white shoes, her ruddy tanned skin glistening in the evening light. With a touch of makeup on, and her wet hair combed back, she looked older and more spirited than the shy neighbor's daughter who all during her visit earlier that evening had kept her schoolgirl eyes riveted to her pleated skirt and her mother's cards. There was even a suggestion of self-conscious elegance in the way she carried herself, holding her champagne glass with both hands, her elbows almost resting on her hips.

Yet the absence of stockings and a handbag and the white outline of what must have been a missing man's watch on her tanned wrist betrayed a hastily dressed or vaguely under-dressed quality, as if after spending all day at the beach, with barely a few minutes to make it to the ball, she had put on the first thing that came her way without drying her hair or feet. Her toes were probably still lined with sand. Somewhere, he thought, watching the dimmed evening lights play off the liquid sheen of her white gabardine dress, was a wet bathing suit, hurriedly taken off and left crumpled on a wooden bench in a friend's cabin.

"Did you come all by yourself?" he asked, making sure he was facing her when he spoke.

"No, with friends." Perhaps she wanted to dance.

"Would I know them?" he asked.

"No, but I'll introduce you," she said, not thinking he had no interest, taking his hand as she threaded what seemed an endless path through the crowd until they reached the other end of the large terrace, where a group of young men was waiting for her. One of them, leaning against the balustrade, was holding a maroon cardigan very much like the one she had worn earlier in his parents' home. Was he holding it for her, or had she borrowed it earlier that day and given it back to him? She made the introductions, describing how she had kept her neighbor's son waiting outside his own home. Everyone laughed—not at her error, this time, but at the way she had closed the door in his face.

"She's done much worse," said one of them.

"We're leaving," another broke in. "People are waiting for us at the British Consulate."

"Want to come?" she asked.

He hesitated.

"You might enjoy it." She smiled again.

"Oh, I don't know."

"Another time, then."

Turning to the young man who had been holding the cardigan, she motioned for the car keys.

"No. I'm driving," he replied.

"My car, I drive," she said peremptorily.

My father followed them mechanically to the end of the garden. She opened the door to her car, got in, leaned all the way across to unlock the other doors for her passengers, and then rolled down her window with jerky, determined motions, one foot still resting on the pavement as she fumbled with the keys. "My respects to your mother," she said as she closed the door and started the engine.

Without budging, he watched the car silently roll out from the consulate grounds, inching its slow, quiet way through the milling crowd and the parked cars and the row of tall palm trees dotting the alleyway, gliding further downhill until, before even reaching the gateway, it took a bold, accelerated turn past the gatekeeper's hut and suddenly shot outside the compound toward the Corniche.

All that remained of her as he stood on the spot where her car had been was the memory of that white satin shoe resting on the pavement, tilting sideways as she struggled to unlock the other doors, then resting back on the gravel as she searched in the dark for the key to the ignition. Perhaps, before closing the door, she had even thought of leaving her shoe behind.

And perhaps she had. For later that night, when he suddenly found himself unable to think of her, or when he felt the memory of her features starting to fade from his grasp, like an anthropologist reconstructing an entire body from a mere bone fragment he would think of that shoe, and from the shoe work his way around her foot, and from her foot, up her legs, her knees, her gleaming white dress, until he had reached her lips, and then, for a fleeting instant, would coax a smile on a face he had been seeing for years across the street but had always failed to notice.

■

A few days later, early one Sunday morning, he saw her walking past his garden.

"Where are you going?" he asked.

"To the beach," she replied, pointing to the north. "Are you coming?"

"Maybe. Who are you going with?"

"No one."

"Wait, I'll get my bathing suit."

They arrived early enough to swim, lie on the sand, talk, and then leave just in time to avoid the churchgoers, who started to arrive after Mass. On their way back, they stopped at a small pastry shop, where he bought her a cake and a lemonade. She had an ice cream as well. She said next time it would be her turn to pay. Amused, he repeated "Next time." When they reached Rue Memphis, they stopped at her doorstep. He waited for her to disappear into the dark, sunless entrance, stood awhile there, then crossed the street, opened the front door to his parents' home, and, to his surprise, saw that he was still in time for breakfast.

At about two-thirty in the afternoon, when the sun started pounding on the veranda floor and he was wondering whether to nap for a few hours or take a chair out under the trees and read a Russian novel there until dark, his mother, looking quite flustered and surprised, rushed out to tell him that Madame Adèle wished to speak with him on the telephone.

Whatever did she want with him, he wondered? And why the telephone? Then he remembered. Would she really have the bad taste to ask him never to presume to take her daughter to the beach again? Would she use that horrible expression "to compromise my daughter"? He began to regret that fateful moment when he had seen her walking holding a large blue-green towel inside of which she had neatly wrapped her bathing suit. Why did mothers have to meddle in the affairs of their daughters, and what could the two mothers have been saying to each other before summoning him to the telephone?

His throat tightened.

"Hello," he said, a cold, leaden weight sitting on his chest.

"Hello, am I speaking to Monsieur Henri?" said the voice at the end of the line.

"Yes, madame."

"Monsieur Henri, this is Madame Adèle, Gigi's mother, calling."

So he was right after all. Might as well sit down, he thought, knowing it would ruin his day now. The woman was clearly about to start an admonitory tirade of the kind parodied so well in English movies. Who knows in what benighted, prudish cell of the Dark Ages these people still lived. Her father, it was rumored, prayed every morning and had even disowned his son for marrying a Catholic girl. Daintily, the Saint cleared her throat again.

"I am calling because of my daughter. She asked me to ask you if you wished to go to the movies with her this afternoon."

"This afternoon?" His voice was quavering.

"Yes, this afternoon. It is somewhat last-minute of her. But that's how she is."

"This afternoon," he mused.

"Yes, this afternoon."

"And at what time this afternoon?"

"Let me ask her."

There was a moment of silence.

"At three, to be exact." He heard mother and daughter conferring in whispers.

"What did she say?" he asked.

"She said she'll understand perfectly if you cannot." Another moment's silence elapsed.

"Tell her I can be ready in five minutes. How long will she need?"

"Oh, she's ready now." Again mother and daughter whispered at their end of the line.

"She thought you'd enjoy seeing *Gaslight*. Personally, I think it is a grotesque movie, but whoever asked an old lady like me?" giggled the mother.

"But hasn't she already seen it?"

"No."

The film was playing at a small neighborhood theater not far from Rue Memphis. In front of the ticket booth, he found her waiting for him with her glasses in one hand and two tickets in the other. "I only wear them for reading," she explained, "and I need to read the subtitles."

Later, on their way home, she looked up at her living room window and saw that it was dark. "My mother must be at your mother's."

He opened the gate, and together they walked past the arbor where he knew he would have been sitting all by himself till now, reading Tolstoy until it got dark, hoping—as he always did on Sunday evenings—to avoid meeting his father, who always urged him to put down his books and go out and "live" for a change. "All these books, and all these clothes, and all these pipes, but never a woman on Sundays!" the old man would jeer. No doubt, on seeing him with the girl tonight, his father would have stepped out into the balcony and whispered, "So, we're flirting with the neighbors now."

The girl said she would be willing to go out another time. When he asked which films she hadn't seen, she almost laughed, she had seen all of them.

■

"The girl is beautiful, but don't forget she is what she is," said his father three months later as they walked along the Corniche one evening.

"I know. And so?"

"Well, if it's going to be 'I know and so?' we're never going to be able to discuss this thing rationally. You see, not only does she have to live with her misfortune, but so will you. If it's marrying you want, there is always Berthe Nahas. She's beautiful, she worships you, she has money, and her father can set you up very, very nicely." His father itemized each of Miss Nahas's attributes on a different finger of his hand. "As for love, well, either it comes naturally, or it comes later, or it never comes at all, in which case she'll be busy with the children and you'll be busy elsewhere.

"There is also Micheline Joanides, Arlette's daughter. You saw the face her mother made when she saw you speaking to Gigi. Or Arpinée Khatchadourian. Christian, that's true, but at least she can hear."

"Not Arpinée," said the son.

"You're right. With her drooping, bloodshot eyes swimming like a pair of beets in white potato soup—you're absolutely right. Ugly outside, ugly inside."

"Whoever said I wanted to get married in the first place?"

"With the Saint's girl, you can only get married," said the father.

"I did see her with others, you know."

"They let her roam freely, but no one's fooled. They're miserly, bigoted, Arab-shantytown Jews imitating the fast-car, cocktail-lounge airs of Europeans. But they're Arabs through and through. He'll live in scrounging misery until the day of his daughter's wedding. Then he'll glow like a pair of patent leather shoes."

"I know what I'm doing."

"And suppose," said the father as they watched the waves break against the beaches of Ibrahimieh, "suppose you want to speak to her in the dark. I don't mean 'Pass me the glass of water,' but other things."

"She reads my mind better than anyone. I can't even lie to her."

"A good quality in a mistress, or in a mother. But in a wife?"

The son did not reply. He remembered his mother's cruel words. "She's a gem of a girl, but cripples I don't want."

The father took out his aging silver cigarette case, removed a small penknife from his pocket, and sliced a cigarette in two. "To smoke less," he explained. He was about to put the other half back into the case when he changed his mind and offered it to his son.

"And so," he said as he took his first puff, pensive and remote, letting his unfinished sentence trail about him like the smoke from his cigarette.

"Does Flora know about the bicycle queen?" asked the father.

"Yes."

"And what does she say?"

"What should she say?"

Flora had said almost nothing when he broke the news to her on their way home from her music school by tram one evening. "I should have known," she had said. "How silly of me not to have seen it." Then, with that note of smiling resignation with which she greeted joy in others' lives when there was so little of it in her own, she complimented him on his choice, and then, as if choking on her words, finally broke down: "Tell me one thing, though. I've played more music in your house than anywhere in the world, and I know how much it's meant to you—at least how much you claimed it did. And yet here you are with a woman who doesn't know what music is, who can't even hear it." She paused a moment. "I swore to myself I would never say this to you." He was about to mutter something in his defense when she broke in: "But why *her*?"

The temptation to blurt out something cruel or flippant was almost irresistible. Then he realized it was the question that had prompted his cruelty, not the woman asking it. "I don't know. I don't even think I know her well enough yet. But she knows me better than I know myself."

When he began to explain what he meant, he had used the word *marriage* to avoid the more obvious word *love*.

"Then it's worse than I expected," said Flora, with thwarted anger quivering on her smile. "I knew I should never have asked. I've already heard—and said—more than I should. I hope you'll forgive me."

As they approached the next station, she put the book she wasn't reading back into her bag and stood up. He looked surprised; this wasn't her station.

"I'm getting off here if you don't mind," she said. "I'll walk the rest of the way. I need to get some air."

She made her way down the crowded aisle, stepped down the tram stairs, and stood on the platform, looking meek and crestfallen, rummaging through her old purse for a match, while a man, wearing a *galabiya*, eyed her intently, clearly about to beg for a cigarette. A pang of sorrow raced through his mind, and he felt for her as he watched her looking at him with helpless submission in her eyes. Revenge always comes too late, he thought, and only after time, indifference, or forgiveness has evened the score.

"Then she was upset," said his father. "She'll never forgive you."

"When I wanted her, she wasn't sure; now that I'm taken, she wants me."

"You'll never understand women!"

"I understand enough."

"You understand nothing. You don't even understand men, for that matter, and certainly not yourself."

He tossed his cigarette into the sea and finally said he was growing cold. He wanted to go home. Blown by the wind, an Arabic newspaper got caught between his feet. The old man struggled to disengage himself. "This dirty city and the dirty people who live in it," he said, watching his son's cigarette spiral like a weak flare and disappear into the water. "From thieving Arabs to Jewish grubbery, it had to be the daughter of a wheel merchant." Then he chuckled to himself. "At any rate, when it comes to marriage, things always turn out for the worst."

■

A few days later, and after several family rows on the other side of Rue Memphis as well, the Saint began to experience terrible pains in her side. Dr. Moreno came to see her and, on his orders, she was taken to the hospital, where they gave her the choice of having her entire gallbladder or some of its stones removed. In typical Levantine fashion, she deferred the decision to her husband. He was for removing the whole thing. "I want to return to my parents, that's all I want, Monsieur Albert," she kept saying.

"I want to go away and be far from everyone and everything," she said a few mornings later when neighbors flocked in one by one to her hospital room only to find that she might not be operated on after all. "See, even operating won't help," she concluded. "Oh, let me put an end to a life that started on the wrong foot."

"But all lives start on the wrong foot—" Albert remonstrated.

"Stop speaking nonsense, both of you," said the Princess. "The important thing is to rest."

"Yes. To rest, madame, to rest for a very long time, believe me," replied the Saint.

The next day, when the Princess's husband went alone to see her early in the afternoon, she lay quietly in her room, the glaring afternoon sun blocked by a thick curtain someone had pulled across while she was sleeping.

"Am I disturbing you, Madame Adèle?" he whispered as he pushed open her door and stuck his head in.

"Who? You? Never, *mon cher*. Come in, and sit here."

He sat next to her bed, and in silence they stared at each other awhile, resigned sorrow limned on their features.

"So there," she sighed, crossing her hands.

"So there, indeed."

"I'm waiting," she sighed.

"You're waiting. Did they say how long—" he asked.

"They won't talk, but things don't look good at all, worse than not good."

"So this is it, then."

"I'm afraid so. This is it. Frankly, Monsieur Albert, I don't at all feel like dying today."

"Courage, ma chère, courage."

"But, Monsieur Albert," she exploded, "I hope you don't feel obliged to agree with everything I say simply because I say it."

"No, no, believe me, I think things are very serious indeed. You don't look well at all. Even Esther said so yesterday."

"You think so too, then? But, Monsieur Albert," she protested after another pause, "I'm not ready to die."

"Whoever is, *ma chère amie*, whoever is?" A moment of silence elapsed.

"Monsieur Albert, I don't want to die."

"Do stop fussing like a child. There's nothing to fear. You'll die and you won't even know it."

"Oh, Monsieur Albert, stop stoking death on me. I said I didn't want to die."

"Well, don't die, then."

"You don't understand. I want to die, but not just yet."

"After the wedding, you mean."

There was instant silence.

"How well you know me, Monsieur Albert."

"All too well. You should have lived with me, I tell you,

instead of clawing your way through life like an old crustacean in a fish tank."

The Saint giggled at the metaphor.

"Gallbladder, my eye," grumbled her husband a few evenings later when he came to visit her after work only to find the hospital room turned into a regular salon. "All this pain, the moaning, and the sleepless nights, and the doctor, and the ambulance, and the hospital, and what does it all add up to: giggling. *Quelle comédienne!* Now, my poor mother, may she rest in peace, she really suffered from gallstones. She died of it, poor soul. And without so much as uttering a squeak. In those days they didn't have painkillers the way we do today —in those days you made a fist, clammed your mouth tight, and suffered in silence so as not to wake up the children."

"The important thing is to eat well," added the Princess.

"But I've lost all my appetite. I eat so little."

"Then why do you keep putting on so much weight?" her husband interrupted.

"Nerves, that's why. You've been in this room two minutes and already I feel the pain starting."

■

She returned to that same hospital many times during the next ten years until 1958, the year she was to leave Egypt, each time dreading the operation she feared might be the end of her. And when, finally, she had her gallstones removed under emergency conditions, it was an Egyptian doctor at the Jewish hospital who performed the operation. Luckily, peritonitis was averted. Her longtime Jewish surgeon, into whose hands she had entrusted her entire life, had been arrested, had his license revoked, and, it was rumored, would be tried as an Israeli spy.

By then she was in her sixties and was already beginning to lose her memory. Her head was propped up by pillows, and

I remember her wearing a shabby flannel bathrobe, a pearl necklace, and her aluminum bracelet, which she claimed helped her rheumatism. Her hair had thinned quite a lot by then and was matted on her head like a lopsided wig. She struggled to smile each time she looked at me. "This is the end, Madame Esther," she said when the Princess took me to visit her one spring morning.

"Not to worry. One more week and you'll be sitting with your daughter on your balcony, enjoying the sun as you always have and as you always will long after I and all of my siblings are gone."

"No, madame, you're made of steel," said the Saint, remembering how the Princess's husband had once complained that his wife's very skeleton was made of steel rods that clanked when she tossed in bed at night. "Besides, we all go when He wills us to go, no sooner, no later." The Saint assumed that characteristic pinched and pious little air of hers whenever she meant to put people in their place.

As we stood up to leave, the Saint remained in bed, producing a lank rosy hand which she placed gently on the back of my neck muttering a string of words in Ladino. Then, full of love, she bit my arm and kissed it, while I threw my arms around her.

"Don't I get a hug now?" interrupted the Princess rubbing my hair. Before she had time to finish her request, I had already put both arms around her and was hugging her very tightly, pressing tighter still, because I wanted not only to reassure the Saint that I was finally complying with her wish to love the Princess more, but also to tease her into thinking that, during her sickness, I had done just that. I waited for the Princess to unstiffen and yield to my embrace as the Saint had done on so many occasions. I wanted to hear her own litany of endearments, the accent of her sorrow, of her love, of her passion—and the less she responded, the more I stiffened my grasp. But she did not know this game and, in the end, all she did was utter a squeamish little cry, half giggle, half squeal.

"Look at all this love," she exclaimed, beaming with joy. "It's not good to love so much," added the Princess as she ran her fingers through my hair.

"I try to teach him this too, but he won't listen."

As the Princess had predicted, two weeks later the Saint was once again sitting on her balcony with her usual visitors, enjoying the late afternoon sun waning into splendid summer evenings. She swore she felt much younger, now that her Egyptian doctor had worked a miracle. "A generation ago he would have been no better than the boy servant bringing us tea on this balcony," she said. "Now he's brought me back to life. He speaks impeccable French. And you should see his office—sumptuous. Not bad for an Arab who is scarcely thirty years old. If he represents the new order here, well, *chapeau* to the new Egypt."

"Just wait until they're all in power. Then you'll see how the new Egypt will treat you, Madame Adèle," broke in one of her Greek neighbors.

"I don't care. This one is a true gentleman. I owe him my life. You'd be surprised, but ever since my operation, I've become quite philosophical. I thank God for everything He's given me; what I don't have, I don't miss, and what I can't get, I don't want. We are not rich, but we are comfortable; I've never loved Egypt, but life has been good here; and almost everyone I love comes to see me at least once a day. Never was I happier I didn't die."

■

"She should have died right there and then," said Aunt Flora twenty years later as she insisted on paying for our coffee somewhere near Ponte dell'Accademia. "For she died worse

than a dog's death, and in such squalor, you'd swear there
never was a God in heaven."

She collected the change but left the waiter no tip. "Because
they're impertinent *fannulloni*," she said. Then, as though to
apologize for the restaurant, she added, "I know the food isn't
very good here, but it's not bad, and I like to sit at this table
in the shade and listen to the water and let my mind drift."
She finally put away the toothpick she had been twiddling.
"Perhaps this is why I've chosen to live in Venice—because
no matter where you turn there's always water close by, and
you can always smell the sea, even if it stinks; because there
are mornings when I wake up and think the clock is turned
back and I'm on the Corniche again."

Summers were long in Venice, she said, and there was nothing she liked more some days than to take the vaporetto and
ride around the city, or head directly for the Lido and spend
a morning on the beach by herself. She loved the sea. I loved
it too, I said, reminding her that it was she who had taught
me how to swim.

I looked at her. At sixty-seven she had the same clear green
eyes I remembered and the same tapered, nicotine-stained fin-
gertips that could race across the keyboard when she played
the opening bars of the *Hammerklavier*. I had not seen her in
ten years, and for another five before that. We spoke about
Rue Memphis again.

"She wasn't a bad piano player at all. Her trouble was discipline. And memory. Memory especially. I, on the other hand,
have plenty of discipline; as for memory, there isn't a thing
I've forgotten. I can still remember the names of all the tramway stops from Ramleh to Victoria."

I took a paper napkin, unfolded it, gave her my pen and
asked her to write them down. She decided I might want those
of the Ramleh–Bacos line as well, so she jotted them too.

"Mind you, I remember the old names, not those newfangled, patriotic names which the new regime adopted: Independence Street, Freedom Square, Victory-this-and-that."

Our waiter, who had been scowling in our direction, turned his face elsewhere and was busily talking to a colleague from across a makeshift hedge separating our restaurant from another. When he sighted a hesitant tourist couple scanning our empty terrace, he went out to greet them and, before they had time to retreat, strong-armed them and asked them to please, follow this way.

She watched the sheepish tourists being escorted to the worst table on the terrace. "I do hate Italy sometimes," she added. "But then there are days when I wouldn't want to live anywhere else."

We crossed the bridge and made toward Campo Morosini. Except for occasional groups of young tourists braving the early afternoon heat that Sunday, Venice appeared deserted. The quiet piazza with its white marble and travertine masonries offered scant relief from the sun. Along its western edge, two establishments that were totally vacant at this time of day sported straw chairs neatly packed, three to a table, all of them baking under closed Cinzano umbrellas that studded the cobbled sidewalk. On the piazza, the shops were closed.

She bought me an ice cream.

"Do you need to buy souvenirs or things?"

I shook my head.

"Your mother spends all of her time buying gifts for everyone each time she visits me. I assumed you would too. How about books?"

"No. I came to visit you."

"You came to visit me," she repeated, visibly pleased anyone should do such a thing.

We threaded our way through the narrow, empty streets of Zattere while the sun, following an oblique path, cast an ochre-hued glow along the stuccoed fronts of the little buildings lining Calle del Traghetto. One could still make out the faint clatter of plates being washed after late Sunday family luncheons. Several corners later, we arrived at her home. She lived on the ground floor, though the place was sunken below street level. Like most Venetian apartments, hers was extremely small, and her bedroom, with its low ceiling and small window, had all the makings of a sparsely furnished monk's cell. On the nightstand was an old portable tape player surrounded by a scatter of cassettes: Callas and di Stefano, Wanda Landowska, Paul Anka. She could have been an undergraduate in a college dormitory. On her dresser I caught a picture that could only have been of me, though I had never seen it before. For a moment I was baffled to see that a part of me had traveled all the way to Venice and had been sitting in someone's bedroom for twenty years before I myself had finally come upon it.

Inside the only other room in her apartment sat two old grand pianos, side by side, leaving little space for anything or anyone else. I had to squeeze behind the first piano to reach the second. The room looked more stuffy yet, because the walls were lined with very old cork tiles. I could not tell how one would go about opening the window.

"I leave the room shut throughout the year. It stinks of cigarettes. But this is exactly how I learned to play. None of my students has ever complained. And if they did—"

She showed me the kitchen where she cooked, ate, wrote letters, read, watched television, corrected homework.

She began to clear the table.

"Can I help?" I asked.

"Sure, just tell me where you propose to put all of these papers." She dumped an entire bundle of brochures, flyers, scores, newspapers, and unanswered mail into my arms. I looked around and acknowledged defeat.

"On top of the first piano." I could tell she was happy.

"Meanwhile, I'll heat up some water and cook the gnocchi. I made them myself. I've also baked some vegetables. If there is one thing I know how to do," she said, kneeling down to light the stove with a match, "it's how to make good gnocchi." She tried another match.

"This may interest you," she said, still concentrating on lighting the stove. "It was your grandmother who taught me how to cook. I gave her piano lessons, she taught me how to cook. 'One day you'll need to cook a man a real meal, and piano music is all very nice, but men need *un bon biftek, vous comprenez ce que je veux dire*, Flora?' So she taught me Sephardi dishes which nowadays even Sephardim have forgotten how to cook. Fish, artichokes, lamb, rice, eggplant, leeks. And red mullet, of course."

At which we both chuckled.

"You may laugh, but your grandmother was no fool. She knew exactly how to manipulate people. And the person she manipulated best was the one everyone thought could easily outfox her. Letting her think she didn't know how to buy red mullet, when she, her mother, and her great-grandmother had been cooking them forever. Or letting her think she thought her a Frenchwoman, which she knew would tickle her no end, when, in fact, they had grown up in the same neighborhood in Constantinople. Or letting her think she was so inferior, and so humble, and so distracted, when all along she knew perfectly well what she was doing.

"To think that I was there with my mother on the very evening they met. That I was waiting to hear from him on the very day they decided to get married. That I, who should have been the first, was in fact the last to know.

"Here," she smiled, announcing dinner. "I've also prepared something I remember you liking years ago. I hope you haven't changed."

She apologized for the stainless steel knives with red and green plastic handles that clashed with the silk-embroidered tablecloth she had placed on top of an old kitchen table. In the thirty years since she had left Egypt, she had managed absentmindedly to throw all of her real silverware into the garbage, piece by piece. "The symbolic end of my brother's fortune," she said, referring to her inheritance from the Schwab. Only these five silver teaspoons remained—and that because she never used teaspoons, otherwise they too would have wound up at the bottom of the Canal Grande. "Five silver teaspoons," she repeated, as if this short sentence summed up the ledger of her life.

"Your father kept it secret from me for months," she said, returning to the subject of my parents. "I can't begin to tell you how shattered I was. I never showed it—I even became best friends with your mother—but it took me a long time, years, to get over it. Even now, there are still days when I think I never outgrew any of it. And days when I'd like to think that neither has he. You know, we were an odd match —we always left our doors ajar, but we never let each other in. We were right for each other, provided there were others to return to. Left to ourselves, we were always evasive, couldn't even stay alone together in the same room without feeling awkward and strained.

"Even today, I continue to live my life that way. I cross the street on the slant, I always sit in the side rows at concert halls, I am a citizen of two countries but I live in neither, and I never look people in the eye," she said, as I, conscious of her effort to do so now, averted my own. "I'm honest with no one, though I've never lied. I've given far less than I've taken, though I'm always left with nothing. I don't even think I know who I am, I know myself the way I might know my neighbor: from across the street. When I'm here, I long to be there; when I was there

I longed to be here," she said, referring to her years in Alexandria.

" 'You see, Flora,' the Saint used to say to me, 'you think too much, and you ask too many questions. In life one must put blinders on, look straight ahead, and, above all, learn to forget. *Débarrasser*. You cannot live and be your own pawnbroker.'

"As you see, I've only learned how to get rid of my silverware. That's all. All the rest is dutifully catalogued and neatly stowed away in the book I carry here," she said, pointing to her forehead. "I forget nothing—not the way things were, nor how I wished they might have been. I'm like old widows who spend hours sifting through objects they suspect may no longer mean much but which they continue to cherish because it takes more time to replace or discard them than to keep them clean." She was silent for a moment. "Perhaps I remember more because I've lived—and loved—far less than my years show."

She stood up, took down something that had been hiding on top of the refrigerator, and produced her surprise, a large Ottoman dessert made with goat cream called "bread of the palace."

"What is so pathetic, now that I think about it, is that forgetting is what the poor Saint did best of all. She forgot so much that in the end she forgot who she was. After the government seized her husband's assets in '58 and they were forced to flee the country, she arrived in France the most pitiful sight in the world: there she was, the *grande bourgeoise* of Rue Memphis—with her grandchildren, her pianos, her tea parties—standing at Orly airport as frightened and confused as a five-year-old child.

"Robert, who had gone to meet her, told me years later how lost she looked as she scanned the crowd for him, even after he came up to her and said, 'Mother, I'm here!' He tried to embrace her, but she kept pushing him away, declaiming, '*Mais je ne vous connais pas, monsieur*,' in that fine textbook French of hers. 'But it's me, Bertico,' he said."

Flora went on to tell me that when the Saint finally did recognize her son, all she did was touch his face and say he looked so old. Then she apologized and said it was because she wasn't wearing her glasses; she had forgotten them at home. But not to worry—she would send the boy servant to fetch them. Only then did Robert realize the extent of the damage. He had left her a beefy-armed woman who could walk about with a grandchild on each hip. Here was an unkempt, defeated old lady who couldn't even string together a coherent sentence. The airplane trip had been disastrous; she had cried the whole way.

When they arrived at the bus terminal in Paris and were waiting to get their luggage, my grandmother did the most unexpected thing: she bolted, wandered off. When Robert came back with a porter and the suitcases, he found his father totally beside himself. "What is it?" he asked. "Your mother's gone."

They immediately contacted the police. But it took them days. Eventually, they found her—at the opposite end of Paris, beyond the Porte de Clignancourt, without glasses, without dentures or underwear. How she had gotten there or what had happened to her during those seven days and nights we'll never know. In the hospital, she refused to speak French and, when she wasn't weeping, would mutter a few syllables in Ladino, saying she had gone back to Rue Memphis as a dog but found no one home.

"I'm told she complained of nothing," Flora continued. "She always said she was comfortable, that the nuns and nurses were kind to her. But she refused to eat. There were terrifying fights over food. At night she howled in her sleep, a long, plaintive, heartrending howl he says he will never forget. She would call for her mother and for her son. Then she would wake up, remember something, mutter a string of senseless words, and doze off again."

Silence filled the kitchen. I looked out the window and saw that it was night outside.

"I didn't know," I said.

"No one knew. Robert only told me years later." After a pause she asked, "And now, how about coffee?"

"Yes," I said. Then, trying to break the heavy silence that had settled over the kitchen, I asked at what time I should take the vaporetto that evening.

She said I had plenty of time. Besides, it depended where I wanted to take it.

"So, then, could we hear the Schubert now?" I asked like a boy who hadn't forgotten his promised treat.

"Is Schubert what you really want to hear?" she asked, alluding to my letter in which, to earn her forgiveness after not seeing her for so many years, I had written that I still remembered her Schubert on those warm summer afternoons on Rue Memphis. She wrote back saying that my grandmother had never liked Schubert. "But if Schubert is what you re-member, well, maybe we did play Schubert then." I wrote back saying it was the B-flat major sonata. "If you insist," she conceded. "Maybe I was practicing alone and you overheard it."

She probably continued to suspect I had made it up. I wasn't sure that I hadn't.

"At any rate, you'll hear Schubert the way I played him when the Germans stood outside Alexandria and everyone in the house thought the world had come to an end. I played it every night. It annoyed them at first, for they didn't know the first thing about music. But they came to love it—and then me—after a while, because Schubert stood like the last beacon in the storm, tranquil and pensive, an echo of an old world we believed we belonged to because we belonged nowhere else. At times it felt like the only thing standing between us and Rommel was a sheet of music, nothing more. Ten years later they took that sheet of music away. Eventually they took away everything else as well. And we let it happen, as Jews always let these things happen, because, deep inside, we know we'll lose everything we own at least twice in our lives.

"I played the Schubert on those nights because I knew that, for me, the war, terrible as it was, was no more than a pretext to avoid facing I'd botched up my life.

"I'll play it now the way Schnabel played it, because this is the way your grandfather, and then your father, heard me play it, and this is how my son, had I a son, would have heard me play it tonight. Sit here."

∎

I did not take the vaporetto at Zattere that night. Instead, I walked across the Dorsoduro to the Accademia. As soon as I reached the ill-lit floating platform, a beggar, the only soul in sight, told me that I had missed the vaporetto to the Lido. "*Bisognerà aspettare*, you'll have to wait," she said.

With a good forty minutes left, I decided to cross the wooden bridge back to Campo Morosini. The bridge too was empty, and, from where I stood, the adjoining Campo San Vidal, which led up to the church of Santo Stefano, was both dark and deserted. I sighted a rat slinking by on a sunken marble step along the canal, his grayish hair matted to his back, something deft and purposeful in the speed with which he waded through the shallow water and nosed his way through a crack.

"So she played her Schubert for you as well," they would say, the men snickering, though everyone would be pleased.

And I thought for a moment of the crowded apartment in Grand Sporting when the Germans stood outside Alexandria, and of all my uncles and aunts huddled there for protection and solidarity, listening to Flora's Schubert every evening after the BBC. "Stay after the others," she had told my father. "There is something I want to say to you."

I looked across to the station platform and saw the old beggar shuffle away.

I thought of Aunt Flora again, and of how she had come to Venice years ago, and why she had stayed here all by herself, her life *thrown away* because she never learned *to bounce back*, not after Germany, not after Egypt. And I thought of her during the war years in Alexandria, riding the tram with my father in the evening, giving small concerts in the city, and how they would walk back home along the Corniche at night, looking out into the dark sea, wondering why, with death so close, it was still so difficult to speak. And I thought of what they might say tonight, walking arm in arm after so many years along these dark and haunted alleys in Venice, where she would show him her favorite café at night, her favorite ice cream vendor, her favorite spot along the Dorsoduro from which to survey the city's starlit canal and watch one water-city summon up another, silent as they always were together, working their way through strands of time like captured shades on the Bridge of Sighs. Why had she bared her soul to me tonight?

As I walked ahead, the slate-blue pavement of Campo Morosini glistened in the dark night. Scirocco weather, I remembered. Nearing the piazza, I made out the fading lights of a trattoria about to close. A waiter with his collar open and necktie undone was rolling up a striped awning with a long pole crank; another was stacking chairs and taking them inside. Farther away, the two sidewalk cafés we had passed earlier in the afternoon were now crowded with tourists. Tall Senegalese peddlers, carrying large duffel bags, were busy winding up toy birds, which they sent flying above the piazza in full view of the tourists.

I left the piazza and returned to the station and for the first time that day made out the hollow sound of water lapping against the city. Soon after, an almost empty vaporetto arrived. Once inside, I made for the stern deck and sat on the rounded wooden bench along the fantail. Then the engine gave a churn, and a boatman released the knot. As soon as we began moving, I put both legs up on my bench, the way schoolboys ride the open-air deck on trams in Alexandria, staring at that vast expanse of night around me and at the gleaming silver-jade sweeps trailing in our wake in the middle of the Canal Grande as we cut our way deeper into the night, gliding quietly along the walls of the ancient arsenal like a spy boat that had turned off its engines or pulled in its oars. Up ahead, scattered light posts studding the lagoon tipped their heads above sea level, while the moonless city drifted behind me as I caught the fading outline of Punta della Dogana and further off the dimmed tower of San Marco looming in the late night haze. Roused by the searching beam of our vaporetto, splendid Venetian palaces suddenly rose from their slumber, one by one, lifting themselves out of the night like shades in Dante's hell eager to converse with the living, displaying their gleaming arches and arabesques and their glazed brocade of casements for a few glowing instants, only then to slip back into darkness and resume their owl-like stupor once our boat had passed.

After San Zaccaria, the vaporetto took a wide, swooping turn and headed across the lagoon toward the Lido, the boat doubling its speed, chugging away loudly, with a cool wind fanning our faces, easing the thick scirocco weather, as I reclined and threw my head back. So we've seen Venice, I thought, mimicking my grandfather's humor as I turned and watched the city sink into timeless night, thinking of Flora and of all the cities and all the beaches and all the summers I too had known in my life, and of all those who had loved summer long before I came, and of those I had loved and ceased to care for and forgot to mourn and now wished were here with me in one home, one street, one city, one world.

Tomorrow, first thing, I would go to the beach.

3

A Centennial Ball

At first, there would be a scuffle of words, someone shouting, another shouting back, then a moment of silence, the illusion of peace restored. And then it came.

For years my father had heard that scream break upon the day and rise above Rue Memphis and the daily clamor of Ibrahimieh, tearing its way out of powerful lungs like an ancient, spellbinding, ululating wail.

This, he would find out one day, was the howl of the deaf, when the deaf are in pain, when the deaf quarrel, when they scream, when words fail them and nothing comes out but this sputter of shrieks that sounded more like a fleet of buses screeching to a halt on a quiet beach-day Sunday than like the voice of the woman he had married.

People in the street referred to her as *al-tarsha*, the deaf woman, and, among the Arabs in the marketplace, everyone and everything in her household was known in relation to the *tarsha*: the deaf woman's father, the deaf woman's home, her maid, her bicycle, her car, her husband. The motorcycle with which she had won an exhibition race on the Corniche in the early forties and which was later sold to a neighbor continued to be known as the *tarsha's mutusikl*. When I was old enough to walk alone on the streets of Ibrahimieh, I discovered that I too was known as the *tarsha's* son. My Arab barber in Ibrahimieh—once Aleco's assistant, now the owner of Aleco's—always asked after my mother, never my father. Sometimes, on seeing me, street vendors, shopkeepers, or those idling about the cafés would discreetly raise an index finger to their ear. They were talking about my mother. But they might just as easily have pointed at their temples, for many confused the deaf with the insane. She had screamed at nearly all of them, and everyone knew her temper.

Some forgave and pitied her with the languid kindness of the Middle East. Others mocked the discordant, grating voice of the deaf, adding twisted faces to twisted hand signals, looking like gargoyles and village idiots. One day, in a crowded grocery shop, my mother caught a young Egyptian mimicking her speech. She could not tell what he was saying, but she recognized the derisive smile that crept over people's faces when they made exaggerated movements with their mouths. It was his insolent gaze as he smirked at her, all the while looking over toward his friends, that must have annoyed her. She stopped whatever it was she was doing, told me to stay put by the cash register, and without giving the young man time to blink slapped him twice on the face, very hard, and then, before he could recover, grabbed him by the head, threw him to the ground, and proceeded to beat him up, first with her fist, then with anything that came her way.

When she was finally pulled away from him, the young man's shirt was torn, and he was bleeding from the mouth, weeping like a child.

"Let's go home now," she said, as she turned and marched out of the store, not letting go of my arm.

The Princess, who heard of the incident, grumbled to my father that his wife behaved no better than the Arabs among whom she had grown up. "How will your son ever learn the right way to act if all he hears all day is her deaf yammering and constant brawling with Arabs?" Discharging a torrent now that she had spilled a few drops, she went on:

"In less than two months we'll be celebrating my mother's centennial, and I want him to know how to behave there. I don't want to introduce Madame Lord or Victoria Coutzeris to the son of a Jewish *tarsha*, understand?"

My grandmother was referring to another incident that had occurred a few days earlier. My mother had been haggling with a butcher when an argument eventually erupted between them. This was not the first time, and everyone in the butcher shop and surrounding stores put down what they were doing and came to watch, looking on as the deaf woman brought down meat prices and, once her price was met, changed her mind and bargained for a lower price still, the butcher screaming bloody murder, telling her never to come back, only in the end to lower his price again, muttering obscenities under his breath as he hacked at his choicest cuts of meat with the wrath of ten Achilles, hurling one steak after another onto the scale, finally wrapping it all up in the thick, gray paper, which she instructed him not to bloody with his dirty hands because her son, standing meekly nearby, liked to draw on it. The butcher, glad to see her leave, obliged with an extra piece of paper, as I slunk out next to my mother, fearing the worst once our backs were turned.

All I was aware of during supper that evening was the echo of the butcher's scream as he threatened to kill the Jewish bitch on the spot, followed by my mother's furious, dizzying shriek as she dared him—if he was man enough—offering to hand him the cleaver from his table. And then, a moment later, the burst of laughter as everyone made up, everyone feeling sorry for everyone else, she putting down the cleaver that she had grabbed in theatrical self-defense, he pointing to his ears, implying that if he had not gone ahead with the murder, it was only because of the affliction God had already visited upon her, because she was a good, pitiful woman after all, a *maskina*. This was the man who would one day weep and embrace her, and rock her in his arms, dirty bloodied apron and all, when she told him we were leaving Egypt.

But the sound of her shriek would not go away that night. It was an ugly, coarse, demented shriek, and no matter how I tried, no other thought, no conjured sound could quite muffle its persistent, frightful ring in my ears.

How I envied other boys their mothers, their sweet, hearing mothers who answered the telephone, who opened the door to you and always said something pleasant about your clothes, or about the day, or about a film everyone had seen. Mothers who met your teachers and didn't need an interpreter. Mothers who played the piano, who shook your hand and listened to what you said, and answered back in chiseled little sentences. Mothers who never brawled with servants, mothers who dismissed them instead, mothers who put you in your place with a few softly spoken words, darting, cutting words, not the yelp of a madwoman, mothers who expected to be apologized to, mothers who said "I love you" as though it were a compliment, not a claim, mothers you wanted to flaunt, not hide.

Louder and higher than most, my mother's voice would travel far, as when she shouted goodbye in the morning, looking out our window, while I boarded my school bus and stared the other way, pretending I hadn't heard her; or when she spotted me coming back from the beach, and, leaning over the veranda rail, screamed out my nickname, while the boys I had just befriended looked puzzled, no one knowing she was my mother, no one suspecting it was my nickname they had just heard, for one had to get used to her speech. I would look up, and smiling at something someone might have said, would use that smile as a way of greeting someone farther away who understood exactly why my smile seemed so vague, who had already forgiven me for it, and who on those summer afternoons when we sat in the dining room eating fruit because it was too hot to eat anything else would let out words of love no one understood, for they weren't even words, just sounds reaching far back into her childhood to a time when she couldn't even speak—half-words which she sometimes yelled out in the water when we swam together, her voice muffled by the sound of waves, thinned of its coarseness, kind as a seagull's.

■

Not knowing how to explain her voice when I introduced her to my friends, I would avoid greeting them altogether. At the movie theater during intermission, I would try to put some distance between us or wrest my hand free of hers, or suddenly stop talking to her when I caught sight of a familiar face from school—which I almost always did, since everyone in Alexandria went to the movies on Friday. Because I lacked the courage to say she was my aunt, all I could do when I spotted a classmate coming toward us was simply freeze, put a vague and absent look on my face and pretend I hadn't seen him.

As soon as the film was over, I always wanted to rush out of the theater, far from the crowded lobby, where people were milling around trying to decide where to go next. But my parents, instead of hurrying, always dawdled near their seats talking about the film or insisting I put on my sweater now, not later, or continuing to look under their seats for something my mother claimed she had dropped, invariably waiting for the aisles to clear before leaving, telling me to stay put, when all I wanted was to vanish.

Then the trembling started.

"Just look at him, he's shaking all over," she would say to my father as she'd help me slip my arms into a sweater. I could feel my chin quiver and my elbows stiffen. "It must be someone from school. He's seen someone from school again." My mother always read my thoughts, my fears.

My father would look on sternly, scanning the crowd for the face I was struggling to avoid. "You can't carry on like this. No one's going to bite you, you know."

"I know," I mumbled.

"Then what is it?"

I did not know. But the worst thing he could do was speak to me in that tone while people from school were within earshot.

"It's me he's ashamed of," my mother would conclude as she buttoned up her cardigan. "I just know it."

"Rubbish, no one is ashamed of you," my father would reply with a listless, exasperated look on his face, which was how he tried to defuse her anger each time, by affecting annoyance and fatigue.

"What do you know? You're ashamed of me too."

"Just lower your voice, will you please!"

" 'Just lower your voice'—what do I have to do, be mute as well?"

"Come," she would say, grabbing hold of my hand. "At least he doesn't know how to lie yet, which is more than I can say about you," she said, throwing a knowing look in his direction. With that, she stormed through the crowd, reaching the exit long before my father, muttering things to herself as people watched her cut through the throng waiting outside the theater for the six-o'clock show.

■

Everyone said I was her ears. Because she could not speak on the telephone, I had to make her calls. Sometimes, to avoid this task, I would lie, saying her friend's line was busy. To tease her, I would swear someone was ringing our doorbell, though I knew she knew I was lying.

My thoughts were her thoughts, just as her thoughts were my thoughts. When, frightened of the night, I touched her hand and woke her up, she knew what I was saying long before she had made out my lips in the dark. And I knew, by the way she laughed at a guest's joke, that she had totally missed his point and was only laughing to be polite, though everyone present would swear she understood him in every detail. Sometimes in the evening, when the lights went out, it was she, and not Abdou, the cook, who would run to the fuse box. And as I heard her tinkering with the wires, pulling things out and putting them back in, answering my unasked questions with the plea that I not move lest we collide when she came down the ladder, all I could think of, as I hoped this darkness might last forever and be like a long night devoid of sleep, was that Mother had lied to me, that others had lied to me as well, that she was never as deaf as she made herself out to be.

Only then would it hit me, this truth about her ears, that she would always be deaf, never hear music, never hear laughter, never hear my voice. Only then did I realize what it meant to be alone in the world, and I would run to find her in this large house that became so quiet, so empty, and so very dark at night, because nighttime in our part of Alexandria was always somber and murky, especially with my father out so late every evening. We would turn the lights on everywhere in the house, not to ward off imaginary thieves, but to look out the window and see our reflected faces on the windowpane.

From that darkness every evening came the ghoulish howl of the yogurt vendor repeating a long, hooting "*Yaooooourt

. . . *yaooooourt*" until he reached the end of the block and turned uphill toward the small barracks where antiaircraft guns were sometimes heard sputtering their practice shots. How grateful, then, when I heard my mother's voice rise above the night as she shouted in the kitchen at Abdou, who was about to go home but was detained an hour more because he had forgotten to clean the oven.

∎

With my great-grandmother's centennial ball fast approaching, the Princess finally decided I was spending far too much time with the deaf and with Arab servants at home. Though Smouha, where we lived, was only a fifteen-minute carriage ride from Ibrahimieh, to my grandmother it still remained the swamp it had once been, and its newly built homes and quiet vistas of fragrant plantations would always remain a bit too *nouveau* for her taste, not an acceptable address.

One morning, she informed my mother that she wanted to take me under her wing, the pretext being that I had been caught mispronouncing far too many words under the influence of my mother's deviant speech. Seeing that she had my mother nearly cowering before such an indictment, the Princess pressed ahead and asked her also to inform her deaf friends that they should curtail their visits somewhat, especially Aziza, a poor, young woman who also served as maid, cook's helper, cleaning lady, and seamstress, and was guilty, in my grandmother's eyes, of the twin crimes of being deaf and an "ignorant Arab."

She suggested I visit her every other morning and then have lunch with her at my great-grandmother's home. Stunned by the proposition, my mother was silent, but I caught her pupils darting about, a sign of impatience and suppressed rage. "And what do I do while he's with you, darn socks with my deaf friends?"

"Not at all. Oh, I didn't mean for you to take it like that at all, Gigi," the Princess replied, beating a hasty retreat with that startled, innocent air calculated to make you feel peevish and unfairly suspicious of her motives. "I just want the child to know my side of the family and hear polite conversation. He must learn how to speak correctly."

"But I already take him to my parents every day for that very purpose," protested my mother.

"That's very good, Gigi. Still, it's not quite the same thing," she said, raising her index finger. The Princess had not invited my mother's parents to the forthcoming celebration, owing to the alleged difference in standing between the two families—not to mention the Syrian question. "I want him to become distinguished," the Princess said. "Like my brothers, who are, as you know, *très comme il faut*."

Without thinking, my mother had already capitulated.

When my father arrived late that evening, the first thing he did was show he was extremely displeased to find Aziza still there.

"I don't want her here all the time. Isn't it enough that most of your deaf friends are here every day, do we need deaf servants as well?"

It took my mother a second to piece together the puzzle.

"Is this going to end up with your mother taking care of him every other day?" she said, pointing at me.

"Why not?" he replied, going on the offensive now that she had found him out. "I don't want him growing up thinking he is either deaf or an Arab."

My mother took this in silence.

"Meanwhile, poor Aziza stayed later than usual to finish ironing your shirts." She flung open a cupboard and pointed to two stacks of neatly folded shirts.

"What do I care about shirts!" he shouted.

He picked up one of the shirts, examined it as though looking for a crease, found none, then brought it close to his nose. He found what he was looking for.

"Let me be very clear: don't ever let me see Aziza again," said my father, losing his temper. "I don't want to hear her toadish croaking in my home, I don't want her nosing around my things, and I certainly don't want that fetid odor of hers lingering in the house after she's done cleaning it. Here," he said, almost thrusting the shirt into my mother's face to let her sample the smell.

"It was washed this very morning," she said.

"Smell again! It stinks of *hilba*! *Hilba*! *Hilba*!" he shouted as he picked up each shirt, sniffed it, and threw it on the floor. "Get rid of her!"

■

My father was right about one thing: Aziza always trailed that pungent odor of *hilba*, an auburn-colored substance that Egyptians drank in large doses for its alleged curative properties and which dyed their palms red and made their bodies exude what Europeans considered a repellent, dirty odor. My father called it *une odeur d'arabe*, an Arab smell, and he hated to find it trapped in his shirts, his linens, his food.

This odor was so unmistakable and so overwhelming that one could immediately distinguish Westernized Egyptians, who used a strong aftershave, from those who affected Western habits but whose minds, homes, and regimens were still steeped in the universe of *hilba*. Even if an Egyptian had completely adopted Western ways, shed his native customs to become what my grandparents called an *évolué*, and wore a suit every day, learned table manners, kissed *mazmazelles'* hands whenever he greeted them, and knew his wines, his cheeses, and the required number of La Fontaine fables by heart, the fact that his clothes gave off the slightest trace of that telltale

scent would make one think twice about his professed inclination for the West and suspect that not everyone in his
household—himself included—had risen above the dark, sin-
ister underside of Arab hygiene.

But there was another reason for my father's visceral aversion
to *hilba*. He, like his mother, disliked all kinds of recognizable
ethnic odors, thinking that the more Westernized a family, the
more odorless its home, its clothes, its cooking.

It would never have occurred to either of them that all homes
bear ethnic odors, and that anyone born in Alexandria would
just as easily have sniffed out a Sephardi household like ours,
with its residual odor of Parmesan, boiled artichokes, and
borekas, as they themselves could recognize an Armenian
kitchen by its unavoidable smell of cured pastrami, a Greek
living room by the odor of myrrh, and Italians by the smell
of fried onions and chamomile. Working-class Italians
smelled of fried peppers, and Greeks smelled of garlic and
brilliantine, and, when they sweated, their underarms smelled
of yogurt.

"It smells as though an Arab caravan camped here over-
night," said the Princess when visiting us late one morning.
"I can smell her, I know she was here." Though my father
had pronounced a ban on Aziza, it was never enforced.

"At least have her confined to the kitchen whenever I'm
here," my grandmother would say. "And while you're at it,
keep that Om Ramadan out of sight as well—or do you want
me to invite her to the centennial ball?" This last was a particularly cruel command, as Om Ramadan, our washerwoman,
had been in my mother's father's family service for forty years.

■

Om Ramadan was a very tall, lanky woman who came about
twice a week and spent the entire morning in the bathroom

with a large steel bucket filled with dirty lukewarm water in which she washed our clothes by kneading, slapping, and wringing them until she had squeezed the very life and color out of them—an exercise that required such vigorous movements that, as with famous conductors, it explained her longevity. She was ugly and old, probably in her seventies. Her hair was not white but fair, with a light auburn touch, because of either henna or peroxide. Her skin was very white, especially her arms and hands, which some said had lost their pigmentation because of the heavy bleach she used in her wash.

Om Ramadan had only one eye. She never hid her bad eye, and, to joke, she would pry open her eyelids with her fingers and show me what was no longer behind them.

"One day this eye will go bad too, and then they'll have to take it out," she would say, as though speaking about a tiny mole on her foot. "But I'll continue washing here all the same." And just to prove her point, she would tilt her head slightly upward, roll up her good eye so that only the white showed, and with a pained, uplifted face staring vacantly in my direction, go on wringing my shirts with mechanical hand motions, intoning, "Alms for the blind, alms for the blind."

Om Ramadan's method for washing clothes was the simplest and oldest. She would squat in front of the large washbasin with both feet flat on the floor and her bony knees jutting up inside her *galabiya*, almost reaching her chin. Sometimes she wore wooden clogs about two inches high and would squat on those, chain-smoking and drinking scalding dark tea from a tall glass that never left her side and which Abdou kept replenishing throughout the morning, while she, without looking up, would bless him for his kindness, and he bless her for hers.

By midmorning, Om Ramadan would start her singing, and though everyone in the household made fun of her voice, with its dirgelike, monotone drone, still, from outside our windows, coming from neighboring homes, another maid or washer-woman, followed by yet another nearby, would echo the same song, as they all plied away at their wash, squatting in their respective sunlit perches, which were filled with the peace that inhabits large Mediterranean bathrooms. Without budging from their places, without seeing the others, they had learned one another's names and would call them out and swap entire life histories like ships exchanging signals in the fog.

After finishing the wash, Om Ramadan would sit in the kitchen and smoke a cigarette with Abdou. Then, with more tea in her system, she would return to the bathroom, load a large wicker basket with wet clothing, and carry the load on her head up the five flights of circular servants' stairs that led to the roof, taking slow, deliberate steps, stopping to catch her breath on the landing above ours, where another neighbor's servant would hand her a glass of water. Then she would resume her climb, I alongside her, and the closer we got to the top, the brighter the stairwell grew, with more and more light shining against the walls of the sixth, seventh, and finally the eighth floor, where a sudden, blinding spell of heat and sunlight dazzled our senses.

Not a sound on the terrace. Only the faraway whir of distant traffic below. Everything I touched was burning hot, and as I roamed about the empty terrace and looked over the tops of all the other buildings of Smouha, there it was, immense as always, that color blue lining the limitless horizon, quiet, se-rene, and forever beckoning: the sea.

A gridwork of clotheslines awaited us. The sagging gray cords were frayed with use and, all along them, abandoned clusters of unused pins sat like little sparrows idling on electric wires.

Now would start the most tranquil and contemplative work

on earth. Pursing a few pins between her lips, Om Ramadan would begin to unwring and uncoil bedsheet after bedsheet, hanging one on the clothesline, then another next to it, then another on a line opposite the first, thus unfurling row upon row of draped and scented passageways where one could run and lose oneself as surely as in heaven's corridors, with the sky above, silence below, and the odor of clean sheets drying in the sun, some still dripping on the gray cement floor that exhaled a salty smell of summer and seawater.

Hours later, Om Ramadan and Aziza would go upstairs, bring back the dried laundry, and proceed to fold what was not going to be ironed. Usually, a large heaping mound of crisp, clean clothes would collect on someone's bed, and, early on those warm afternoons, I would throw myself into that large pile of scented sunlight and half-nap to the quiet flutter of two women folding large white and light-blue sheets, each tugging from her end as hard as she could—there was bad blood between them—folding and tugging, until, picking up the last sheet, on which I lay, they would have to wake me up.

■

"Om Ramadan gives me the creeps," said the Princess. "Every time I come here it's as though I've walked into an asylum. There is always a deformed person roaming about. This isn't a bestiary, it's my son's home."

In addition to Om Ramadan, there was in our domestic asylum Hisham, the *sofraghi*—the waiter—who, as irony would have it, had only one arm and could never hold a large platter long enough to serve eight persons without having to rest awhile. Then there was Abdou, the cook, an alcoholic. And his much older cousin, an albino, also named Abdou, who spoke fluent Turkish and who came as an extra sometimes but who had a terribly ulcerated leg, which my grandmother suspected was leprous. And Margherita, our Italian neighbor's retarded daughter who came to do the ironing. And finally there was Fatma, the errand girl, who one day, in trying to help the two Abdous dust a carpet by hanging it from the balcony, had lost her balance and fallen to the sidewalk, as a result of which she limped on her way up and down the service stairway until finally, unable to find a husband, she went back to the Said in the south.

But the person my grandmother most despised remained Aziza—Aziza, that invidious, evil-eyed jinxer who smirked all to herself in her corner of our living room, casting a spell on you when you least suspected; Aziza, that insidious factotum who knitted all of our sweaters, darned all of our socks, and helped with injections, cupping glasses, and enemas, and who, once a month, performed *halawa* on all of the women. "A barbaric ritual!" the Princess said in disgust, referring to this Arab practice of boiling sugar-water until it formed a thick, caramelized paste which was then applied to women's bodies to remove body hair. Before "doing *halawa*," Aziza, who by common consent was an expert *halawiste*, would knead the paste, spitting into it several times until it had achieved the desired consistency. Seated before her, the women would put forth their legs as Aziza bent down and applied the paste. Then, with short, determined pulls that sounded like paper being ripped from a notebook, she would tear off the paste as if it were a huge bandage, leaving behind a smooth red blotch. She would knead the paste again and apply it elsewhere.

Nothing seemed more painful than *halawa*, especially on women's underarms. I once saw my mother in such pain that she bit her knuckles hard enough for them to carry a weeklong bruise. The Princess, finally persuaded to try the procedure, yelled in agony. Aziza laughed and said, "It's nothing." "Barbarian!" shouted the Princess.

A Centennial Ball

■

Aziza originally belonged to a coterie of friends my mother had made while a student at Madame Tsotsou's boarding school for deaf girls. Under Madame Tsotsou's vigilant egalitarianism, no one was permitted to distinguish between rich and poor, Greek and Arab, and since none of the girls were allowed any pocket money, there were no privileges to be had, except for the occasional jar of marmalade, whose contents were equitably spooned out to all in the dining room. The school was quite successful, and well-to-do pupils came from all around the Mediterranean with no other goal than to speak and behave like the hearing—preferably in French, and through French, to free themselves from this terrible *corvée*, this burden of silence.

An obdurate middle-class idealist, Madame Tsotsou defined a successful graduate as one who befriended the hearing over the deaf, who felt less deaf than she truly was, and who experienced an instinctive revulsion toward those who knew no better than to speak with their hands, not their mouths. Her most cherished success stories were girls who had married the hearing; it was the romance of the servant girl marrying the landowner's son. But of the seven in my mother's class who married, only one had a successful marriage, and she was the only one to disappoint Madame Tsotsou by marrying a deaf boy.

A few times every week, four or five of these young women would be in for tea—to the revulsion of my grandmother, who, more than ever now, deplored the world in which I was growing up. She would sit and fidget, complaining she had to share her visits with survivors of malnutrition, amputation, and meningitis, not one of whom was worth the two cents she paid the coachman to drive her to her son's home after visiting with her sisters. Even their conversation, when she was able to fathom it, was insufferable, since it usually devolved into slapstick, gossip, and recipes. Sometimes they began shouting and screaming at each other, made peace a few moments later, and resumed their confounded cackling with greater vigor yet, forcing her to conclude that of all the people she knew none spent more time talking than the deaf-mute.

Among my mother's friends was a young woman named Sophie who came from a patrician Greek family that had lost everything in Smyrna and now retained nothing but the vestiges of distinction in their obligatory afternoon tea where you tasted oversweetened Greek jams on a spoon. Sophie and my mother often recalled their dreadful boarding-school days when Madame Tsotsou locked them up in the dark whenever they forgot to turn off a water faucet—a frequent mishap among the deaf, who cannot hear the water running. "But look at what women I've made out of two spindly little girls who couldn't read or write, much less speak, when I got them," Madame Tsotsou would say.

Sophie married a Greek auto mechanic, a hairy, cocksure sailor-type with greasy hair and dirty fingernails who roared about Alexandria on his motorcycle on Sundays, sporting gold bracelets, a tank-shirt, and the nymph Sophie on the backseat. Costa had the boisterous familiarity of Alexandrian Greeks and was a jack-of-all-trades dabbling in twenty more, a *sale débrouillard*—"Impresario," he would say with a tiny wink in his eyes, meaning a trader in stolen, black-market, and counterfeit goods.

The only person who took a liking to him was, of all people, the Princess.

"He's a true savage, but a heart of gold," she would say. Unbeknownst to my mother, Costa would often visit my grandmother and bring her presents, ranging from caviar and champagne to perfumes and foie gras hijacked from Beirut. In return, he asked nothing but the ear of an old woman who, he said, was like a mother to him and understood him far better than did his Sophie, who, during mating season—as he called it—could think of nothing better than to squeeze the pimples on his forehead. "Can a man live that way, madame? Tell me, can he?" he would ask, exasperation bubbling in his voice.

"What can you do? These are unfortunate women."

"But I can't anymore." He would get worked up, choke a moment, and suddenly break down sobbing.

"Now, don't get angry like this, Costa," my grandmother would say, pretending to mistake his weeping for anger so as not to embarrass him.

"Angry? These are not tears of anger. These are tears of shame, tears of stupidity, mine, hers, and everyone who watched this happen to us and said nothing."

"Patience, Costa, patience," my grandmother would urge.

"And what for?" he would shout, truly furious this time. "I am Costa, and Costa is a man, and Costa needs passion, fire, spices, madame, not this—" he said pointing to a pimple on his forehead. "I don't like speaking in front of children," he went on, looking my way, "but she has shown me the passion of a tapeworm—and Costa, madame, needs a tigress."

∎

My grandmother had met Costa one evening just as he was arriving to pick up his wife, Sophie. Since the two of them were the only hearing people in the room, they began to talk and soon discovered that both were born in Constantinople. The man showed all the requisite deference a sailor is expected to extend to a princess from Constantinople, and she found in the garrulous *palikar*—warrior—a gentle soul yearning for kindness.

When she heard that he owned a motorcycle, and that he

ran errands in Ibrahimieh every morning, I saw my grandmother give a start and say "Achhh, Kyrio Costa—" and beg
him to bring the boy to her house every other morning. The
man consented easily.

"Kyrio Costa, your soul is blessed in heaven."

He blushed.

"No, madame," he said seriously, "Costa has done many bad
things in this life, and for some, madame, you don't even know
their name. Costa will pay."

Thus every other morning, Monsieur Costa would arrive
with the loudest motorcycle in the world. He would whistle
with both fingers in his mouth, and as soon as I was saddled
on his backseat, would order me to hold him tight by the waist
and off we went, roaring through Sidi-Gaber, past Cleopatra,
then Grand Sporting, racing with the tram, beating the tram,
leaving the tram behind us, finally reaching Petit Sporting,
and slowing down toward Ibrahimieh, all of it in a matter of
minutes as he kept taking sharp and ever more intricate turns,
veering left then right—growling "Hold tight, *pedimou*"—and
leaning the bike as low as he could, his boot grazing the asphalt,
always congratulating himself with "What reflexes, Costa,
what reflexes!" speeding all the way out to Camp de César,
almost to Chatby, and then turning back again toward
Ibrahimieh—"for the fun of it"—and slowing the vehicle to
the equivalent of a regal canter down Rue Memphis, finally
depositing me in front of my grandmother's house, where she
waited for me with a piece of fresh fruit already peeled and
ready to be eaten as soon as I hopped off the motorcycle.

An hour into my visit, my grandmother would never fail to
observe that I already looked much better. "Look, he's laughing," she would tell her husband as we sat around a table in
the garden. "Isn't it true that he only laughs when he's with
me?"

"Come, we'll take a walk around the garden," my grandfather would say, always eager to be away from his wife, taking me into the arbor where birds sang and where the air was thick with the parched, dry, cloying scent of rosemary and sweet, overgrown rhododendron. Away from my grandmother's gaze, he would finally reach into his pocket and produce a present: a keychain, or a pen, or a penknife—our secret, he'd say, for she always disapproved of the things he gave me, claiming they were dangerous or unseemly. "Soon I'll have to teach you billiards," he said one day, producing three smooth ivory balls from his striped bathrobe pocket. Then, using his cane and a billiard cue, we would pluck guavas from one of the orchard trees.

At around half past ten, my grandmother and I would hire a carriage and ride all the way to Stanley Beach, where her siblings and her mother had a summer cabin. Sitting next to her in the carriage, I would make out the wholesome, soothing fragrance of Madame Anèle's almond creams, tea rose ointments, and cucumber lotions—all three forever laced into the memory of those sunny mornings. Sometimes we took the tram at Ibrahimieh, stopped at Rouchdy, and only then hired a carriage. The carriage would struggle uphill along a quiet, tree-lined avenue, taking forever to reach the top, as my grandmother went on with her chilling tales of the Armenian massacre and of the Armenian priest whose hand was cut off as he struggled against three janissaries who then lopped off his head along with that of a grocer who had come to the old man's rescue—when, suddenly, without warning, greeted by the rising clamor coming from the beaches, we knew we had reached the top of the hill and there, shimmering right before us in a dazzling expanse of turquoise and aquamarine, was the sea, extending from as far back as Glymenopoulos to the mighty fortress of Kait Bey.

"Ah, but the water is wonderful today," she would exclaim,

tapping my thigh with excitement, for until coming face-to-face with the sea, you never really knew whether the water was going to be rough or quiet.

The cabins at Stanley were located on three tiers of board-walks; each had its own porch, or vestibule, resembling more an opera loge than a changing area, and was separated from adjacent porches by lateral cloth dividers, while overhead, a long white awning fastened to the parapet along the common boardwalk was always fluttering, so that on crowded, sunny days, all three boardwalks were almost entirely hidden from view, beaming white in the sunlight, squeaking and fluttering like sails on a Spanish galleon.

At the beach, my great-aunts were persuaded they still lived in fin-de-siècle Alexandria, far from the world of Smouha, of querulous maids and crippled manservants. The women never put on bathing suits but wore white or cream-colored short-sleeve linen or cotton voile dresses with plenty of lace, and large, ornate hats, which they held in place with their hands whenever a breeze came up. On the beach, all four sisters, their mother, friends, and Madame Victoria Coutzeris, whose villa overlooked the bay itself, would sit on multicolored, striped folding chairs, forever repeating how important it was to avoid the sun, their swollen feet crammed into tight shoes, and each heaving a happy sigh whenever the wind stirred the large, striped umbrella. Every morning, the lifeguards would put up their umbrella in their favorite spot some distance from the water. Some of these lifeguards knew how to fasten awnings particularly well and were highly regarded, with the sort of reverence the landed gentry will extend to an otherwise insignificant gatekeeper who happens to have a special talent for trapping rodents. Others, however, were not so skillful and were shooed away as soon as they offered to help.

I was never allowed to drink or eat anything, certainly not

Coca-Cola or those hazelnut biscuits sold by grubby vendors along the sand. My grandmother always insisted that nothing agreed with the sea more than fruit, and plenty of it, which is why she brought a thermos filled with lemonade. To my great joy, however, I found out that ice cream could be had simply by sneaking up one flight of stairs to the upper deck, where Aunt Flora had her cabin. There I would usually find her reading in her reclining beach chair, ask her for ice cream, and return, rather pleased with myself, to confront my angry grandmother, who stood waiting, like God after Adam had eaten the forbidden fruit.

Once, by chance, I found Aunt Flora sitting quietly next to another woman whom I did not immediately recognize, although she seemed quite interested in me. The surprise and sudden joy were such that I immediately forgot everything that had stood between us that day—Monsieur Costa, my grandfather, the dizzying rides through the nameless side alleys of Alexandria, the Armenian massacre, the billiard balls, even my grandmother's joyful tap on my thigh as soon as we had sighted Stanley that day—everything vanished when I heard the woman's voice. Minutes later, she reminded me that my clothes were still downstairs in my great-grandmother's cabin and that we would have to tell them I was going home with her instead.

My mother waited for me to finish my ice cream, then took me by the hand, went downstairs to greet her in-laws, and, with a tone of voice that admitted no discussion, said she was taking me home.

"But I had planned to take him to visit Albert at the billiard hall. We always stop there, don't we?" the Princess asked, trying to enlist my help.

I nodded.

"No, he's coming with me," said my mother.

I thanked my good fortune that my mother had spared me yet another confrontation. But when my grandmother was drying me off before dressing me in clean clothes, the silence between us was intolerable. I wished I had not been so visibly eager to leave her, for the old lady seemed on the verge of tears, and as she bent down to buckle my sandals, which must have been difficult for her, I knew that, given the chance to do it again, I would have forfeited the mango ice cream altogether and not run into my mother. I kissed her on the cheek, saying something I seldom said to her. I told her I loved her. But I said it in Arabic.

On our way home, my mother hailed a carriage along the Corniche, and Flora and I got in. "No, wait," she told us, and with hand signals and her poor knowledge of Arabic asked the man how much he would charge to take us to Rue Memphis. "Too much, the man's a thief, come down," she ordered, whereupon both Flora and I went through the motions of getting off. The man relented, which meant that the haggling was about to commence, and soon she was raising her voice. Then she began to shriek, which we knew would subdue him. People were looking in our direction. And suddenly I understood, as I watched her gesture the price she was not going to budge from, that she was yelling not because the driver was being too stubborn—everyone knew he would relent in the end—nor even because she was exploding with the rage she had had to suppress in seeing how her role as mother was being so cunningly undermined by my grandmother. She was screaming because she already knew that with a few oblique hints of outrage whispered in my father's ear later that day, my grandmother would succeed in painting her as spiteful and vindictive toward a benevolent old woman whose sole wish in life was to devote the few years left her to grooming the son of an overly suspicious Arab Jewish ingrate. She would never be able to counter such allegations—for to do so she would have to crawl under and around her mother-in-law's verbal barbed wire. And this, Madame Tsotsou's old pupil had not been taught to do. She could sniff out guile with the cunning of a fox, but she could not avoid the snares of sophistry. Arguments turned against her, because she knew how to shout, not how to argue, because, in the kingdom of words, she would always remain a stranger. Hers was the frustration which an innocent man feels when confronted by a gifted prosecutor.

■

To placate his mother, my father personally took me to his parents' the next morning. But to satisfy my mother, he decided perhaps we didn't have to go to the beach. Instead, he suggested that he, his father, and I go to buy shoes at a closeout sale. We drove along the Corniche on this clear summer day, parked the car near the Cecil Hotel, and walked toward Boulevard Saad Zaghloul. We stopped to take in the view and listen to the sound of the water licking the huge, ugly boulders lining the city's waterfront. And there we were, the three of us, before the parapet, looking over beyond the bay, beyond the seawall, past the fortress of Kait Bey, where the water was always rough and dark by the ruins of the fallen lighthouse. There was a pause in the conversation.

"You know," said my grandfather, turning to my father, "I don't think I need new shoes."

My father said nothing at first.

"But you know how difficult it is to find good English shoes nowadays. Do you mean to walk in worn down moccasins for the rest of your life?"

All this was said as both stared out into the shimmering morning sea.

"I don't know." And as though he hadn't been paying attention to his son and was merely following his own train of thought, he added, "All this sky and all this water—what do you do with so much blue once you've seen it?"

Then, catching himself, he asked, "Don't you have plenty of shoes already?"

"Yes, but when I wear them out, can you see me wearing flimsy made-in-Egypt shoes?"

We proceeded to walk along the Corniche toward the Boulevard.

"Walk faster," said my father to his father.

"But I'm walking fast."

"No, you're walking sluggishly. You should walk briskly, energetically. Like this." And suddenly my father began to outpace us. Seeing that he had walked far ahead, he came back at the same pace.

"See, it's good for you," continued my father, saying something about Monsieur Politi, his gymnastics instructor who came every morning at six.

"Like this?" mimicked his father.

"Somewhat. Move your arms as well, and breathe deeply."

"Like this?"

"Yes."

"And by doing this, I'm to live how many more years? Enough to outlive your mother? Thank you for the demonstration. But I'll walk the way I've always walked."

My father changed his mind about the shoes. "Perhaps we don't need ready-made shoes after all," he said, implying that he was rich enough to afford custom-made ones. Instead, he suggested coffee at an establishment overlooking the bay. "I've had an excellent year. Things are going very well. I'm even building an annex to warehouse more goods. So I can afford a cup of coffee at La Côte."

"I don't understand," said my grandfather, as though talking to himself. "One day he's the impoverished son of a pool hall owner, and the next he's splurging on the best cars, best clothes, best this, best that. This can't go on. You're only doing well because all the other large textile manufacturers have sold their businesses and moved back to England. It doesn't bode well. You should be saving more," added my grandfather.

"Both you and Gigi have only one thing in mind: save, save, save."

Meanwhile, we had reached La Côte and my father opened the heavy glass door, letting both of us in ahead of him. The place was crowded but almost silent.

The waiter, who recognized my father immediately, knew that he liked a table next to the window.

"You shouldn't be spending your money so frivolously. I'm not the first to say it." My grandfather was looking out the window. "The entire city knows. There are even rumors about other things as well, if you follow my drift."

"Your drift sticks out a mile."

My father picked up a cigarette, let it rest between his fingers as though trying to remember whether he hadn't already just smoked one, then, staring at it still, seemed to change his mind. "You were hardly any better yourself," he added.

"It's easy to accuse me. But I was married to a witch."

A waiter wearing a turban and traditional Egyptian garb poured coffee for the two men, while another, a Greek, brought me a large ice cream soda.

The old man sighed. He looked at the table next to ours, where two women were drinking tea.

"Look, don't think I don't know these things. We are all like that, us men, and I've known it about myself ever since the day I became a man, more than half a century ago."

"But—" the son began to protest.

"Just promise me this," added my grandfather. "As long as I'm alive, be good to her, and no more women."

The son swore.

"And when you're gone?" he asked, trying to liven the mood.

"When I'm gone, I'll be gone, and what you do will be your business."

The waiter brought two large glasses of water and a tiny slice of Turkish delight.

"You know you shouldn't eat sweets," said my father. "My doctor—"

"*My doctor, my trainer, my walking, my breathing*—please!" interrupted his father. "Coffee, cigarettes, and sweets. I'm not even seventy, yet these are the two or three pleasures left me." He sipped the coffee, holding his demitasse and saucer in the same hand. "There," he interjected. He had already given me a piece of the Turkish delight and was already cutting me another.

My father, who was sitting across from us, had put down his demitasse and was staring at us in silence, as though not wishing to break the spell.

My grandfather cut me yet another piece and watched as I put it in my mouth, almost purposely avoiding his son's gaze.

"And what are you staring at?" he finally asked.

"I'm looking at you."

"He's looking at me," mused the older man, as though there were something terrifically moving about staring at one's own father—which I suddenly realized there was.

A few minutes later I caught sight of my mother, Aunt Flora, and my two grandmothers standing at the doorway of La Côte.

"What a surprise—and Flora as well!" exclaimed my father, as soon as the women were escorted to our table.

"Dr. Katz said she is perfectly healthy," reported the Princess, who had run into the three women that morning at the tramway station and, on impulse, had decided to join them. "The gallstones are far better, she's got the liver of an ox—"

My grandfather muttered something to his son.

A breeze fanned our faces as we ordered another round of coffee.

"A day meant for the beach," said Flora with that joyful, expansive air her voice acquired whenever she spoke of the sea. "Why isn't the boy at the beach today?"

"It's about time he spent time with grown-up men," explained my grandfather, offering her a cigarette from his cigarette case.

Flora, who hadn't seen my grandfather in a while, asked him how he was.

"I'm getting older," he said. "I stay home a lot. I'm bored when I stay home, I'm bored when I go out. Voilà. And I sleep a lot," he added, as though he had forgotten a significant detail. "When it'll be time for me to show my face above, I'll walk up to Saint Peter and say, 'Excuse me, Holy Father, but I've slept so much these past few weeks that I couldn't possibly sleep any more. Perhaps I could come back in a few weeks.' "

Flora laughed heartily, repeating my grandfather's last words several times, indeed, never forgetting them.

"Ah, Flora, I'm so happy to see you."

"And I'm glad to see you, because, frankly, I needed to smoke one of your cigarettes."

"Ah, Flora, if all women were like you—if you only knew."

"What's with him today?" asked Flora, turning to my father.

"I don't know," answered my father. "He's been like this all morning."

"Your grandfather is a wonderful man," she said, "but he can be more *malheureux* than earthquake victims."

Soon everyone decided it was time to break for lunch. My mother and Aunt Flora had planned to have lunch at the

Saint's. My father invited my grandfather for lunch. The Princess, not daring to say anything, just looked at me.

"Can you take him to lunch at Rue Thèbes today?" my mother asked, turning to the Princess. My mother explained she was busy that afternoon. First, the tailor was due to arrive to measure her for a dress for the centennial. And Aziza was going to "do" her *halawa*.

"Stay with her," whispered my mother, indicating the Princess.

My grandmother's face suddenly beamed like a sunny day in June.

■

My father knew it as soon as he picked up the receiver that same night and heard the flustered, officious tremor in the Saint's voice. She kept trying to convey the news obliquely, with a notion of dignity and fortitude. His mother, she said, was sitting right in front of her, crying. She was drinking a *fortifiant*, the Saint's euphemism for schnapps. Then, while trying to comfort my father—yet also hint at the forthcoming ball, to which she had still not been invited—she reminded him that not everyone was meant to live to be a hundred.

My father immediately woke me, not as he usually did, by sitting at the edge of my bed and whispering my name, but by tapping softly on my shoulder. A sense of cold, almost mechanical urgency seemed to govern each of his movements, as though he had been rehearsing this for months. He washed my face, dried it with swift, perfunctory dabbing motions, and, for the first time, it was he and not my mother who got me dressed. He was not talking. When we came out the front door to go to the garage, there was no one on the street. Only dogs. One came closer. My father picked up a stone and threw it, and the dog quickly scampered away. Inside the front lobby of the building across from ours, someone had left the light on. It was still nighttime.

We drove in silence.

"You shouldn't have brought the boy," said my grandmother, tucking her crumpled handkerchief inside the left cuff of her shirt.

"I want my father to see him, and I want him to see my father."

Mother and son whispered.

It had happened after he came back from the pool hall.

"Who knows!" she said, biting the point of her diamond ring anxiously to keep herself from sobbing again. "I call it the pool hall in order not to call it other things. Do I know where he goes wandering late at night? He never tells me, I never ask." She was silent an instant. "He doesn't want to move. Doesn't even want to take his clothes off." When they finally took me in to see him, he was lying on his bed, still wearing his tie, jacket, and trousers. Only his shoes had been removed. His socks were too long for his feet and dangled past his toes.

As soon as he heard the door, he thought he was speaking to his wife:

"Don't come in."

"It's me," whispered my father.

The old man's voice immediately mellowed.

They spoke in Ladino. Then he spoke to me. "*Tu vois ça?*" he said, meaning, "Can you believe this? Do you see what's happening to me?" The Saint came in and took me away.

■

A few weeks later, Monsieur Costa deposited me at my grandmother's house as usual. She shut the gate behind him and, together, we watched his motorcycle roar toward Camp de

César. She then looked at the sky and with her usual enthusiasm said, "Just look at this blue! We'll have a beautiful day at the beach today."

As I walked into the house, I felt an unusually cool draft running through the corridor. The voices of Greek merchants and Arab vendors on Rue Esnah crept into the house from the back windows in the kitchen, and the sun beamed starkly upon the kitchen tiles. Even the stuffy smell around the pantry seemed gone, and from the garden the scent of basil filled the house. Something had changed. "I'm going to put this on," my grandmother said, displaying a light-blue linen and cotton dress with buttons running all the way to her ankles. Nothing had pleased her more than when I asked her in front of everyone at the beach not to wear black.

When I made to open my grandfather's door, she whispered he was sleeping, that I should not disturb him. "We should pick fresh fruit for the beach," she said. But I had heard the faint crackle of my grandfather's old radio from behind his closed door, and I went to open it, knowing that he was not sleeping now but sitting at his little table listening to his news broadcast. Perhaps he had already heard me come in the house and was about to open the door to meet me. I pressed down the handle to push his door open and felt him pull at the same time.

I said good morning to him, and just the sound of his name spoken out loud in his room told me he was there. The room was unusually bright, with its windows wide open, overlooking a street I had never before seen or even suspected existed. From one of its shops came the loud sound of a radio I had mistaken for his. The wind had pulled open his door as soon as I had touched the door handle.

The round table with the radio had been pushed against the wall. His ashtray was sparkling clean for the first time ever, and the mattress on his bed was folded back on the bed frame, like a man performing a back exercise. A bedspread was thrown clumsily over the whole thing, no sheets, just the frayed faded stripes of the ancient mattress. Over the bedstand was a large mound of suits, neatly piled, while in his closet all one heard was the chime of hangers dangling from the metal bar.

I saw a row of shoes without trees, stashed like limp and lifeless sloughs, under the dresser. He had always said they were older than I was.

At first everyone had said he was sleeping. Then they said that he was resting. Then that he was gone. "Don't disturb him" evolved into "Don't disturb his things." His cane, his tobacco case, his deck of cards, his dentures floating in solution, his penknife, his loose things that not even the passage of time could tidy. Then his things began to disappear. I noticed Abdou wearing his shoes. And Mohammed, Abdou's nephew. The servants did not appreciate shoelaces, so they would pull them out, walking with the instep wide open, their shoe tongues sticking out insolently.

I recognized one or two ties on my father. Then he stopped wearing them. He said they had been his long before he had handed them down to his father, which was his custom with clothing he no longer wore. The ties, he said, made him think of himself years ago, when he would come home late every evening to listen to his father's recurring plea that he do something with his life other than read books and dream away his days over an embittered spinster whose love was a field of nettles. Each tie was invested with stirring reminders of distant faces or unspoken hopes that had made its extravagant price worthwhile. "You're wasting your money, your life, your time," his father would shout, "and a week's salary for a tie is criminal." Then he would agree it was a lovely tie. "Where will you ever wear it, though?" When the son told him he didn't know, the father replied that neither did he at his age.

When, several years later, we moved all his garden furniture to our summerhouse at Mandara, something of those hot, peaceful summer mornings came to stay with us as well. Much of the garden furniture had been painted over, but what lingered there was not his presence, not even his memory, but that vague sense of well-being that would fill his sunlit garden when I came looking for him, hoping to hear his cane or his billiard cue, so that we might pluck guavas.

For years, every time I passed by his garden on Rue Memphis or looked into it from the Saint's balcony, the thought would flare through my mind: What if he happened to be there right now?

One evening, just days before leaving Egypt, as I was walking around Ibrahimieh with friends on our way to visit a woman called La Léila, I suddenly stumbled upon the house at 48 Rue Memphis. I was thinking of other things then and had drunk too much wine, but the thought had come so naturally, and with such persistent urgency, that from the man I was about to become that evening, I would gladly have borrowed five minutes to go ring his doorbell and check one last time.

■

Impatient with my constant questions about my grandfather, the Princess instructed Monsieur Costa to take me directly to her mother's at Sporting, where she had moved so as not to be alone in her house on Rue Memphis. The Greek produced himself under our window one morning, and my mother, who by now had accepted that I would be spending a part of every day with the Princess, got me dressed, brought me downstairs, and set me on his motorbike.

This was Monsieur Costa's first visit to my great-grandmother's home on Rue Thèbes. I watched him park his motorcycle as neatly as he could and enter the building with marked reluctance and unease. "Are you sure it is here?" he asked me, knowing that it was.

"I bring the child," he told the maid who opened the door, speaking the shortest of sentences to conceal his shortness of breath.

"And who are you?" asked the Greek maid in French.

"*C'est moi que je suis le Monsieur Costa*—it is I which am the Monsieur Costa"—his way of speaking elegant French.

My grandmother, who happened to be passing by the entrance, shouted his name when she saw him and kissed him as if he were a son returning from a long journey. "What a pleasure to see you, you have no idea," she said in Greek. "Sit here, I am sure my brother wants to speak with you. I have to go. As you see, the house is upside down."

The whole apartment seemed as if hit by a hurricane. Furniture was scattered about the rooms, the sofas in the entry and the main living room were disordered, and carpets had been rolled up and heaped against the walls, one on top of the other. All my aunts were cleaning the apartment and the maids were on their knees waxing and scouring the parquet floor with a product so strong it was almost impossible to breathe. Everyone was shouting. They were to start cooking for the centennial that afternoon and, according to Aunt Elsa's plans, the cooking would take many, many days. Aunt Marta, who had poked her face into the living room, was shouting at the top of her voice, almost sobbing; the seamstress had sewn the wrong buttons on her mother's dress.

I was told to sit quietly in a corner and not move. I strained my eyes to catch sight of Sporting Beach.

"Let's go," said Uncle Vili after his brief meeting with Monsieur Costa.

I got up and gave him my hand.

"No hand-holding. We're men," he said with his usual sharp voice. "Where's your bathing suit?" he asked peremptorily.

I hunched my shoulders. I didn't know. I never used bathing suits. At the beach I would walk around in the shorts I was wearing and when it was time to go into the water, my grandmother would take them off.

"Don't tell me he goes naked at the beach like an Arab."

"That's how they do it in their family. Do you think I'm about to teach them how to live their lives?"

"Arabs! Something must be done."

Aunt Elsa, overhearing the conversation, came up to me, took a tape measure from her pocket, measured me, went into her room, pedaled at her sewing machine, and, five minutes later, came out with an antiquated version of a bathing suit. She had even decorated it with colored tassels. "I always said I never liked this business of swimming naked. Here, it's a present," she said, extremely pleased with herself. Elsa's presents were known to have led a previous life in her possession. In this case the cloth had come from an old bedspread she did not have the heart to throw away.

"Don't bother to try it on now," she added. "If it's too large, use this safety pin."

"Come on, *giovinezza*," said Vili with the sprightly vigor of vitamin takers.

When we got to the beach, Vili changed in a jiffy and insisted we exercise first. He began with jumping jacks, while my grandmother looked on in silent admiration. I had watched my father exercise every morning with Monsieur Politi but had never done it myself. Vili said I was flabby. I was not holding my shoulders straight, my posture was altogether wrong, awkward, unseemly. Men did not hold their chest in and tummies out. Chest out, tummy in, like this, he insisted, showing me. "No sense of exercise, or of hygiene either."

"Stop it, Vili, you'll give him a complex," said my grandmother, who was beginning to grow worried.

"What complexes? If your posture is bad, how can you swim? How can you swim if your posture is bad?"

After our warm-up exercises, Uncle Vili said we should race the length of the beach. As we sprinted along the shore, I fell and scraped my knee on a broken shell. "Not to worry," he shouted after examining the wound. An Englishman who happened to have been sitting where I fell volunteered to go to his cabin and fetch a bottle of alcohol. Scarcely had we refused his offer when a look of sudden horror crossed the Englishman's face as he witnessed Uncle Vili wet two fingers with spit and apply his saliva quite liberally to my wound. "What alcohol! All animals lick their wounds, and there are more of them than there are of us," Vili told the appalled Englishman.

It was a hellish morning, filled with shouting and screaming. After lunch, I broke down and cried, telling my father on the telephone that I never wanted to see my aunts or uncles again. My father remembered all too well the bite of Vili's tirades, especially before his wedding, when my mother's deafness had been a subject of frequent dinner squabbling, with Vili leading the pack against her. "Tell Vili to go—!" he said.

When, after my telephone call, Vili asked me whether the crybaby had reported everything to his daddy, I told him he was *un grand idiot*. His mother overheard the remark, as did Aunt Elsa, as did my grandmother. "The son of a *tarsha*, what did you expect," said Uncle Vili.

"Poor Esther."

Everybody was on edge. Vili threatened to hit me. My grandmother pleaded with him to stay calm. He said he would, for her sake.

To prevent further clashes that day, my grandmother decided to take me with her to Ibrahimieh, where she wanted to pick up a few more things—her embroideries, creams, spices—and tend *a bit* to her garden, which she was reluctant to abandon.

The house at 48 Rue Memphis was dark, the windows tightly shuttered, and most of the furniture draped with drop cloths, with only the feet of chairs and armchairs showing beneath the covering. All the lightbulbs had been removed, and the Persian rugs were gone. I remember my mother's father saying once, "You watch, the first thing to disappear will be the rugs." My mother later reported she had seen two of the rugs in the living room at the centennial. "I knew it," replied her father who hadn't been invited. "They're like piranhas. As soon as someone dies, they tear down everything he owns, bring it to the Gypsy queen mother, and there parcel it out among themselves like Ali Baba's thieves."

Before leaving my grandmother said she had to go to the bathroom. "Come with me," she said, not trusting me alone in the house. "Close the door. Just turn around and look the other way." I heard her undress. I did not shut my eyes but I averted my face as she had asked, when suddenly, past the soap dish, past the tiny bowl on the glass shelf containing moistened quince seeds that she set her hair with every morning, there, just inches from my nose, was my grandfather's striped bathrobe hanging from a hook on the bathroom door, smelling so much of him that I could almost touch him. So he was here, he was here, after all, I thought, and turned around.

I will never forget what I saw: my grandmother perched on top of the toilet bowl. Instead of sitting on the seat, she had lifted it up and was squatting with her bare feet on the rim, her seventy-year-old body in a precarious balance. I must have looked appalled, for she immediately tried to reassure me.

"I can only do it the Turkish way. Since this house lacks a Turkish bathroom this is what I have to do." Later she said it was also the healthiest way to go.

On our way back to Rue Thèbes, she urged me never to tell anyone. "It will remain our little secret."

Before the day was over, hardly anyone on my mother's side of the family had not laughed at least once at my grandmother's expense.

"I shouldn't even be speaking with you, but I will," she told me the next morning on our way to the beach. "Don't pretend you don't understand—you know very well what I mean."

I never found out who gave me away. But when the Saint heard that the very Princess, who had still not invited her to the centennial, squatted no better than a washerwoman when nature called, she probably couldn't resist.

■

Only very few days were left before the ball, but there was no sign that the Saint or her husband or anyone in their family, with the exception of my mother, had been invited. Having heard, however, that the celebration would last three days, the Saint, still unwilling to accept the snub, secretly hoped that the Princess's family might change their minds and invite her at the last minute, if not for the first night of festivities, when the wealthiest members of the Alexandrian establishment were to gather, then for the second, or possibly the third day, when friends, fellow club members, and minor business associates would be allowed to sample leftovers. If the neighborhood Copt pharmacist and his Syrian-Lebanese wife and other *évolués* were invited for the third day, and if her husband's Greek accountant and the impoverished Silvera sisters were also invited, then surely she would have to be invited as well.

But she never was. "Because of Jacques," said the Princess

many years later when I asked her why. There was no compunction in her reply, but she was probably annoyed that her grandson couldn't have figured it out himself. Except for the rabbi of Cairo, who was an Egyptian Jew, Arab Jews had not even been considered as possible guests.

The Saint and her husband would hear of preparations for the festivities only indirectly each day as my mother paid them a short visit.

"Blasphemous pagans, the whole lot of them," said my grandfather on the eve of the centennial, as the tension between Rue Memphis and Rue Thèbes reached an unprecedented high. "The poor man doesn't have time to turn in his grave, and they're already celebrating his mother-in-law's longevity. Mind you, he was no better. He was so sure he would end up outliving his wife that he even asked me once, 'Monsieur Jacques, do you think I will live long enough to forget I ever married her?' "

"And what did you reply?" asked his wife.

"I told him no one had ever lived *that* long."

"At any rate, he hated her family so much that he probably would have refused to go," Monsieur Jacques added.

"He wouldn't have been invited," said the Saint.

"Which is why our daughter shouldn't accept the invitation. It's a matter of principle."

"You don't want me to go because you haven't been asked," retorted his daughter.

"Even if I were invited, I would say, 'Madame Esther, I am touched by the invitation, but in honor of your husband's memory, I feel I cannot accept. Another time, perhaps. But right now, no.' And that would put her in her place."

"And if she doesn't invite you?"

"If she doesn't invite me, I will still find a way to thank her for already knowing why I would have refused her invitation."

"If they invite me, I'm going all alone, then," said the Saint.

■

At lunch on the day of the centennial, in honor of the man who had ridiculed them all of his life, both Uncle Vili and Uncle Isaac read eulogies for my grandfather. The seat would have remained empty, said one of them, had it not been filled by his grandson. Because of the number of guests, dining tables were moved into my great-grandmother's bedroom, a huge corner room with two balconies and plenty of sunlight. While one of her sons was speaking, my great-grandmother, seated at the center of the table, had taken a small decanter of olive oil that stood in front of her and poured a few drops on her empty plate. She sprinkled some salt on the oil, tore a small piece of bread, dunked it into the oil, and, holding the bread in place with one hand, pricked it with the fork she held in the other and brought it to her mouth.

"I can't help it—I'm hungry," said the old woman as she caught an admonitory gaze from one of her septuagenarian daughters.

After the speeches were over, someone toasted the memory of my grandfather. Everyone said, "Amen." My grandmother, who was seated next to me, turned to her neighbor, Madame Victoria, and said, "I used to tell him, 'Your head is in the clouds'; and he would say, 'And you, Esther, your feet are underground.' Look who's underground now." Madame Victoria smiled philosophically, remarking, "My husband used to say I looked old enough to be his mother. And yet, I buried him, remarried, and outlived a second husband." The smile disappeared from my grandmother's lips as she cast another look at her mother's chin, which was shining with oil. "Elsa, wipe off her chin before the oil drips on her dress," she said.

My great-grandmother wore a black lace dress that day. Next to her was seated her older brother, who had come from Turkey purposely for the occasion of his younger sister's centennial. I remember shaking his big, fat, miller's hand and staring at that gruff immobile mass of flesh, only to hear the man produce the sweetest strain in his *"Bonjour, jeune homme."* For the pictures that were taken that day, my great-grandmother posed standing, very upright and very alert, her thin dark lips tightly pursed, which was how she smiled, a restrained, cunning, murky look in her eyes. In her hand she's holding my grandfather's cane.

She was asked to make a little speech to the thirty or so family members who had gathered for lunch that day. Since she did not know French or Italian well enough to speak for a minute without making at least ten mistakes, she gave a small blessing in Ladino which ended with the cheerful though rather flat *salud y berakhá*, health and blessings. But urged by her sons, she finally yielded and began to speak in a halting, heavily accented French, saying that she had lived in Egypt for exactly fifty years, that half her life had been spent in Egypt, and the other half not in Egypt, and that the part not lived in Egypt was lived abroad—and yet in all these years, she went on proudly, she had never learned more than fifty words of Arabic. "One for every year," snickered her elder son Nessim. She knew Arabic so poorly, she explained, that one day she had asked an Arab servant to help her make a bed. The man suddenly blanched and grew flustered and asked her to please reconsider. She had no idea to what he was referring and insisted they go and make the bed together—until a Greek chambermaid informed her that what she had told the servant in Arabic was, "Come with me together in the bed." The irony, which escaped no one in the room, was not that the extremely old matron could make such a dreadful mistake but that had she insisted, the poor servant would have had to comply. Everyone burst out laughing.

By late afternoon, guests had begun to arrive. When I awoke from my nap, the house was filled with noise. By evening, they were crowding the corridors, the entrance hall, and the two living rooms. Many of the men sported rows of medals, emblems, and rosettes on their chests, some with larger medals hanging from striped bands around their necks, everybody looking like retired members of a small brigade meeting on the anniversary of a significant battle. Someone took me into the kitchen, where the maid Latifa got me dinner. Members of a musical quintet had just finished eating and were busy brushing the crumbs off their dark suits and wiping their mouths with handkerchiefs, which they put back into their pockets. They were not due to start for a while yet.

My mother also came into the kitchen to see how I was doing. She wore a jet-black dress that sparkled under the kitchen lights and gave off a dark greenish tinge when she opened the refrigerator door to inspect its contents, one hand holding her cigarette far away from the food, the other feeling about in the back of the refrigerator, because she had finally penetrated the mindset of her in-laws and knew that if there was something good to eat they would of necessity be trying to conceal it from one another.

Having found what she was looking for, she gave me the first spoonful herself and walked out of the kitchen, promising to return soon. "If he wants more, give him more," she said, already suspecting that the maid would do everything possible to hide once again the jar of whatever it was as soon as my mother had turned her back.

After my dinner, my grandmother came and took me by the hand, and, walking about the house, introduced me to friends of the family, most of whom were very old and portly and spoke with the same slow, stuffy, melodiously well-articulated French. To my surprise, I caught sight of Hisham, our servant, standing in the middle of the crowd, wearing a fez and the traditional waiter's garb of which he was so proud, holding with one arm a giant silver platter that was decorated with flowers. He winked when he saw me, and I shouted "*Ya* Hisham!" but my grandmother quickly tried to hush me up, for not only was I waving a friendly greeting to a servant but, to her dismay, I must have sounded like an Arab. She took me into another room and introduced me to the wife of an English lord whom everyone called Madame Lord. I exchanged a polite greeting with the woman who spoke with clenched teeth and a high-pitched voice, all the while speaking through clenched teeth myself. This infuriated my grandmother, who shook my arm, saying she would absolutely not permit me to do what I had just done. Madame Lord, who didn't understand why I was being reprimanded, asked if I would kiss her. I turned my face the other way, watching a man wearing a monocle pick peanuts from a bowl. "Doesn't want to kiss me, then?" asked Madame Lord, with a mock, coquettish pout. "Oh, just one kiss," she implored, bending toward me and pointing to the exact spot on her cheek where she wished me to place my kiss. "A man must never refuse," she said, looking very pleased and petulant in her fumbling impersonation of a French bawd.

Suddenly the lights went out. Everyone gave an astonished "Ah," and for a brief moment there was a hushed, expectant hubbub. Then came the sound of a gong. Holding a tall lighted taper in his hand, old Uncle Nessim stood on top of a dinner chair and, with the look of an amused scarecrow on a moonlit heath, announced that one hundred candles would be lit throughout the house and that everyone was welcome to help light them. "But this is absolutely divine," mouthed Madame Lord, no longer interested in my kiss. Everyone began queuing up as the servants passed out the tapers. Gradually, the north-west corner of the room, where we all stood, grew lighter and lighter. "Come," said my grandmother, "we'll be the first to light these here." And without thanking Hisham, who was handing out the tapers, she grabbed one from his tray. "How beautiful," said someone looking out the window. "Just fab-ulous," said another. "I've lighted four, and I'm going to light another and another—oh, so much fun, so much," squealed Madame Lord, who now looked like a besotted fairy god-mother trying to coax her older, paunchy husband to join her as she flitted through the hall looking for unlit candles to touch with her magic wand. She was breathless with excitement. "Here," said my grandmother, holding the taper in my hand as my mother hovered behind me, kissing me. "Light these two. This one and that one." She pointed at two candlesticks.

"Three," I overheard one of the Ayoub brothers say. "We each lighted one. And we are very happy."

"We're honored, messieurs," said my grandmother.

"No, it's we who are honored," they insisted.

My grandmother turned to me and, pointing to an unlit candle, said, "This one is for grandfather, because he will be happy you remembered him tonight." She lifted me up as my father and my mother guided my hand. "And now this one you light for—"

"I'll light it for her"—I indicated my great-grandmother; everyone was extraordinarily pleased—"for when she'll die."

There was a chilly silence. "Children," exclaimed Uncle Vili, who knew how to smooth all sorts of ripples.

"He is not a cruel boy. He just doesn't know how to keep his mouth shut," my grandmother apologized to those who had gathered around to watch me light the second candle.

"A diplomat he'll never be," hissed Uncle Isaac.

A photographer roaming about the room asked my grandmother to hold my hand. She did, resting her other on the edge of a mantelpiece with the dreamy nonchalance with which she normally affected contemplative, patrician plenitude.

"A diplomat I don't see him as either," agreed my grandmother after thanking the photographer. "There are certain people in this world who talk a lot and cannot keep secrets." She looked at me reprovingly.

My father took the taper from my hand and then handed it to my mother, and I watched him help her reach for an unlit candle in the back. "This is for your father," she said. He kissed her on the cheek. She smiled, and placed a palm along his.

By now all the rooms were aglow with candlelight, and when the servants opened the windows and balcony doors to let in fresh air, a mild autumnal breeze lilted through the house, swaying the lights ever so gently, as everyone marveled at the effect of the light against crystal.

"This we'll never forget," said Mr. Khatchadourian.

"Thank you, thank you," said Aunt Elsa, who immediately turned and complained to Madame Victoria of the awkward way in which Armenians spoke French.

"Even when in Europe we'll be, of this we'll think each year on this one same day. This I promise."

"Can't they ever speak correctly?" she whispered to her sister. "*To Cairo we went, from the theater I came, to America we'll go.*"

A bang was heard in an adjacent room. "*Evviva lo sciampagna,*" said an Italian gentleman. Uncle Nessim announced that, as the eldest of the siblings, he had uncorked the first bottle. Apologizing for the noise, he wiped his hand with a napkin and let one of the waiters take over.

"I'll keep this forever," he said turning to his mother, staring at the cork as if trying to decipher the precious inscription on its head. "We usually say 'May you live to be a hundred,' but now I don't know what to say."

"Don't get all worked up now, Nessico," she replied, tapping him on the arm. "You've done enough already."

"But there won't be another," he protested.

"No, there won't."

"If only we could start again."

"*Evviva signora*," cheered the Italian gentleman who had overheard the mawkish conversation and who suddenly began singing "*Viva il vino spumeggiante*" in a loud stentorian voice, motioning to the band and to all those around him to join him in a chorus, as everyone, even those only vaguely familiar with the aria from *Cavalleria Rusticana*, joined in the song. "But it's Ugolino da Montefeltro," said my grandmother as she blew him a kiss from afar. "He has just returned from France," she told guests around her, "just back from France."

No one had heard Monsieur Costa arrive. But suddenly I saw him standing in the middle of the hallway, looking like a baffled hermit who had strayed into a pagan orgy, scanning the room for a familiar face, dressed as always in his bombardier jacket, his shirt collar wide open, his hair greased back, the trimmed black mustache about to touch his upper lip.

"Please excuse the disturbance," he said as soon as he saw my grandmother, "but I must see His Excellency your brother immediately."

Uncle Vili came walking quickly, muttering "Ay, ay, ay" to himself, knowing that such a visit could only mean trouble. "Come into the kitchen—no, in here," he told Monsieur Costa, pointing to a junk-filled room next to the kitchen that sometimes doubled as the maid Latifa's. "You, out," said Vili pointing at me. "I want to come in," I insisted, promising not to utter a word. I was on the verge of crying. "Come in, but not a sound or I'll kill you."

"They caught my brother," said Monsieur Costa in one breath.

"That was a risk. Everyone knew that," replied Vili.

"Well, yes. They have the money of course. But they also know the numbers of the bank accounts in Switzerland. And they have a list of names."

"You mean the fool carried a list of names on him?"

"Apparently."

"But it's all over, then."

Monsieur Costa did not say a word but kept his arms crossed with a look of helpless consternation, as though trying to avert a blow by looking prematurely mortified.

"I am in as much trouble as you, Your Excellency," he said in the end. "There is a ship leaving tonight. It's a Greek merchant vessel, I can guarantee passage on it. I will be on it as well. Now, if Your Excellency will permit me, there are a few other people I must warn as well." Monsieur Costa took the service entrance and was never heard from again, not even by his wife.

"Call Nessim and Isaac now—and don't look so worried, for God's sake."

This was my first secret mission, and I waited for the right moment to tell each of my uncles that they were urgently needed in the *chambre des karakibs*—which in Arabic meant bric-a-brac. Once I escorted both, I was told to stay outside.

I tried to listen at the door, but all I heard were exclamations of distress. They opened the door and asked me to bring in my grandmother only. She must have sensed something was amiss, and by the look on Monsieur Costa's face she knew it concerned the police. Uncle Isaac was advising Vili against taking the ship. Costa could no longer be trusted. Instead, he would arrange for a car to drive him directly to the Cairo airport that same night, from where he could catch a dawn flight to Rome without anyone asking too many questions.

None of this caught Uncle Vili by surprise. For years he had been liquidating his assets in Egypt and secretly smuggling money to Switzerland in defiance of the Egyptian government's ban on all shipment of currency abroad. The punishment for the crime was imprisonment and eventual expulsion. Those holdings still in his name in Egypt were kept for appearances' sake and could easily be sacrificed. He had even managed to ship his clothes as well as his antique furniture to Europe. All he was leaving behind of value was a poorly kept villa filled with junk, rugs, and a Treccani encyclopedia set, given to him by, and bearing the signature of, none other than Il Duce himself. Many years later, that coveted set fell into my hands, only to be sold to a dealer for less than a dollar when we left Egypt.

Presently, I saw my grandmother come out of the junk room tucking her handkerchief into her left sleeve, shutting the door immediately behind her.

"What is it?" asked my father.

"We've decided to start the waltz now," she replied.

At that moment, the quintet sounded a few notes and everyone cleared the space in the middle of the room to watch Vili, the youngest son, dance a Verdi waltz with his mother on the occasion of her hundredth birthday. Together they took a few rehearsed turns around the room, pretended to stop a moment, and then resumed the dancing, everyone applauding as the couple spun in the light of the hundred candles, until Vili brought her back to where she had been sitting and where my mother waited to help the old lady regain her seat. Without asking, Vili reached out for my mother as he let go of his own, took her into his arms, and suddenly accelerated the pace of the waltz, taking dizzying swirls around the room, the exinfantryman from the battles of Val Maggio and Sant'Osvaldo wheeling the wheel merchant's daughter from Ibrahimieh, showing the world that a sixty-year-old rake could still ignite the heart of a thirty-year-old belle.

When the waltz was over, everyone applauded. Vili returned my mother to my father and said, "I owe your wife many apologies. I should have married her myself." He took my mother's hand in his and brought it close to his lips and, still holding it there, whispered, "I won't see you for many, many years. Goodbye." My mother blushed and, unsure of what he had just said, smiled and said, "Thank you."

Vili rushed to the kitchen, where his brother's chauffeur had been waiting for him with his brother's raincoat, his brother's suit, and a battered suitcase wrenched out of the junk room which his sisters had filled with old clothes so he would not arrive at the airport looking suspicious. The service door was opened, and from the landing outside, an unmistakable smell of *zibala*, refuse, wafted into the kitchen.

There, so as not to arouse suspicion among the guests, who had no notion of what was taking place at the other end of the apartment, his sisters had come one by one to bid their most cherished brother farewell. Each wept, washed her face, put on a smile, and went to mingle with the guests while another took her place, exhorting her youngest brother, as each had probably done before both world wars, to behave, be good, and be careful. My grandmother, his senior by almost fifteen years, was the last to say goodbye. "You won't start now," she said, "because if you do I will." "I won't, I won't," he promised. They hugged and kissed, after which Vili asked, "Esther, bless me." Unable to hold back her tears now, she began weeping aloud, placing a shaking palm upon his head, sobbing the Hebrew words out loud until she had said "Amen."

"Come, enough of this," she said as she kept caressing the

lapel of his jacket. "Promise to write. Don't just disappear." Unable to speak, he nodded.

The chauffeur picked up the suitcase and proceeded down the winding service stairway. Vili followed him, but he had not taken two steps before he suddenly collapsed against the banister. My grandmother exclaimed *"Santa Madonna!"* A second later, seated on one of the grimy metal treads of the stairway, Vili exploded in a loud sob.

"I'll never see Mother again," he began weeping, swaying like a drunkard, his face resting in both hands. "How can I go without saying goodbye, how can I do that to her, how?" I noticed that his lip was bleeding. "Blood!" I shouted. "It's nothing," he said, brushing the blood away with his palm as he resumed crying. The chauffeur had left the suitcase on the floor below and had come back upstairs to help him. "No, leave me here a second." My grandmother asked me to fetch a glass of whiskey. "Ask Elsa, she'll understand." I asked Hisham instead, who immediately poured a glass for me. I walked back along the corridor with the huge glass. No one asked me anything. When I made it into the pantry, I stopped. There was no one. I hid behind a pillar and spat into the glass. Then I stirred the spit with my finger.

"What a dog's life," Vili said after drinking the contents. "All these years, and now this."

"Adiós," he said.

His elder sister and I waved at him until the shape of his gray hat and of his hand disappeared all the way downstairs through the half-lit concentric turns of the winding banister.

"And now we must tell no one," warned my grandmother.

We shut the door of the kitchen behind us, walked through the pantry, shut the pantry door, and suddenly we were back among the guests. "Where were you?" asked my father. "Don't ask," gestured my grandmother. Then, seeing he was beginning to look perplexed, she said, "Vili left." "So soon?" he asked. "He left for good. *Understand?*"

The only one who did not know the truth for the next two days was my great-grandmother. She had been told a lie so the festivities would not be disrupted.

"He's in Cairo," they said in the end. "The king wanted to see him." No one had ever told the old lady that the king had been deposed a few years earlier.

Still, she knew something was amiss.

"He isn't dead, is he?"

"Dead? Who, Vili? He's as indestructible as Bismarck. Not like the other one."

The "other one" was my grandfather.

"No, the other *wanted* to die," added Dr. Alcabès, our relative and family homeopath. "I told him we could save him," he added as we were sitting at the third and last luncheon of the centennial. "But when he heard what the cure involved, he wanted no part of it. 'Cover me that I may die,' he said, quoting a Turkish proverb. So I told him, 'Albert, this can lead to only one thing!' Do you know what he said? 'Well, that's got to be better than letting you open me up, scrape me clean of my favorite organs, and leave me as hollow as a bell pepper. No thanks.' "

■

"He was a poor soul," said my grandfather to my mother as we made our way through a narrow passage in between the graves on Yom Kippur a few weeks later. We had just been to lay flowers on his mother's grave and were now headed toward my grandfather's. The Saint had not come with us, perhaps because she feared to run into the Princess with whom she was still quite angry.

I knew the way to my grandfather's tomb from previous

visits to the cemetery with my father and sauntered ahead, avoiding the low slabs. When we arrived, I saw my father waiting for us at his father's tomb.

He was all alone. The Princess had not come either.

"The poor man," said my grandfather after reflecting a moment. "We never got along, though God knows I never nursed any ill will toward him. But—" he said, meaning all that was water under the bridge.

"Can I recite a few words?" he asked his son-in-law, careful not to seem at all pushy when it came to religious matters.

"Yes," said my father, with a look of forbearing irony that almost said "if you really must."

My grandfather spoke the words softly, slowly, almost meekly, with diffidence and an air of mild apology one never expects from the faithful. He reminded me of my mother, who despite her anger, her fierceness, her blustering cry when she lost her patience, would always remain meek, uncertain, and kind.

When he was done, he gave his daughter a look and she immediately spoke two or three words of Hebrew, after which she said "Amen."

"*Voilà, Monsieur Albert*," said my grandfather, staring at the stone. Then, with the timidity of a man who had never felt at ease with his son-in-law, he touched my father on the shoulder once, a gesture of hindered sympathy that he did not wish to prolong for fear of overstepping his bounds.

"I feel for you," he said. "None of us is going to stay much longer in Egypt, and, frankly, it hurts when I think we'll have to leave our loved ones behind, me my mother, and you your father.

"They would have been happier to lie where they were born, with their loved ones. Your father had once asked me, 'What did I come to Egypt for if everyone will be leaving soon, leaving me stranded all by myself, twiddling my thumbs in my grave, the last Jew on this parched, half-baked strip of dust teeming with dirty feet?' He hated Egypt and he's buried in Egypt. 'What could be worse than being buried in a cemetery where you know nobody, Monsieur Jacques?' he would ask.

"And I tell you what. Worse than dying is the thought that no one will ever come to your grave, that no one will come wash the letters of your name. Everyone remembers for a few months, a few years, on anniversaries, and then, a generation later, they forget you. And the earth might as well make dust of you, for you're as good as unborn—you never *were* born— even if you live to be a hundred."

My father did not reply, though the allusion to the centennial did not escape him.

On our way out of the cemetery, the four of us greeted other Jewish families who had come to pray for their dead. My grandfather was going to synagogue and had asked whether we would join him for the service.

"Not today," said my father.

"I'll come," said my mother.

This pleased her father who, otherwise, would have had to go alone.

It was a typical Alexandrian autumn weekday morning. One could even have gone to the beach. My father said we would take a walk in the city; it was still too early to sit anywhere for a cup of coffee.

And then it must have hit him like an inspiration. "Come," he said, and we walked faster along the Boulevard and after a few turns finally ended up on Rue Chérif, where we stopped at an antiques dealer. My father looked inside, hesitated, then opened the large glass door. We heard the sound of chimes as we walked into a store filled with objects that reminded me of my great-grandmother's home. Two saleswomen were busily laying out velvet pads bearing coins in the shop window.

"May I help you?" asked one of them.

My father hesitated, then said, "Well, not really."

The woman, who could not have been older than thirty, seemed baffled. My father was nervous.

"Frankly," he started, looking out the window, "I am here because you knew my father and I know he used to speak to you about my son, so I thought maybe you might want to see my son."

"*I* knew your father? I don't think so," she said with an almost haughty ring in her voice as she arched her eyebrows. And then, before I quite knew what had happened, I saw her face redden, and a misty dampness swell in her eyes.

"Of course," she said, finally laying down the black velvet pad she had been holding all the while since seeing us walk into the store. "Of course," she repeated, nearly slumping on an antique chair, the backs of both hands flat against her thighs. "So this is the small boy. Let me see," she said, kneeling down to my level. "But he looks just like him." And turning to my father, "How nice to meet you too," she said. "You've no idea how happy this visit makes me."

"I thought perhaps it might. He would often say you wished to meet his grandson, so this morning, seeing we were free, I thought why not, and, well, here he is."

"What a coincidence, though. I was speaking about your father only yesterday," she continued as baffled as ever, touching my hand with her finger. "Wait, I must tell my brother Diego. Diego," she called out, "come and see who's here."

A man a touch younger than his sister appeared from a back room.

"Yes?" he asked.

"Take a good look before saying yes like that," urged his sister.

The man screwed his eyes on both of us.

"I'm sorry, but I don't understand."

"But this is the grandson."

"What grandson?" he exclaimed as though losing his temper.

"You sent him the ivory balls and you don't recognize him."

"Oh, my God!" he exclaimed, bringing a palm to his mouth. "He mentioned the boy several times, but who would have thought—"

He asked me whether I played billiards. I shook my head. He asked if I still had the balls he had given my grandfather for me. Yes, they were in my room, I said. What color were they? I told him.

"What a man, your father! I'm sure you know." Then, upon silent reflection, he added, "No, I suppose you can't know. One never knows when it's one's father," he said. Then, as though spurred by a sudden whim, he asked, "May we give him something?"

My father, still unable to believe there were people who venerated his father without being related to him, was growing more strained and uncomfortable, as though he suspected the brother and sister of bad faith, or simply of having been so easily duped by his father into loving him so much that they could only have been dolts.

"I'd prefer not," he said.

"Oh, a little something hurts no one."

"Please don't."

"But, monsieur," said Diego, "I am making this present not only to your son but to your father. Please allow me."

He pulled out an old brown drawer bearing a lion's mane on each knob and opened a small jeweler's box in which lay a gold tie clip studded with a rounded turquoise.

"It's for you," said the sister.

She handed me the small box.

"May I kiss him?"

"Of course," replied my father.

"He was a very special friend, you know."

My father did not reply. He began to show an interest in an old clock. But the young lady interrupted his inquiry, saying he should not feel obliged to purchase anything simply because we had received a gift.

"But the next time you happen to be here and have a free moment, please bring the boy."

Brother and sister saw us to the door and we exchanged goodbyes. On our way to the coffeehouse on the Corniche, I clutched the little box tight, refusing to hold my father's hand when we crossed the street for fear he might ask me to let him take it. Which is exactly what he did.

"Here, I'll keep it in my pocket for you," said my father, gently taking it from my hand. "It might be better not to tell anyone about it."

Then, trying to sound casual, he looked up at the clear sky, thought a moment, and, looking straight ahead, said, "I hope they'll give us the same table."

4

Taffi Al-Nur!

◧

My mother noticed something strange about the city as soon as we stepped out of the wool shop that evening. An unusual darkness hung over the crowded bus terminal in the main square; people fretted about the streets, cluttering the sidewalks as they waited for buses that arrived more overloaded than usual, tilted under the weight of passengers who were hanging onto doorways, some holding on to fellow passengers. Suddenly, the lights of Hannaux, the city's largest department store, went out, followed immediately by those of the Hannaux Annex to the right. The crowd gave a start as someone remarked that even Hannaux had put out its lights. Then St. Katherine's lights went out.

Everything was dark now, and we guided our footsteps by the unsteady, sporadic illumination of car headlights. Other people seemed to be doing the same. Suddenly, men wearing *galabiyas* came rushing, almost bumping into us. They were chanting slogans.

My mother held my hand and began to hurry toward Rue

Chérif, walking faster and faster along the sidewalk until we caught sight of a grocery store on an adjoining street. Its Greek owner was standing outside the doorway holding a long metal crank in both hands, as though about to fend off looters with his improvised weapon. When I looked through the open door, I saw that the shop was packed with customers, most, like us, having wandered in seeking shelter.

From outside, the Greek lowered the rolling shutter till it reached knee level. Then, bending under the shutter, he crept back into his store, rested the long crank against the doorjamb, tugged at his apron, smoothed its crinkles and, rubbing his hands together as though all this were just another rainstorm that might as well be weathered in good cheer, proceeded to take the next order.

The grocer had no intention of closing early on this autumn evening. Shoppers normally filled the streets after work, when the sidewalks throbbed with a chaos of lights spilling out of busy coffee shops and stores, especially now that the days were shorter and shops stayed open long after it got dark. Through the store windows you could watch women trying on gloves, and salesgirls forever folding and stacking sweaters in rainbow assortments of colors. I felt the nap of my sweater rub against my chin, there was something warm, wholesome, and kind in this soft, autumnal smell of new wool that presaged long, tea-room evenings, holiday shopping, and Christmas presents. I let the wool rub my chin again, thinking of tarts and hot chocolate at Délices, Alexandria's largest pastry shop, where Aunt Flora was to meet us that evening, and my father a while later, and where we would huddle together under the muted orange spill of evening lights at our usual table overlooking the old harbor while waiters delivered family orders on very large platters.

We had gone to buy my first winter uniform. That afternoon,

my mother had come to pick me up at school. She had waited in a taxicab parked on Rue des Pharaons, outside the school grounds, and as soon as she saw me had asked the cabdriver to honk a few times to draw my attention. I got in the cab as everyone else was lining up for the school bus. Mother let me sit on the jump seat in front of her. She kissed me from behind once the driver had closed the door.

We ordered the uniform in less than an hour. Most everyone at school purchased their uniforms from the school concession. Mother wanted to have mine made by her mother's tailor. The Princess suggested a compromise. Hannaux, apparently, sold school uniforms, less ostentatious than tailored clothes, but not those lopsided things others wore. We also had to buy a winter coat. I wanted the kind everyone else in class had, a coarsely woven cavalry twill trench coat whose belt came with a large leather buckle with two prongs and two rows of holes. My mother examined some of the coats and decided our tailor made better winter coats. We were not poor, she said.

Then, as the sun was setting, we had gone to an Armenian store to buy hanks of wool for sweaters that Aziza would knit for us in the weeks to come. I was told to choose my own colors. I hesitated awhile. Then I chose salmon. My mother said the color was not right for me, she wanted me to choose navy. But the owner of the store congratulated me on my choice of color. "Like father, like son," he said to my mother. "My husband never wears salmon," she protested. "That may be, madame, but it's his factory that dyed this wool, and look," he said, taking another spool from one of the lower bins, "no one but your husband can get these colors out of wool, no one," he said as though my father were a Michelangelo, able to free the most resplendent hues from an ordinary Egyptian fleece. Pleased by the praise, my mother decided I should have a salmon-colored sweater as well. Compliments were paid back and forth. Then we said goodbye, left the store, and had barely taken a few steps toward Place Mohammed Ali when suddenly the lights went out.

Ten minutes later we were packed inside the crowded Greek grocery store. At some point, the owner was forced to turn off all the lights in his shop; an Egyptian running the length of the side alley, banged on the rolling shutter, screaming "*Taffi al-nur*—put out your lights—*taffi al-nur!*" Everyone had to obey. "I don't want trouble," said the Greek as he implored his customers to forgive him.

In the dark, I held my mother's hand. She did not know about the wail that had cut through the evening clamor of the city and hovered overhead, a loud persistent blare that had come from around the Attarin district, one of the poorer neighborhoods of the city, and which someone said was a siren.

"But what's all this," complained a woman in Italian, "one can't see a thing in the dark."

"Wait," said the grocer. We heard the rattle of the shutters and the sound of the metal lip finally striking the ground. Seconds later, someone turned on a weak light in the rear of the shop.

"*E bravo!*" shouted one of the customers. Everyone else joined in the clapping, and business resumed as usual.

"Soon it'll be over and we'll all go home," said someone.

"At any rate, how long do you think it could possibly last with *them*," said someone else in French, mocking the Egyptian forces.

"A day or two at the most?" guessed another.

"If that," said a fourth voice. "The British will clean this whole mess up for us, give the Egyptians the well-deserved hiding they've been begging for ever since nationalizing the Suez Canal. And in a matter of weeks things will be back to what they always were."

"*Inshallah*," said a European in Arabic—"If it please God."

We made our way to the cashier, where my mother asked if we could use the telephone. The cashier said others were waiting in line for it. "We'll wait too," she replied. She gestured to the man in line ahead of us—could she possibly call first, seeing as she had a child with her and so many packages. The man shrugged his shoulders, saying the situation was urgent for everyone, not just her. "Imbecile!" muttered my mother under her breath.

After the present caller paid for using the telephone, the "imbecile" took hold of the handset and began dialing. He listened intently and looked extremely worried. Suddenly, relief and a flustered smile lit up his features. "Hello, Mammaaaaaa?" he shouted in the middle of the crowded grocery store.

She obviously couldn't hear very well because he had to shout. He made jerky movements with his head each time he warned her to stay put till he got home. "Go downstairs to the shelter. Nowhere else, understand?" I could hear her yammering in the earpiece. "Understand?" he repeated louder. Still she kept jabbering away. "Understand? Yes or no?" he yelled. At which she must have remembered to say yes, because he blurted out an exasperated "Finally," ending his conversation by whispering, "Me too."

He paid the cashier and our turn came. My mother, as was her habit, waited a moment as she held the handset before dialing. As soon as she dialed a number, she handed me the telephone. It was busy, I said. "On your word?" she asked with menace. "On my word." She tried another number. This time it rang. I never knew whom we were calling until they answered the telephone. But no one answered. "No one's at the office then," she said. She tried a third number. "But where are you?" the Princess exclaimed. "We've been looking everywhere for you. We even called Hannaux."

"We're in a grocery store," I said.

"In a grocery store! What are you doing in a grocery store at a time like this?" she yelled.

"Why are we in a grocery store?" I asked my mother.

"Because there's a *blenkaw*. Tell her it's because of the *blenkaw*," insisted my mother.

"She says it's because of the *blenkaw*."

"Because of the what?"

"The *blenkaw*," I explained.

"What in God's name is a *blenkaw*?"

"What's a *blenkaw*?" I asked my mother.

"It's when they shut off the lights and you're in the middle of a war."

"*Blackout*," corrected my grandmother, bursting with anger. "Will she ever learn to speak correctly before the boy ends up talking like a deaf-mute?" she commented to herself. When were we coming home, she asked.

"There are no taxis," answered my mother.

"And what is the name of the grocery store?"

"Miltiades," said my mother.

"But that's at the other end of the world. Why did she have to go to Miltiades of all places? I'm coming."

"She's coming," I said.

"She's not! Tell her not to come. Tell her we'll go to her house."

My grandmother began to argue when, in the course of the debate, the all clear rang over the city. My grandmother heard it too at her end of the line. "Come immediately," she ordered. The Greek and his wife turned on the main lights and almost simultaneously raised the rolling shutter. Blackout rituals from the Second World War were still very fresh in everyone's mind. "You may leave now, ladies and gentlemen—courtesy of Miltiades," he said as he stood at the doorway, wishing all of his customers good evening like a doorman expecting a tip. I had grown to like the warm, stand-up fellowship inside the store and was almost sorry to leave so soon, for there was something reassuring in being herded with so many people who smelled of cigarettes, perfume, and damp wool coats.

It occurred to my mother that we still had no way of getting home from where we were. By the time we reached Rue Chérif, all the shops had closed and the streets were emptying fast. There were no taxis available and the carriages normally parked along the sidewalks of Hannaux had disappeared.

The only choice was to reach Ramleh station by foot. From there we hoped to catch a tram to Grand Sporting, where my grandmother lived. But Ramleh was not close. "Can you walk?" she asked. "Because we'll have to walk to the station, and we have to walk fast." She gave me two of the smaller parcels and began to march forward, as I held on to her hand. She cursed herself for buying tea and pickled scallions at Miltiades.

The city was very dark. We turned the corner at Rue Toussoum, hugging the walls of the Ottoman bank as we tried to stay clear of the traffic. Mother stopped to judge whether, without knowing it, we might have missed Rue Phalaki in the dark. But no, Rue Phalaki was up ahead, she said. When we finally found ourselves walking along the dark and narrow sidewalk of the street on the way to the Boulevard, the wail of a siren once again tore through the city. People behind us began to run and the few lights inside the adjoining buildings immediately went out. Men were shouting in fear, invoking Allah. We too began to hasten our pace toward the Boulevard. Once we reached the intersection, we made out a large crowd massing around the tramway station. "This is worse than I thought," Mother said, as she stopped to catch her breath. The underground shelter would be crammed with people by now.

I had seen the Boulevard Saad Zaghloul late in the evening

before, with its shops closed for the night, but this was different. All the lights were gone now. People in *galabiyas* were racing around us, running toward the station as, a woman shrieked a boy's name. In between the dark outline of the buildings along the Boulevard, starlit, silver-flecked patches flashed in the distance, the old harbor.

Not two yards from Délices, we ran into Kyrio Yanni, the chief pastry cook, who immediately recognized us and offered us shelter in the Délices annex that housed the kitchen facilities. In the dark kitchen where we stood, Kyrio Yanni warned my mother that we should not go back to Smouha. "The guns of Smouha are sure to draw enemy fire." Mother explained that we were not planning to go to Smouha that evening.

Meanwhile, one of the Egyptian pastry chefs who had been smoking a cigarette in front of what looked like a large oven brought us two freshly baked pastries, which we devoured on the spot.

"Two more," insisted Kyrio Yanni. "Two more." And before Mother had a chance to refuse, he produced two of the creamiest *mille-feuilles* I had ever seen. He went back into another room, where I heard him fiddling around with paper. Then he reappeared with a small package. "For the family," he said. "And now we must go. Come."

Too impatient to wait for the all clear, Kyrio Yanni put on a winter coat over his white overalls and turned off the light in the stairway. "Slowly, slowly," he whispered. Then he opened the door to the street. By now there was not a soul on the sidewalk. It was cold. "Are there any bombs?" I asked. "Quiet!" snapped Kyrio Yanni. He was superstitious and did not want me to tempt British bombs. "We'll first go to the Hotel Cecil," he said. "It's close to the station." He peeked out again. "Come," he ordered, imitating what he had probably seen in movies of English prisoners escaping from a German camp. Mother pushed me forward and hurried behind me. When I turned and looked back, I saw her holding a half-eaten piece of cake in her hand.

Everyone in Alexandria must have had Kyrio Yanni's idea, for the hotel lobby was packed with people anxiously watching for the next tram to come into the terminal, at which point they all planned to dash across the street and jump on board. No sooner had we arrived than I thought I heard the tired old metallic clank of a tram bell. "*Yalla*, let's go," whispered Kyrio Yanni, who had seen the tram—one of those bearing the red *Victoria* sign on its front—well before anyone in the hotel and wanted us to be the first ones on.

My mother immediately understood why the Greek, who had grabbed me by the hand, was already racing across the street. She followed with packages in both arms. He and I climbed onto the car and ran to the very end of the first-class compartment. "Here, you sit here," ordered the pastry chef, "while I keep an eye out for your mother." He lowered the window, stuck his head out, and started to wave in the dark night. There was no sign of my mother on the platform. "But where is that one?" he muttered to himself. Then I heard her voice. She had raced all the way to our door along the siding.

"She could have gotten herself killed," yelled Kyrio Yanni who had never thought of using the tracks to get to a seat first. Our rescuer then closed the window, hoped we did not lack for anything on our perilous journey home, and asked my mother to pass along his regards to the family. "Until next time, then," he said as he gallantly strode out of the jam-packed tramway car with the heroic self-mockery of a man who might have been a daring resistance fighter in another age but who in ours was, and would always be, the chief pastry chef of whatever establishment he deigned to bake in.

I heard the rhythmic clatter of the steel wheels. We were

moving. I looked out the window, watching all of Ramleh and then Mazarita pass by under the moonless sky like an eerie forest in a dark nightscape. Sometimes I saw no farther than my hands. There was only the sound of the wheels, and the tossing within, and the ghostly call of the conductor's voice from the very back of the second-class car naming invisible stations.

An old lady sitting next to me was pressed against my side. Someone nearby began coughing. Mother tapped me on the shoulder and gave me a candy. I heard her unwrap another for herself.

Soon would come the second stop at Chatby, she said, followed by Camp de César. Then came Ibrahimieh, Petit Sporting, and finally my great-grandmother's stop. But when the conductor named Chatby, I realized we had not gone far, and that what I had mistaken for regular station stops were no more than erratic stalls and halts along the congested tracks.

And then it happened, and everyone gasped. The all-clear siren must have sounded some minutes earlier, but no one had heard it. For suddenly, as though roused from a long sleep, night began to lift from the city, unveiling bright bustling pockets of light all across Sporting and Cleopatra. Presently the lights within the car were turned on.

We opened the windows to look outside. The lights along the Bacos and Victoria lines, which bifurcated at Grand Sporting, could be seen dotting the tracks all the way to Cleopatra like a giant V-shaped landing strip. On the deserted platform, a lone, bowed figure stood anxiously watching our tram inch to a stop. It was my grandmother.

She was squinting at our tram, while a few steps behind her, Latifa, the maid, was already waving at us.

"Thank God you're safe," the Princess said, kissing my mother. "I've been waiting forever."

"We kept stopping every few yards," explained my mother. "What happened?"

"*What happened?* What happened is that there's a war. The baker called your mother, who called us. Everyone is worried."

I asked where my father was.

"Here," she said. He was standing halfway in the station-master's hut, listening to the latest news bulletin in Arabic.

"Not good, not good," he repeated as he walked toward us. "There's a blackout all over Egypt. The British, French, and Israelis have attacked. Who knows what will happen."

This was the first time I had ever seen him anywhere close to a tram. He always had a car—never took a bus, a tram, or even a cab. On the platform now, he looked humbler, like an ordinary commuter, like other fathers who took public transportation every day on their way to work. I liked him better this way.

∎

Kyrio Yanni was right to suggest we stay far from the guns of Smouha. That night my father decided we should spend the war days at Sporting, at my great-grandmother's home. Two other families had already moved in that afternoon, bringing their servants as well, with the result that the otherwise dark, grim, old Victorian apartment had become festive.

"But didn't you know the war had already started this afternoon?" asked Uncle Isaac with an unconcealed reprimand in his voice.

"How was I to know? No one told me," said my mother.

"The important thing is that everyone is here," interrupted my great-grandmother. "Let's have dinner, I'm starving."

Aunt Elsa, who was in charge of the household, always insisted on sounding the gong to announce dinner at exactly eight o'clock.

At the sound, more people came out of the smaller living room, people I had not seen since the centennial, two years earlier. "So many people," interjected my grandmother, "what joy." At which my mother remembered the groceries she had bought and, above all, the cakes.

"And cakes no less," shouted Aunt Marta on hearing the good news. "How many?"

"Twenty-four!" exclaimed another.

"What an idea—to go buying cakes on the night of an air raid!" grumbled Isaac.

A siren began wailing.

Immediately, a loud, burly voice along the street bellowed "*Taffi al-nur!*" into our dining room. "*Taffi al-nur!*" it repeated, followed by a string of thuggish curses as it trailed down Rue Thèbes, threatening other households.

"Do they know whom they're shouting at?" asked an outraged Uncle Isaac. "I could have had them flogged and impaled once."

"And now it's their turn," replied Uncle Nessim.

"Just wait for this war to be over, and we'll show these savages. I've suffered their nationalistic claptrap long enough."

"Ah, if only the king were still around—"

"What we really need is another Moses, a modern Moses," said Aunt Marta.

"And the only Moses we've got is Vili, and Vili is busy lording it in England. There!"

"Lucky Schwab is no longer with us," said Uncle Isaac, lighting a cigarette.

"Leave Aldo out of this, poor soul," replied his widow.

Aunt Elsa rang the gong a second time. When I entered the dining room, one of the servants was busily pulling the heavy curtains shut while another was struggling to lower the wick of a kerosene lamp that had just been placed on the buffet. It was dark. The grown-ups were busily conferring around Uncle Isaac, who was opening a wine bottle, everyone worrying, trying to outguess the course of events. There was a hubbub of voices.

Young Cousin Arnaut, Aunt Marta's son, was clearly on the verge of panic. "Above all, let's stay calm," said Uncle Isaac lifting his glass. "*Prosit*," someone else rejoined, "we've been through this many times before."

Children sat at the end of the table and were told not to make noise. I never liked the food in that house. I looked over to where my mother was sitting. In the dark, she could not read lips. I watched as she dreamily eased a bone from the fish, looking at no one in particular, talking to no one, yet obviously thinking about something, because, after bringing her fork to her mouth, she stopped chewing an instant and let an imperceptible shrug escape her shoulders. Mother caught me looking at her. "Why aren't you eating?" she asked merely by shaking her head at me. "It's horrible," I grimaced.

"What is it?" interrupted my grandmother, who saw we were communicating. My mother seized the opportunity.

"If you don't mind," she whispered so as not to interrupt the men, "I'll have him call my parents. They must be very worried."

"As you wish."

Mother signaled me to follow her out of the dining room.

In the dark, she held my hand as we picked our way through the long, furnished corridor. I guided my steps by the kerosene lamp in the dining room and by the voices of servants sitting in the dark kitchen.

We found the telephone. Mother dialed the numbers, feeling for them in the dark. As soon as the Saint heard my voice, hers began to warble and finally throw out that familiar string of Ladino words whose meaning I completely failed to comprehend but whose savage caress could reach through the telephone wire. "Why didn't you call any sooner?" she asked.

"Why didn't we call any sooner?" I asked my mother.

My mother hesitated a moment.

"Tell her it's because of the usual reason. She'll understand."

"You'll understand. It's because of the usual reason," I repeated.

"I'm her mother, of course I understand," said my grandmother.

I stood quietly a moment, thinking she had been speaking to me only.

"You didn't tell her. Tell her I'm her mother, that I'll always understand her, that I think of her."

"She thinks of you, she says," I repeated, bored and careless as always when relaying messages on the telephone for my mother.

"And that I'm her mother, that I understand," insisted my grandmother at the other end.

I said nothing, hoping my grandmother might think I was silently mouthing the message to my mother.

"What did she say? Tell her I want to see her tomorrow," said the Saint. I relayed the new message.

"But there are bombs, she says," I said.

"I'll come anyway. Or she should come to me. Tell her!"

Mother and daughter agreed to call each other the next day.

When we returned to the dining room, everyone, with faces half glazed in the kerosene light, was still talking about the war, all looking like anxious conspirators meeting in the underground.

■

At five to nine that evening everyone moved into the smaller living room and crowded around the radio to listen to the news. Someone placed the small kerosene lamp on top of the radio.

The Egyptian news bulletin in French announced a decisive victory over the enemy. England, France, and Israel had been thoroughly defeated by the intrepid forces under the command of Colonel Nasser. The crushing march to Haifa and Tel Aviv was already under way, and by midnight of December 31, 1956, the combined Arab armies would celebrate their victory on the shores of the Galilee.

"Pure claptrap!" muttered Uncle Isaac.

Through our living room windows, I looked at the surrounding buildings sitting in sullen, silent darkness. All of the streetlights were turned off. The few cars traveling up and down the avenue kept their headlights off, some already painted cobalt-blue to avoid being spotted by the enemy.

Shouts were suddenly heard along our street. "Perhaps we should put out our kerosene light as well," suggested Aunt Elsa.

Uncle Isaac lowered the wick of the lamp. My father was busily fumbling with the shortwave knobs on the radio, but all the frequencies had been jammed, which irritated Uncle Isaac even further. He motioned to my father to move away and began turning the knobs back and forth himself, humphing away under his thick mustache, only to find that he too was unsuccessful. "Bastards!" he shouted. It was Aunt Marta who, with the diligent persistence of a blindwoman trying to thread a needle, finally locked onto Radio Lebanon. Radio Lebanon was fulminating against Israel, the treacherous neighbor, the knife in the back, the puny ganging up with the mighty. The announcer said something about a war on Egypt; the British had landed in Port Said.

That was good enough for everybody. "It's already over," said someone.

"If Vili were here, we'd be uncorking champagne right now," said Aunt Marta.

Overjoyed by the news, my grandmother began jumping up and down in the large entrance hall.

"Bravo, Esther," joined Aunt Elsa who also began clapping and skipping about on her septuagenarian legs.

Behind the half-parted curtains leading into the main corridor, I caught sight of Abdou listening in on the news bulletin. He was standing and leaning forward, half concealed in the dark, his glinting eyes peering out from the heavy folds of the old brown curtain like those of an inquisitive fox frozen momentarily in the headlights, something guilty in the manner his eyes darted away as soon as I caught him staring at us.

I immediately told my father, who dismissed it the way he always dismissed my grandmother's complaints about her servant's petty pilferings. "In their place I'd do the same thing," he said.

"Yes, but think of it," rebutted Uncle Isaac who always claimed to see things from a far broader perspective. "You may understand their nationalistic aspirations, but remember that without us Egypt would still be a desert."

"Softly," said my grandmother, who did not want Abdou to hear any of this.

"Softly-who-cares!" interjected Cousin Arnaut, who was constantly reminding everyone that the entire family should move to France. "If we can't say what we think under our roof, then we have no roof!"

"Spoken like a true poet, *ya salam!*" exclaimed Uncle Isaac, using an Arab expression denoting profound admiration. "*If we can't say what we think under our roof, then we have no roof.* Fear brings out the poet in you."

Minutes later a dead silence filled the room as everyone, including the seven or eight children, sensed something solemn in the sonorous voice that suddenly spoke from the old Philco in a stately French accent so different from ours. Radio Monte Carlo! It was the French of movie stars, the French my uncles mimicked but never mastered, the French one made fun of but secretly envied, the French one claimed one didn't care to speak, the way some might say they didn't care for certain cheeses because no Brie or Saint André could ever compete with a good, hearty slice of fresh Greek feta. "I always come back to my feta," Uncle Isaac would say, the way he might have said that he always came back to Aunt Lotte. It was a French that made us feel remote, dated, inferior.

The voice that spoke to us from far across the dark Mediterranean seemed to come from light-years away, lofty, polished, and unshaken, declaiming the old promise that France would always stand against the forces of darkness. The joint forces had launched strategic air strikes against Egypt. Port Said had fallen. Allied paratroopers had taken Suez.

"That's the end of that!" said Uncle Nessim.

"They'll be here in a matter of days."

Moments later someone was pounding at our door. Uncle Isaac immediately turned off the radio, took the small kerosene lamp, and went to answer it himself, his swollen shadow sweeping across the ceiling as he finally reached the entrance door. It was the porter. He did not wait for the door to open before shouting out curses at us for waiting so long to turn off our lights.

"Do you want us to get bombed?" he asked in Arabic.

Uncle Isaac looked at him, stunned. "Of course I don't want us to get bombed," he replied.

"Then turn off the lights, you old Jew, or I'll have you arrested for spying."

The porter did not give my uncle a chance to slam the door

in his face, but pulled it shut behind him. In the hallway, I heard him yell the same thing at poor old Madame Silvera.

■

That same evening most of the living room and entrance furniture was moved against the walls, mattresses were laid down, and when my grandmother saw that there were not enough mattresses for everyone, she had old blankets, some dating as far back as the Crimean War, taken out of the storage room, and put down for the children to sleep on. All my cousins and I would share the living room for the next few weeks.

Early the next morning, my uncles asked one of the servants to buy every local newspaper at the main Sporting newsstand. The news was unbelievable.

"Victory again!" quoted Uncle Nessim.

"Victory here as well," replied Uncle Isaac. " 'Not a single prisoner, hardly a wounded soldier among the men defending their motherland.' "

"How could this good-for-nothing upstart Nasser defeat the combined British and French forces, tell me?" asked Aunt Marta.

Breakfast at my great-grandmother's was always served *à l'anglaise*, a custom I had only seen practiced in the movies and which made me feel as though I had entered the most luxurious hotel in the world, where the fresh morning air is always tempered by the welcoming smell of exotic flowers, buffed floors, and hot beverages, butter, toast, and eggs. You helped yourself to whatever you wanted on the buffet and then sat down, while a servant poured coffee, tea, or chocolate. The butter was curled into neat oyster-shaped shells. The dried toast was covered with an embroidered purple cloth, the eggs were kept warm in a large bowl, there were plenty of cheeses and jams. As for the brioches, there were so many of them

lumped together in a basket, it was clear you could help yourself to many more than just one.

"Are you going to eat all this?" asked my grandmother who
was helping me with my breakfast.

I nodded. I watched my mother shake her head at me—I
didn't have to show I had never before seen so much food at
breakfast. But I insisted, telling my grandmother, who had
intercepted the look on my mother's face, that I was very
hungry.

"If you say so, then," said my grandmother, who wanted
everyone, particularly those of her sisters who had their children and grandchildren present, to notice that if she let me do
as I pleased it was not because she doted on me with the
smoochy fondness of Sephardi grandmothers, but rather because ours was a privileged relationship between an unusually enlightened grandmother and her unusually precocious
grandchild.

As always, my grandmother sliced little bread fingers for
me, cut the larger tip off the soft-boiled egg, and then sprinkled
salt into it. I looked up from my seat next to hers and saw the
sun beaming into the dining room. My grandmother's lavender
dress caught the light of this beautiful, quiet morning. I had
stepped into a realm of magic and legend.

When the servant came to pour my hot chocolate, I said I
wanted tea instead and, mimicking my grandmother, asked
him to please add some hot water after pouring the tea into
my cup.

No one allowed me to live it down. During the ensuing few
days, whenever anything was served in the dining room, someone was always bound to ask the servant not to forget to please
add hot water to it. Did I need hot water in my soup? Or in
my salad perhaps? Or did I want some poured into my glass
of water, was it too cold? Uncle Isaac, who loved Aunt Marta's

homemade ice cream, could never refrain from asking whether I wanted hot water in my ice cream.

"We've joked enough. Now leave the boy alone," snapped my grandmother after the third day. "And from now on," she said, turning to me, "drink what you're given without putting on airs, understand?"

Gone was the enlightened liberalism she had affected earlier.

"Wants to be a *petit monsieur*," teased my uncle. "All he needs is a monocle, a top hat, and off goes our *jeune flâneur* through the *grands boulevards de Paris*."

Uncle Isaac asked me what I wanted to become when I grew up.

"An ambassador," I replied, eyeing my grandmother, who had planted the idea in my head.

"And of which country?" he asked.

I said I didn't know yet.

"Which country are you a citizen of?"

I had never thought about it before, but the answer seemed so readily obvious to me that I failed to see why he asked. "France, of course," I said.

" 'France, of course,' he says. Doesn't even know what country he's a citizen of, and his grandmother wants him to be its ambassador. Do me a favor, Esther, do me a favor! You're not French, I'm French," he said to me, with something like venom and a sneer warbling in his graveled voice. "You, on the other hand, are Italian, and not even that—Turkish, to be precise!"

He looked at me for an instant and then giggled.

"Didn't even know it, see? And doesn't look too thrilled, either."

Everyone in the family had talked almost daily about a faraway, gaslit world called Turkey, where ignorance, dirt, disease, theft, and massacres prevailed. It never occurred to me that I was Turkish because of this. I felt sullied, mocked, betrayed. Amid the general laughter, I stared at Uncle Isaac, unable to fathom his twisted loops of irony, not realizing yet that he had the wit, good cheer, and playful devotion to children that mark the cruelest people.

■

Early one afternoon, while everybody was napping, I heard the sudden grief-stricken cooing of a turtledove who had lost her young to a kitten. She was dizzily circling the inner courtyard, rending the afternoon silence, telling everyone in the kitchen of her sorrow, while her mate watched her swirl around the courtyard, almost smashing into the masonry at each turn.

I opened the glass door that connected the living room to the dining room, stepping into the place where, scarcely an hour before, the grown-ups had loudly debated our prospects. "There is nothing to do but wait," Isaac had said. "The banks are closed. They've sealed the doors to my office. The only person willing to extend me credit is my tobacconist."

He was worried. The British and the French forces had undoubtedly won. Yet there was not a sign of them.

"If it worries you so much, why not ask someone in the cabinet?" suggested my great-grandmother.

Isaac, the Talleyrand of the family, had never found the courage to tell his mother that such a cabinet hadn't existed in years, and that, as a consequence, he no longer knew anyone in government. "I'll see," he had said, looking down as he peeled an orange, slowly, suddenly slipping a strip of the rind flat against his front teeth to imitate a monster's mouth, which he knew would scare me.

"If they've taken Suez and Port Said, why aren't they in Cairo or Alexandria?" asked the old courtier.

"The Germans took France faster than this!" added Aunt Marta, looking duly perplexed.

"I must see Ugo," replied Uncle Isaac. "He will know."

Not a sign of our lunch remained now, only a vague scent of citrus, laced into the perennial stuffy odor of cloves, cinnamon, old cloth, and old people that greeted you whenever you wandered into the house. My great-grandmother liked ginger biscuits. She liked tea. She was always cold. I heard her cough in the next room. One of the maids was stoking embers in the old stove. The servants were eating leftovers.

Once I had shut the glass door behind me, the dining room became as peaceful and quiet as Aunt Marta's timeless still lifes along the wall. The dead partridge, the Anjou melon split in two, the emptied wine flask with wildflowers, the trapped pheasant strung on a noose sitting next to dried fruit and autumnal hunting gear in a small English country house. Everything was brown. A sad, sodden, dreary brown filled the room with its beige curtains, faded sheers, and its pale oak furniture and yellow-stained walls on which a muted cast of light gave the day a languid quality between noon and early evening, in a month that was no longer fall but not quite winter either.

Part of the reason the room had an oppressive dun shade was that every piece of cloth in it, down to our napkins, had been dyed in tea, which gave otherwise yellowed, stained, aging white cloth a perpetual tan shade. Everything that had lost its color was ultimately dyed in tea. Even hard-boiled eggs at Passover were dyed in tea.

Aunt Marta's forest scene portraying the tale of Actaeon hung above the buffet, displaying the metamorphosed hunter fending off his own dogs, while fellow stag-hunters begin to close in from around a tawny grove, eyeing the frightened stag as they hurl their spears. An old, tawdry piece of dark embroidered cloth had been placed on the dining table, with a bowl of walnuts to hold it in place.

"So," I heard Uncle Isaac's voice from the entrance hall. He had taken his walking stick, his hat, and his coat and was asking his sisters whether any of them might want to join him for a long walk. None would go. Uncle Nessim had already gone off to play golf. Everyone else was sleeping.

"Then *he's* coming," said my uncle, pointing at me. My grandmother hesitated.

"Where are you going?" she asked with wide-open, suspicious eyes.

"I'm going for a walk."

I could tell she was struggling not to ask again.

She helped me put on my coat and forced me to wear an old, smelly, borrowed scarf.

As soon as we were out of the building, we headed for the tramway station. On the tram, I felt uncomfortable watching Uncle Isaac arguing with the conductor that I should pay a reduced fare being so young.

We got off several stops later at Bulkley. As we walked up an incline, I looked through the trees and saw a row of villas with large gardens and wrought-iron gates. We continued to head east until we reached a narrow, empty road, littered with dry leaves that crackled underfoot.

Uncle Isaac stopped in front of a villa whose porch was lined with imitation Greek caryatids supporting an upper terrace covered with ivy and jasmine. He rang at the gate. A maid eventually opened the main door and, on seeing him, immediately came rushing out to open the front gate. "Your Excellency," she exclaimed, "what an honor."

Uncle Isaac pushed me awkwardly inside the villa grounds and reminded me to walk properly. "We'll only stay a moment," he said. From inside I could hear the strains of loud operatic music.

"Isaac," came a shrill man's voice. "Isaac. Our dear, dear

Isaac. Come in, come in," said the man, extending both hands, with which he shook my uncle's right hand.

When we entered the house, we noticed that all the windows had been covered with thick cobalt-blue paper.

"We haven't started doing this," said my uncle, indicating the covered shutters. "I suppose we should."

"Absolutely must," said the elderly gentleman, who wore a maroon ascot and a beige cardigan. "The police came yesterday and were so terribly rude that, naturally, the first thing we did this morning was to have all the windows covered." His wife was just coming out of the library.

"Isaac, but you're really unforgivable," she shouted in the marble hall. "Staying away from us so very long—really, *tesoro*."

Uncle Isaac kissed her.

"Ali!" she hollered at the top of her lungs. *"Tea!"*

"So tell me, *caro*," said the man wearing the ascot.

"I don't know what to make of it yet," answered my uncle. Perhaps he was being evasive or, as he would say, diplomatic: say less than you think and mean more than you know.

"*E finita*—" said the gentleman, "that's what you should make of it. *La commedia è finita*," he crooned with blithe consternation as he lifted up an arm with the operatic flourish of someone looking for the slightest pretext to break into song.

"But *siamo seri*, let's be serious," said his wife.

"*Siamo in due*," rejoined her husband, breaking into song yet again, whereupon his most devoted and compatible wife, heeding her husband's musical inducements, joined him in singing "*O soave fanciulla*," in which my uncle joined as well, adding his warbly basso.

"Aaahh," sighed the man after the trio had sung and laughed their way into a fit of coughing. "We've lived far too long, *caro*, and have too many wonderful memories to let a bunch of turbaned hooligans frighten us now." He reflected for a moment. "Hooligans, schmooligans," he added. "I've built this house out of nothing"—he pointed to the marble floor, the marble paneling along the marble staircase, where a creamy afternoon glow graced a pair of marble statues standing inside a sculptured wooden door—"and I'm not about to leave it to them. This here, my friend, is where I plan to die many, many years from now, like old King David in the arms of his sprightly, young, desirable Bathsheba," he said, holding his wife by her waist and rubbing his hip suggestively against hers.

"Ugo!" protested his wife with mock reproof.

"*Ugo!*" he mimicked with the rakish petulance of an Old World *charmeur*. "*M'hai stregato*, you've bewitched me," he whispered, his mouth rubbing her neck. Then, holding his wife in both arms, he turned to my uncle and winked at him, wearing a crafty, naughty-boy smirk that seemed to allege an air of impish complicity between fellow womanizers. This was Egypt's most powerful stockbroker, the man whom the country's European and Egyptian elites trusted with their dreams of fortune.

"Ugo, tell me, what is happening?" asked my uncle.

"What is happening?" repeated Signor Ugo with a sprightly look darting from his eyes. "What is happening is that whatever the British and the French take from Nasser they'll have to give back. The Russians won't allow them to keep anything, not the canal, not Port Said, not anything. And the irony is that the British already know it, as do the French, though they'll continue fighting awhile to save face."

"But it's the end, then," muttered Uncle Isaac.

"Isaac. I've heard—" then he stopped and stared in my direction.

"Talk. He doesn't understand."

"My friends," he started, meaning his high-powered clients in the Egyptian government, "my friends tell me that Nasser won't forgive this attack. There will be serious reprisals against French and British nationals once all this is over. Nationalizations. Expulsions. This includes Jews."

"Jews?"

"In retaliation for the Israeli attack."

"But we're not Israelis—" Uncle Isaac began to protest.

"Tell that to President Nasser!"

"But then we're done for. No wonder they've closed the banks. If they don't take everything I've got and throw me out of Egypt for being French, then they'll do it because I'm Jewish."

"*Questa o quella*—" added Signor Ugo, alluding to the aria but tactful enough not to sing it.

My uncle said that this was worse than anything he had ever imagined. It was worse than waiting for the Germans to march into Alexandria.

"Ugo, just in case anything happens to me, remember this name. Monsieur Kraus. Geneva. Vili knows."

Signor Ugo took out a white pack of cigarettes and began scribbling something on the back of it.

"Are you mad, Ugo!" exclaimed my uncle. "Don't write anything. Just remember it."

Signor Ugo gave a quiet, significant nod, put away his pen, and, meaning to stop further dark thoughts from clouding his perennially cheerful disposition, put on a lively face, seemingly for the child who was present, and reminded us that tea would be served in the living room. "*Che sciagura*, what a disaster," he said, revealing a strangely melodious accent when speaking Italian.

Ugo da Montefeltro was born Hugo Blumberg in Czernowitz. Like many gifted Rumanians of his generation, he had emigrated to Turkey in pursuit of petty business ventures, none of which got him anywhere except to Palestine, where he arrived as a correspondent for a Yiddish publication in the Ukraine that folded before he had even written his first article. His next stop was Egypt. The charming young man had a gift for languages and song, and soon enough became a stockbroker for Egypt's French and Italian communities. In a matter of four years, he had become a very wealthy man. Always wary of dangers facing Jews, Signor Ugo and his wife changed their surname in the wake of a series of anti-Semitic incidents in Cairo. They had intended to change Blumberg, which in German meant mountain of flowers, to its Italian equivalent, Montefiore, and would have lived quite happily with that name, had a good friend not reminded them that nothing was more Jewish than the House of Montefiore. Ugo shrugged off the borrowed name and soon after picked a French equivalent, to which, this time, he decided to add the ennobling *particule*. He became Hugo de Montfleury.

But that project did not last long, either, for someone else told him of two French playwrights—a father and son—called Montfleury but whose real names were Antoine and Zacharie Jacob. From this it was inferred that the Montfleurys, the target of Cyrano de Bergerac's most pernicious satires, probably were "like us." Blumberg hastily cast off Monsieur de Montfleury and took a name that sounded quite like it, and which had, as he would always say with an amused quiver on his lips, a certain charm and a long lineage to go with it. He became Ugo da Montefeltro, "domiciled," as his illegally purchased Italian passport showed, not in Leghorn—where most Levantine Jews alleged their ancestral home—but in Montalcino, whose wines he fancied.

To tease him, some of his friends called him Ugolino da Montefeltro, which pleased the Rumanian fop no end, because the name conferred a doubled aristocratic provenance, with brooding reminders from Dante—hence Uncle Isaac's nickname for him: Dantés de MonteCristo.

In later years, few were the European boys in Alexandria whose path did not cross Signor Ugo's. In his impoverished old age, he earned a living as a private tutor of history, literature, and mathematics, while his wife, Paulette, worked as a seamstress to emerging Egyptian families. On Sundays both could still be seen at the Sporting Club, walking arm in arm along the main alley or on the polo fields, he always in the same ascot and tweed jacket, and she wearing loud, colorful designs that she cut and sewed herself, after patterns copied from *Burda*, with the flashy cloth then fashionable in Egypt. My father noticed that the smile was gone from her face, and her husband crooned a bit less when he had us over for dinner, rubbing his hands in excitement before opening an old bottle of Bordeaux that he had cleverly smuggled under the very nose of the Bureau of Nationalization.

"Not the last, but among the last. When these are gone, we'll go—right, *cara*?"

"Always so gloomy," she would say. "Open the wine and let's enjoy it. *Libiam—et après nous le déluge*," she would say, invoking the words of Verdi and Marie-Antoinette, as we all sat in their small pension bedroom-dining room on Rue Djabarti, a far cry now from the opulence of their house in Bulkley. Never one to fail to pick up his cue from Verdi, Signor Ugo would sing one aria and then another and yet another from *La Traviata*, ending with a male rendition of *Addio del passato*. On these occasions, my mother, who had no idea what he was singing, would sit with a glass of wine in her hand, half-bored, half-smothering a giggle at the fustian old gentleman who hid his sagging dewlap under all manner of scarves and who she knew would be weeping any moment now. And indeed, having reached the end of his aria, he would burst into a boyish sob, which never failed to steal the most tender and compassionate *"Tesoro!"* from his wife, who, more than ever now, was forced to liven the atmosphere by holding out her glass to offer a toast: "To the most beautiful soul in the world."

It occurred to very few that the Signora da Montefeltro had lost her smile not only because she was wretched with grief inside, but because she was ashamed to let people see the deteriorated state of her front teeth, which she could no longer afford to fix. When, on rare occasions, she would run into her old dentist with friends at the club and everyone sat at the same table, he would confront her and ask, "Let me take a look at this." She would resist, alleging decorum and propriety, calling him an unregenerate rake for asking a woman her age to show him her mouth in public. But, after much resistance, she would finally consent to a peek at her gums. "Just as I imagined. Come tomorrow, understand?"

By being so unusually brusque and peremptory with the ex–grande dame, he was hoping to spare her the embarrassment of hearing that she would never be charged for her visits. "One day, Doctor, one day. But tomorrow I play bridge."

Tomorrow I play bridge was a famous Montefeltro half-lie intended less to deceive than to display a failed attempt to deceive—a passe-partout phrase everyone quoted when they wanted you to know they were probably lying.

"Tomorrow we're playing bridge," Signor Ugo said out loud as soon as he saw Ali walk in with tea and hot chocolate. It was his way of misleading the servant into thinking we had been talking about cards.

"I play for Paulette's sake. Personally, I hate bridge," Montefeltro went on, quite pleased at the deftness with which he had changed subjects on hearing the kitchen door open. "Especially when it's gray, as it's been these days. And on gray, autumnal days, what better than to drink hot tea and listen to Brahms." This was a hint to his wife to play something on the piano.

"Not now, Ugo. Put on a record instead."

Signor Ugo disappeared into the living room, whistling debonairly. Moments later, with a sound that reminded me of a persistent gardener raking dead leaves, came the piercing strain of an old, scratchy 78 recording of the horn trio.

"Here are some little chocolates," he said, producing a very large box of mini Toblers that were individually wrapped and neatly arranged in a dizzying mosaic of multicolored bars.

"Which will you have?" asked Uncle Isaac.

I took one with a hazelnut on the wrapper, slowly unwrapped it, placed it in my mouth, and, to my dismay, found that, before savoring or thinking about the chocolate or even dropping its crinkled wrapper into the large ashtray that stood next to box—I had already swallowed it. Trying to hide my desire for another as best I could, I pointed out to Signora da Montefeltro that these were really exquisite chocolates. "You must have another, then," she insisted, and when I had finished that one, "and another yet." I chewed that one as fast as I could, hoping she would offer me another. But my uncle intervened after the third, saying I had had three and that was plenty. "Oh, well, if you say so," said Signora da Montefeltro. "But I want him to take some home with him."

When my uncle said it was time to leave, Signor Ugo and his wife insisted we stay longer, which we did—for another five minutes—after which my uncle repeated that we really had to leave, though without standing up this time, knowing he would yield to their inducements once again. At his third reminder, however, they too stood up and gradually walked us to the back gate by way of their huge patio. On our way through a narrow corridor toward the French windows, I caught sight of rows upon rows of empty Elmas cigarette boxes lining the entire wall. There must have been thousands of cigarette packages there. Signor Ugo saw me staring at them. "Sometimes an idea pops into my head. And I immediately jot it down on the back of my pack of cigarettes." He claimed he still remembered exactly where to find each idea, which is why everyone in the house was under strict orders never to touch, move, or even think of dusting what, to most, must have looked like a cemetery of stray thoughts.

"The hooligans can take anything they please, but these, never."

His empty packs were eventually confiscated and examined by the secret police, and never returned.

On our way out, seeing that Signora da Montefeltro had forgotten, I reminded her that she had promised me some chocolates.

"Oh, what an absentminded fool I am," she said as she hurried back into the room.

"But that's appalling behavior," my uncle scolded. "Whoever taught you manners, Arabs? I've never heard of such a thing, never. I'm never taking you anywhere.

"That was humiliating," he kept repeating as we started to walk away from the Montefeltro house, the blessed pair waving at us with exaggerated, Old World, cruise-ship hand motions.

"Humiliating," he repeated, stabbing his walking stick into the pavement each time he said the word. He sulked all the way downhill, while I clutched the small chocolates in my hand, not daring to open a single one until his mood had changed. Silently, my uncle and I turned as we had been advised to do by Signora da Montefeltro once we had reached the bottom of the hill. Uncle Isaac had wanted to visit another family, but on our way we ran into two Egyptian youths who sprung out in front of us. "Are you Jews?" one of them sneered, holding a stone in his hand. My uncle, whose sister Elsa had been asked that same question during the Second World War by two policemen in Paris, remembered her reaction. He slapped one of the youths hard on the chest and asked him how dare he think he was Jewish. "Do I look Jewish?" he yelled.

"We thought you were dirty Jews."

"Look for dirty Jews elsewhere, then."

Uncle Isaac led me away in silence. "*Cammina*, keep walking," he told me in Italian. "I don't want to turn around," he said when we were about fifteen paces away, "but you turn, and tell me what they are doing." I turned around. Both were standing still, as though beginning to doubt my uncle's words.

We took a shortcut through a back alley and headed to the tramway station as fast as we could. "Don't worry, we'll be safe," said my uncle as we began to walk faster and faster. We sighted a carriage waiting and hailed it at the top of our lungs.

"Sharia Tiba," said my uncle in Arabic once we sat down, Rue Thèbes. He haggled over the price; the coachman relented. He gave his horse a slight lash on the mane, and the carriage pulled off. As we began to circle back toward Sporting, passing villa after villa, passing even the Montefeltros' garden with its counterfeit caryatids and its broken fountain spout that had never worked, not a sound could be heard on the empty road except a faraway dog and the rickety squeaks of our carriage, whose horse, for some unknown reason, knew Brahams's horn trio well enough to let his leisurely footfalls stamp to the rhythm of the music.

Suddenly, far, far beyond Bulkley, from an angle I had never seen before, rose all of Sporting, with its distant polo fields and its endless row of palm trees studding the giant racetrack. The air was thick with the gathering rainstorm, and the buildings and churches lining the tramway tracks as far as the eye could see sat under a darkening sky flecked with scattered orange stains. We heard the familiar gong of the Ambroise Rally church strike five o'clock in imitation Big Ben chimes.

"We'll be in time for tea," Uncle Isaac said. Then remembering—"About these chocolates, are you going to hoard them all to yourself?"

I handed him one in a green wrapping. I didn't like pistachio.

■

When we arrived, tea was just about to be served.

Latifa had fainted again.

"Each time the siren sounds, she turns as white as aspirin. It scares her," explained my grandmother.

"Scared of the alarm, scared of men, scared of anyone who raises his voice at her. What isn't she scared of?" grumbled Uncle Isaac.

My grandmother told how she had brought her to: a rag was placed on top of a flame long enough to stink of smoke and then was brought to her nostrils.

Everyone was gathered in the living room, while Abdou and Latifa brought tea and light pastries. "Latifa, I heard you broke the floor," jeered Uncle Isaac when Latifa brought in a second round of pastries. Latifa smiled modestly and deposited a large platter on the tea table. My great-grandmother called Latifa back. She liked her ginger biscuits served on a separate dish. Our Abdou had mistakenly lumped them with other petits fours.

I noticed that the windowpanes in the entrance and the living room had been coated with a cobalt-blue dye. Abdou and Ibrahim and two other servants were in the process of lining the remaining shutters in the house with large strips of thick blue paper which they thumbtacked to the wooden sash frames. They had already painted everyone's headlight covers with the blue dye.

Aunt Elsa rang the buzzer and Latifa's rounded form appeared behind the glass-paneled door. She walked in and softly began clearing the china. So tea was over, I thought, already missing the spell of that moment when my uncle and I had opened the door to find everyone already seated in the living room, the sun just barely set over the horizon, and everyone hurrying to make room for us. Sitting quietly next to my parents, my cousins, my aunts and uncles, everyone's thighs cozily glued to mine, I knew that even if I disliked almost everyone in this room, it was good to be with them, good to hear the ritual hubbub of tea, good to look and be looked at.

And then, after everything had been cleared away, and Uncle Isaac had poured out the first scotch of the evening, while his sister Elsa, who held all the keys in the house, had opened the small Chinese cabinet in which peanuts were hidden away from the children, suddenly, punctually, as though this were why we were gathered in the living room all along, we heard it, rising above Sporting, over the city, wailing and warning, as voices immediately started downstairs—*"Taffi al-nur! Taffi al-nur!"*

Someone would stand up, walk over to the corner of the room, and peek through the curtain, while someone else, just as swiftly, would turn off the lights. A deep, premature night filled the room. When I looked out the window, I saw all the lights of Sporting go out one by one, accentuating the sudden darkness that had settled among us.

"What I don't understand," Aunt Marta would say in her shrill voice, "is that there hasn't been a single bomb dropped on Alexandria."

"And what I don't understand is that you keep repeating the same thing each time there's an air raid," my grandmother would snap.

And thus, for almost an hour, as we sat together in the dark, occasionally interrupted by an irate *"Taffi al-nur!"* rising from within the courtyard in our building, or by my great-grandmother asking what someone in the room had just said, or by Latifa who would tiptoe her way in to retrieve some cups ever so discreetly so as not to disturb those listening to the radio, someone would always remind us that our days in Egypt were numbered, that most of us would be spending New Year's somewhere else in the world, that we would never sit together in this same room again.

For the next day, and the days after that, I would go out with aunts and cousins, sensing that what gave our days their unusual luster was less the walks we took together, or the places we visited, or the peculiar, old-fashioned games we played, or even those improvised visits that made the Saint so happy, but the strangely comforting certainty of coming back to a stuffy room full of stuffy people bound together by the need to huddle in the dark.

■

One evening, ten days after the beginning of the war, the porter came upstairs with a man wearing a police uniform. Apparently, someone from our apartment had been sending Morse code signals to enemy ships at night. We explained that there must be a mistake; besides, no one in our home knew the Morse code. My grandmother had Uncles Isaac and Nessim swear on their honor.

Latifa's face was white. My grandmother asked her to sit down and began fanning her head.

"Are you going to faint?" she asked.

"I don't know, I think so, maybe," said Latifa.

"She's fainted," whispered an exasperated Aunt Elsa, while the policeman looked around one last time and said he was sorry to have disturbed us.

My grandmother immediately called Dr. Alcabès. Minutes

later, my mother, who performed injections for everyone in the family and who, when begged, would describe the shape and condition of anyone's buttocks, administered Latifa with an injection of a certain "revitalizer" of which my great-grandmother had a large supply, jealously guarded by Aunt Elsa. Years later I found out that it had belonged to Uncle Vili and was nothing more than a shady elixir used by near-impotent men.

"But does she need it, or does she just want the evening off to go cackle with the maids upstairs?" asked my great-grandmother.

"Take a good look at her face and tell me if she doesn't need it," snapped my mother.

"You're sure she's not exaggerating?" the old woman persisted.

"Old miser," my mother muttered.

Latifa hated injections and begged not to be given a shot. My mother ignored her pleas and, seeing she was resisting her with erratic kicks, had Abdou and Ibrahim hold her down as she bared her bottom. Latifa let out a violent scream, in which she invoked her mother and all her sisters to come to her rescue.

"But what on earth are you afraid of?" asked Uncle Isaac losing his temper, stomping into the cluttered maid's room as though on the point of striking her. She was lying on a make-shift bed, surrounded by ancient *karakib*. "Do you have to faint each time you hear bad news?"

"It's the pain here," she sighed, pointing to her stomach. "It's because I worry."

"But what do you worry about?"

She did not say. Instead she told us how a midwife in the building had punctured a hole in the side of her belly and inserted a string which she then pulled out to expel the bad things from her body.

"Egyptian sorcery! What *bad things*?" asked my uncle.

"Do I know what bad things? Bad things," she insisted.

She blessed my mother for giving her the injection. Allah had seen her kindness. Then she got up, saying she was feeling much better already.

While some had been attending to Latifa, the others went on speaking about the most recent turn of events. Someone was confirming rumors that the British were already pulling out of Port Said. The doorbell rang. We heard Abdou's slippers trail on the marble floor all the way from the kitchen to the entrance. I heard the door close. Was it going to be the police again? I heard Aunt Flora's voice greet Abdou.

Flora would stay for dinner. She too had heard rumors that the British and French might ultimately cower before the Russian ultimatum. Yes, she too would have to think of leaving, but where to, she didn't know. Probably France, though it still wasn't clear whether German Jews would be just nationalized or also expelled, as it was rumored would happen soon to other Jews.

Everyone in the living room was speaking of France that evening, with Cousin Arnaut advocating immediate migration. An argument broke out between him and Uncle Nessim. Uncle Nessim was for staying put—"We've had a good life here." "Then why not go back to Turkey? You used to have a good life there too," said his nephew.

For dinner we had a huge poached fish in mulled wine and vegetables. Hassan, the chauffeur, who was a reservist in the Egyptian navy, had caught two bluefish while patrolling the Alexandrian coastline that night and at the end of his shift had shown up in his uniform with two very large fish wrapped in newspaper. There was such dissension among the sisters on how to cook the fish that my great-grandmother had to intervene, proclaiming that they had not had a good poached *pa-*

lamita in ages. The vegetables and the fish had also produced a delicious and very thick soup, which that evening my grandmother decorated with sprigs of fennel. Even Aunt Elsa, who despite her lean years in Lourdes had never lost the touch of the *bonne vivante*, decided the occasion merited opening the good wine.

After Latifa had removed the soup dishes, Hisham came in carrying a very large fish platter, which he deposited on the buffet. By common consent, he and Latifa had divided the dining room between them, with Latifa serving the elderly women and the children, and Hisham everyone else.

Suddenly I heard Aunt Elsa call on God and heaven and the Mother of Christ, her jaw dropping as if she had seen death beside her.

Latifa was nowhere in sight.

My father and Uncle Nessim immediately got up and rushed to the corner, tossing their white napkins with summary gestures.

When I looked, I saw large cuts of fish steak scattered over the dining room carpet, a huge pool of unabsorbed fish stock, and, next to the fish, the meek, crumpled figure of Latifa rising to a crouch, one hand clutching her stomach. She cried and apologized profusely, saying she hurt everywhere, she would clean it up.

"But what did you trip on?"

She could not remember.

"Did you break an arm?"

No. A leg? No. Her back? Maybe, no, not her back. Had anyone said anything to frighten her? No. Was she better now? Only if she did not move. And even then, it still hurt.

"But where, my girl, where?" asked Uncle Isaac, losing his patience.

"Here," she said, indicating her stomach, her belly, her liver, her kidneys, her back.

"I don't understand!" he snapped.

"Leave her to me," said my grandmother as she signaled to my mother to help. I heard them laying Latifa down on a sofa in the sitting room. And then I heard a weak, beseeching voice. She was imploring my mother not to give her another injection. Aunt Elsa and Aunt Marta were busy picking up slices of fish and throwing rags on the carpet, muttering to themselves, "How will this ever clean, how will this ever clean?" while their mother, looking down from her seat like a bird from its cage, gave directions on how to dab the sauce without rubbing it into the carpet. Cousin Arnaut proclaimed it did not matter in the least, since we were probably leaving Egypt in a few weeks. "It matters, yes!" shouted Uncle Isaac, losing his temper. "The carpet is still ours, and a very valuable one at that." The mess on the carpet troubled him less than the prospect of having to leave the carpet behind. In years to come, that corner of the rug always remained darker than the rest, and if one tried hard enough, as I did almost a decade later, one could always make out a distinctly pungent fishy odor hovering about that entire area, which, in the fashion of cartographers, we dubbed Latifa's Corner.

When Dr. Alcabès finally came, he walked straight into Latifa's room. "Latifa, *oumi*, sit up," he ordered in peremptory Arabic while he felt for her pulse. Latifa refused, trying to pull her wrist away from his hand, all the while clinging to my grandmother. Hisham, who had seen her faint, said she had never been to a doctor before and was more frightened of doctors than she was of butchers. "As well she should be," said Dr. Alcabès.

"She's such a comedian, though," interjected Uncle Isaac.

"But can't any of you see she's almost green! Where are your eyes!" thundered the doctor. "Her face is greener than a zucchini." Then he held her hand a moment. "Does it hurt here?" he asked, indicating her right waist. She nodded. "And sometimes here?" he asked touching her belly. Again she nodded.

"And when does it hurt?"

She looked around to second-guess whether he too was trying to catch her lying.

"But it always hurts. More and more and more."

He told her she had to lie down. Then he said he would give her an injection. She began to struggle. He told her it was to kill the pain. "You'll see, you'll see," he said in Arabic as he held her hand, waiting for my mother to boil the syringe. "You'll feel better."

"Well, Ben?" asked my great-grandmother after the injection, turning to the doctor.

"She's finished."

"Finished by what? Fear?" exclaimed Uncle Isaac.

"Really, Isaac, sometimes you're as thick as a mule."

His Excellency bristled at the doctor's remark.

"I don't understand this at all. One moment she's fainting and shaking and turning yellow each time there's an air raid, and now she's finished? Just like that?"

"Isaac, let Ben speak," said my grandmother.

"Indeed, let him speak. Because I'd like to know who's the real mule here," said Uncle Isaac.

Dr. Alcabès paid no attention. "It's a tumor blocking her liver. When the growth touches the spinal nerve, the pain is so unbearable, she faints. Simple."

"And what will you do now that it's so simple?" asked Uncle Isaac.

"Do? Nothing."

"Surely they operate on these things nowadays. We're not in the Middle Ages, I hope."

"There's nothing to do, understand!"

Dr. Alcabès finished his coffee and said he had to rush to see another patient. He took my mother to the side and gave her something from his pocket.

"Morphine," said my mother after he was gone.

"Morphine, I didn't know it was morphine," exclaimed Aunt Marta, who had missed the earlier exchange between Uncle Isaac and Dr. Alcabès. "But then, if it's morphine, it's cancer, it's cancer," she whimpered as if death were suddenly knocking at her door as well. She feared pain, doctors, and injections so much that she had sworn everyone—and would always remind them—to let her die should she be stricken with an unbearably painful disease and ask to die—which she never did as she lay writhing with Latifa's sickness years later in a hospital ward in Paris, battling to live on despite the pain, which in her case lasted more than nine months and in Latifa's barely two weeks.

■

The next morning, my grandmother and Aunt Elsa decided to officiate at a ritual to ward off further misfortune. The ceremony, called *faire boukhour*, from the Turkish word *buhur*, which means incense, consisted of placing a smoking censer on the floor and having everyone in the household take turns jumping over it—first the men, then the women, then the servants. My grandmother and great-grandmother said a prayer in Ladino, and all the men, including Uncle Isaac, who was the most Westernized of the family, and my father, who hated ceremonies of any sort, leapt in turn, like children forced to play hopscotch.

Then came the women's turn. Women always jumped with a bashful smile, some lifting up their skirts awkwardly. My great-grandmother was helped in her leap by her two eldest sons, Nessim and Isaac; next came her eldest daughter, and then the others, down to my youngest cousin. Abdou's turn followed, then Hisham's. Ibrahim, whose voice was so deep and stern, suddenly broke into an embarrassed, high-pitched giggle as he covered his face with both palms. Then, lifting his *galabiya* up to give his legs greater freedom of movement, he backed up all the way into the pantry and came dashing into the corridor, leaping over the censer, nearly crashing into Aunt Elsa's glass bedroom door. Finally it was poor Latifa's turn—Latifa, who would rather have been left alone in bed but who, in typical Egyptian manner, managed to perform the ritual with good cheer and a broad smile, leaning on Abdou's shoulder.

A few hours later, Latifa screamed again. We found her with her hand pressed against her waist. Here she was, she said, thinking she was better, and now the ache was back again, only worse. "*Ya satir ya rab, ya satir, ya satir ya rab*," she called to God. My mother reassured her that she was about to give her the same medicine the doctor had given her last night. "Not in front of the boy," said Latifa. My mother asked me to leave the room. As soon as I heard Latifa gasp, I turned around and peeked through the half-open door. Latifa had white skin. She continued to complain that the injection wasn't working this time, that the pain was still there. I heard her whining the same words—"*Ya rab, ya rab, ya rab, ya rabbi*" —repeating God's name with the drowsy modulation of children who go on crying that they're not tired long after closing their eyes.

Mother shut the door quietly behind her. Abdou was waiting outside. "How is she?" My mother bit her lip. Abdou almost tore off his apron by the neckstrap, which is how he would threaten to quit each time he was accused of stealing, and buried his face in it, sobbing, "She has nobody, nobody," as he walked to the kitchen. Latifa had a son, but he had taken up with a bad crowd and never came to see her.

At three o'clock in the afternoon, Latifa woke up and was given diluted chicken broth. She complained it lacked salt. Then she said it had too much lemon. Then she said it was probably her sickness playing tricks on her mouth. But she was better now, she just wanted to sleep.

During dinner that evening, she was shouting again. At first it seemed as though a violent argument were raging in the servants' quarters, with Latifa shouting as she did when she argued with a neighbor, everyone's voices squawking in the courtyard like ravens in mad flight. But Abdou and Hisham were in the dining room, and Ibrahim had taken the evening off. Then it struck me that she was screaming at no one at all, that she was screaming all by herself, which made it all the more terrifying, for it was a fiendish, demonic howl which cut into the late November night. My mother, who quickly understood from our expressions that something had happened to Latifa, stood up and went to see what was the matter. My grandmother followed her into the corridor. Then it occurred to both of them there was no more morphine in the house. An urgent call was placed to Dr. Alcabès. He was not home, his wife said, but she would relay the message.

When we entered Latifa's room, she was flouncing on the bed. She screamed that twice she had tried to stand up but had fallen back on the bed each time. She had coughed up a large worm and this time trapped it in a glass. "Here," she said, pointing to a glass covered with a saucer. My grandmother examined the coiled brown worm and told my mother it was because Latifa never washed the salad properly. "Well, don't worry, you won't have any more worms," my grandmother said. Latifa refused to believe her, swearing there were legions of them, biting, squirming, nibbling away at her insides, for each time they bit she could feel it, and she could feel it right now. And suddenly, in the most stridulous Arabic, she shouted frenzied, scattered words of prayer, yelling like a raging madwoman capable of wielding a knife against anyone who crossed her path.

My mother assured Latifa the medicine would come, but no sooner had she said these words than Latifa uttered another one of her heartrending howls. "*Hayimawituni*, they'll kill me!"

she yelled, *"Hayimawituni!"* She meant the worms. And suddenly, from the inner courtyard, came an equally piercing wail
from another apartment—"What is the matter with Latifa?
Latifa's dying! Latifa's dying!"—which sent a panic running
throughout the building as maids and servants from various
apartments shouted their support, their pity, their invocations
to the Almighty, their prayers for mercy.

Uncle Isaac rushed in, fearful the yelling might attract too
much attention. There was a ring, and my father went to open
the door. It was Dr. Alcabès.

"God sends you, Ben," said my grandmother.

"You can hear her all the way downstairs."

"Give her something fast, Ben, people will think we're killing her," said Uncle Isaac.

Dr. Alcabès made his way into the maid's room, which he
opened without knocking, and, after having had water boiled,
administered the injection himself.

"You'll make us deaf if you go on," he jested.

"Well, Ben?" asked my great-grandmother afterward.

Dr. Alcabès had consulted with other colleagues. It was
too late to operate. Morphine. Perhaps even too much
morphine.

"Maybe we had better send her to the hospital, then," said
Uncle Isaac. "We don't want trouble."

"In her state?" asked Dr. Alcabès. "She may not last the
night."

"But does she have to scream like that? Isn't she overdoing
it a bit?"

"Isaac, she's already no longer with us."

The following morning, the porter escorted two men dressed
in civilian clothes to our door. They had come from the police
station; one of them spoke French, which he had studied, he
said, at the École de la Communauté Juive, a Franco-Jewish

school for poor Jews and middle-class Egyptians who wished to give their children a French education.

"Do you know why we are here, Docteur?" he asked my uncle, who was still in his bathrobe. I was sure they had come because of Latifa's screaming.

"I would like to know," replied Uncle Isaac. His answer was meant to sound peremptory; it came out beseechful.

The men sat down on the sofa. They were there because of a letter addressed to him. What letter? A letter that was sent from Paris a few weeks ago and which the Egyptian censor had intercepted and decoded. A letter in which an alleged niece announced the birth of a girl "whom we received last week," he quoted, holding the letter in his hand, "and who is all gold to us."

"Well?" asked the officer who spoke French.

"Well what?" asked my uncle, sounding respectfully peeved. "My niece in Paris gave birth to a girl."

"To a girl *who is all gold to us*. What does that mean?"

"A girl who is very, very dear—I suppose."

"You suppose. And does one give birth to a baby—is a baby born, or does one *receive* a baby, as it says here?" asked the shrewd officer.

"If one believes in God, then one receives what God sends," interrupted my grandmother, who until the officers' visit had been reading Alberto Moravia's *Gli indifferenti*, a volume she continued to hold in her hand, a finger tucked between the pages to mark the spot where she had stopped reading.

"It is true in your religion and it is true in ours," she continued. "Where is all this leading, anyway?"

"It is leading to the fact that we have proof you have been sending currency and jewelry abroad, and that you, and your brother Aaron before you, have been doing so for many years."

Uncle Isaac denied the charge. He rubbed a finger hastily

past his upper lip and, a second later, pinched that same lip between his index finger and his thumb. When I looked at his forehead, it was glistening.

"I am afraid you will have to come with us," said the officer.

"How do you mean, 'with you'?"

"You are under arrest."

The second officer gripped my uncle's arm.

"Please get dressed."

"Absolutely not!"

"Then we're taking you as you are."

"Never. What is the charge?"

"Treason."

"Egyptian claptrap! I am eighty years old."

My uncle tried to free his arm, and, it seemed, would have fallen to the ground in the struggle had the other officer not held him in place.

"You can't arrest people like this," my grandmother protested.

The men did not answer.

"And where are you taking him?" asked Cousin Arnaut with a breathless pant in his voice as if to suggest he had put up a good fight before abandoning his uncle to his fate.

They were taking him to the police station.

It was then I began to smell a terrible odor. I looked around me, looked at my grandmother, who seemed equally perturbed, and then saw something on Uncle Isaac's slipper and down his ankle. He had turned white. He leaned against the mantelpiece as though about to look at his face in the mirror and, turning around to the group of us assembled in the living room, he whispered, almost without breathing, "*Mamá querida.*"

He asked for a few minutes to change.

Aunt Elsa insisted that as a foreign national he should refuse there were miracles even he could not work, that he too could be as scared as Latifa.

■

A week after Uncle Isaac's arrest, we received a telegram announcing he was safe in *sweet* France. "Lucky Isaac," everyone said.

Then, just as suddenly as they had started, the air raids stopped, as did the sirens, and the blackout. The war had ended.

There was no rejoicing at the news, though a general air of relief had to be affected for the benefit of neighbors and servants. But everyone worried. We worried more without the sirens and the blackout than when we banded together in the dark, fearing the worst every evening. My parents decided not to leave my great-grandmother's apartment. Better to stay together, everyone said.

Then came rumors of the expulsion of some French and British nationals, and other rumors followed of the summary nationalization of factories, businesses, homes, bank accounts. It was said the fate of the Jews would be no different. We worried. Even my great-grandmother began to talk of moving to France. But she would have to take Latifa, she said.

Anticipating the worst, everyone in the family spent the ensuing weeks shopping for things we could afford in Egypt but might find expensive in Europe. Since the period in question coincided with Christmas, the frantic, heady rhythm of shopping cast a holiday spell on our days.

I remember the joy of those December mornings when my mother and I stepped out into the crisp, clean, foggy air of Rue Thèbes as we rushed to catch the tram at Sporting, meeting Aunt Flora a few stations up and spending the rest of the morning going from one shop to the next.

to leave the house. That would only exacerbate matters, he said.

Ten minutes later he came into the sitting room wearing his dark astrakhan-collared coat, with his walking stick in one hand and his monocle slung about his neck. He opened his cigarette case and proceeded to fill it with as many cigarettes as he could from a small inlaid box on one of the end tables in the sitting room. Then he went to say goodbye to Latifa, who had sensed trouble and was already weeping. On hearing her sudden wailing, everyone in the room burst out crying as well. As they flocked to follow him onto the landing, he turned around and said, "Please, everyone! Can't I leave in peace without all of you milling at the door like vultures?"

My great-grandmother, who had just embraced him, stood impassively in the hallway, more dazed than saddened, leaning on her elder daughter, who began waving the handkerchief she had been using on her nose. Aunt Elsa and Aunt Marta did the same. "Ladies, sisters, ladies, please!" said Isaac as he turned around, pushed his youngest sister inside the apartment, and slammed the door behind him.

"He won't last a day if they put him in jail," wept Aunt Elsa. "He's finished," said Uncle Nessim.

After a moment of silence outside, I heard a thud of people stepping into the elevator, heard the metallic gate rattle shut, followed by the snap of the wooden inner door, its loose glass panel shaking in place. Then I heard the grinding wheeze of the motor and the whine of the counterweight cables in the inner courtyard.

Morning gradually began to fill the house. Everyone sat in the living room wearing their bathrobes, their hair down, their breath still filled with sleep, stunned as never before, except at news of death. It had never occurred to anyone in the family that Isaac was as vulnerable as everyone else in the world, that

Store windows were heavily decorated with gift-wrapped boxes, tinsel, and fake snow, with *Merry Christmas* and *Joyeux Noël* written in thick cotton letters glued to the back of display windows. The smell of pine hung over every floor of Hannaux and Chalon. At Hannaux, a bearded Santa sat me on his lap and asked whether I had been a good boy. I told him yes, except for the time when I played with the lights during an air raid. He said I need not worry, the war was over. "*Ne mens jamais*, never lie," he urged, waving a finger. He let me down, and an Arab boy took my place. Santa spoke Arabic too.

Both my mother and Flora bought woolen clothing. Winters were fierce in Europe, and they both agreed it was wise to stock up. We bought three very large thick wool blankets, one for each of us. When they were delivered at Sporting early that afternoon, my father screamed, saying that each blanket was so huge it would take up an entire suitcase all to itself. My grandmother agreed with my father. But then she touched the wool and said it would last a lifetime, a good purchase, she would buy one herself. These blankets were impossible to come by in France.

■

Meanwhile, Latifa was on morphine all the time. Moments after the injection, she would lie down and, eyes wide open, stare at the ceiling, drooling a bit from the corner of her mouth, a dreamy sigh wheezing out of her half-pursed lips each time she breathed. She would bring her right palm to her chest, slowly pick up some imaginary object there with her fingers, and then, raising the same arm as though pointing to the ceiling, offer to the lamp the clump of air she had just picked from her chest. This went on for hours every afternoon. No one knew why she persisted in this silent mummery, or whether it had any meaning whatsoever. My grandmother eventually brought my mother into the maid's room and asked her about Latifa's gestures. My mother understood them immediately. She is offering her soul to God. She is asking God to take her. She wants to die.

Latifa's son finally came one afternoon. He was let into his mother's room by Abdou, who stood watch outside in case the young man decided to wander about and pilfer things in the apartment. He was sixteen but looked no older than twelve, and wore Western clothes. I saw him come in from where I was sitting in the family room.

"Who is it?" whispered my great-grandmother.

"Latifa's son."

"And what does he want?"

Overhearing this exchange, my grandmother put aside her needlepoint and went to meet him. She knocked at the *karakib* door, walked in, and said she was *enchantée* to meet him. The young man simply stared at my grandmother and, at his mother's prompting, finally stood up to offer her the only chair in the room, which she refused. He nevertheless remained standing, shifting about nervously, finally locking his hands over his groin.

"You will talk to your mother now. Then you will come and see me," she said leaving the room.

A few minutes later, the maid's door squeaked open and the irresolute boy came out, his hands still locked over his groin. I looked at his face to see if he had cried. He looked calm, almost bored. He had not cried.

"I have talked to my mother," he said, remembering my grandmother's exact words.

"Come, then," she said, as the boy reluctantly approached the family room. He had probably never been in a living room before in his life and was intimidated by the apartment, the faces, the prying eyes.

"Your mother tells me you steal," said my grandmother. "Is that true?"

The boy did not answer.

"Answer me!" she said.

The boy shook his head, then bit his lip and said, "Yes."

"Do you want to go to jail?"

He did not answer.

"Don't you know it is wrong to steal? Do you know what they do to people who steal? They bind your feet together, pull them up, and beat them till you can't even stand when you go to the bathroom. My brother Isaac was very angry when he heard that Latifa's son is a thief, and next time we hear it, he will tell the king, and they will come and put you in jail."

She had almost believed it herself.

The boy stood expressionless and said nothing.

"Now, go home. Then, I want you to go to my son's factory tomorrow. He will give you a job."

Latifa must have heard my grandmother's diatribe, for as soon as her son opened the door to her room to say goodbye again, I heard her bless my grandmother. He stepped into her room again and before shutting the door made an obscene gesture.

Two days later, Latifa died. My mother and I had left the house to go shopping that morning. Before leaving she had asked me to wait outside the *karakib* door while she gave Latifa her daily injection. But I felt something was different. There was a flurry about the servants' quarters, and Abdou's eyes were bloodshot. When I asked him, he shook his head and made a gesture to signify that only Allah knew.

We returned from shopping earlier than planned. As soon as we arrived at our building and took the elevator, I heard screams such as I had never heard in my life. When we opened the door, everyone at home was in tears, including my great-grandmother, who had finally realized what had happened. The screaming was coming from the service entrance. My grandmother told me in Ladino not to go into the kitchen, but I immediately disobeyed her. When I opened the pantry door, the screaming suddenly grew louder. I stepped into the kitchen and saw Latifa's body laid out on the table. Abdou and Ibrahim were wrapping it up from head to foot in what looked like gray sackcloth, while neighboring servants stood about the service door to see her for the last time. They looked at me but said nothing, though I sensed they disapproved. I did not move from the doorway. Then Hisham, who despite his missing arm was the strongest of the three, hoisted her up on his shoulder and proceeded to carry her down the service stairway.

As he started down the stairs with the body, I heard the screams soar into an almost predatory chorus of piercing shrieks echoing in the inner courtyard. All the maids in the building were leaning out of windows, waving handkerchiefs, sometimes two or three women crammed in one window, howling after Latifa, begging her to come back, imploring Hisham, as was the custom, not to take her away from them, not to take her away, some even tearing the clothes they were wearing, slapping their faces, banging their heads against the wall, screaming, "*Ya Latifa! Ya Latifa!*"

■

The next day, my grandmother asked to take me for a walk. We went to Petit Sporting, bought a penny's worth of roasted peanuts coated with salt, and ended up in Ibrahimieh. From there we headed to Rue Memphis, where we met a lame beggar sitting on the curb of a sidewalk. "Here, give him these," said my grandmother, handing me a few coins. "For Latifa's soul," she added. We paid a short visit to her old house, which she had recently rented to a Copt family. I waited outside while she went in to pick up an envelope. A boy immediately came out and stood without saying a word, eyeing me suspiciously.

Then we walked across the street to visit the Saint. She looked tired and sad, said she had not slept in over a week. The government had just frozen all of their assets; their son and his family, who were French nationals, had already received their expulsion notices. Her turn was sure to come soon. Meanwhile, she just hoped her husband had a way of finding money, because otherwise there wouldn't be any left to buy food or pay the servants.

"But I did not know you were French," interrupted the Princess.

"We're as French as you are Italian, Madame Esther. A lot of good that does us!"

"At least Italian Jews are allowed to remain," answered the Princess. I had heard her say to Uncle Nessim, "Thank God we're Italian."

The Saint was beside herself; she might never see her son or granddaughters again. Whoever wanted to go to France? Why couldn't they stay in Egypt, even as paupers?

The two ladies bid each other a happy Chanukah.

That evening before dinner, Cousin Arnaut welcomed the possibility of expulsion from Egypt, saying that we should all move to an equally large apartment in Paris and, from there, "start again." No one had died, no one was hurt, and no one was too old to start anew, he said, as though enumerating the positives. Uncle Nessim stared at his mother and at my grandmother, saying nothing. Nor would anyone be allowed to starve in France, continued Cousin Arnaut. After all, everyone knew someone who was somebody in Paris, and if we didn't, we had the looks and the talents to aspire to any circle of our choosing.

Taffi Al-Nur!

But this was a counterfeit Vili speaking. Elsa and Nessim had determined they weren't budging for the moment. My father, too, refused to go. Business couldn't be better, he said. His now ranked among the best textile mills in Egypt. He was thinking of building another factory in Cairo. "Build one on Mount Etna too," said my great-grandmother.

A totally unexpected event occurred during dinner. A siren suddenly started to wail. Everyone froze on the spot. "This time it's an atomic war, I know it," whimpered Aunt Marta, bursting into tears as she buried her head in her son's chest. No sooner was the siren heard than the lights began to go out in clusters all over Sporting. People were running down the street screaming *"Taffi al-nur! Taffi al-nur!"* all over again. "But the war's been over for weeks now," protested Dr. Alcabès, who was visiting that evening. "It's a hoax, keep the lights on, I say."

"Ben, we don't want trouble—let's turn off the lights," said my grandmother.

"It's a hoax all the same. They're doing something under cover of darkness and they don't want anyone to know."

Out came the kerosene light. Aunt Elsa pulled the curtains over the windows of the living room, shut all the doors, and thanked her frugal good instincts for not removing the sheets of blue paper that had lined our windows only a week or two earlier.

Presently, we began to hear a strange rumble, not of distant antiaircraft guns, as I suspected at first, but of armored vehicles and many, many trucks being mysteriously convoyed through Alexandria. At one point our house began to tremble under the loud jolts of tanks thudding and whining their way past Rue Delta onto Avenue Ambroise Rally.

"What did I tell you," said Dr. Alcabès, who was peeking through the opening between the curtains. "This has nothing to do with air raids. They're redeploying men elsewhere and they don't want anyone to know it. I bet you these trucks are filled with prisoners and wounded soldiers whom the Israelis have just released, and now they're being ferried back home under cover of darkness."

I noticed it was growing progressively darker in the dining room as the pungent odor of burning oil rose from the ever-feeble wick in the kerosene lamp. My father had noticed the same thing, for he said, "Elsa, next time, please, a bit more oil in the lamps, at least to tide us over an entire meal."

I knew then that as soon as the pounding noise of engines receded, we would hear the all clear, and everyone in the neighborhood and everyone in the room would heave a sigh of relief and finally turn on the lights. If only we could have five, ten more minutes in the dark together. I didn't even mind not seeing well, and I suspected that everyone, including my father, wouldn't have cared much if we went on with our meal in the dark, now that our eyes had gotten used to it.

I would miss these nights, I thought, not the war itself but the blackout, not my uncles or my aunts but the velvety hush of their voices when we turned off the lights and drew closer to the radio, almost whispering our thoughts in the dark, as though the enemy were listening in on us as well. It was the blackout that spelled our evenings together, lengthening our dinners because it was so dark in the dining room we could hardly see what we were eating and were forced to eat slowly. The blackout interrupted tea, cards, conversations, quarrels, crying, visits, only to confer upon our lives a ceremonial, almost liturgical air sanctified by the smell of kerosene and burning oil which hovered over our evenings like incense.

"Latifa!" called my great-grandmother. She wanted more biscuits.

"Poor Latifa is gone," said my grandmother.

"But where could she have gone to at this time of the night?" she asked.

A week later, several members of the family were expelled from Egypt.

Three months after that, four more left voluntarily.

Followed almost immediately by six others. Everyone settled in France.

Eighteen months later, the Saint and her husband left for France as well.

By then only eight of us remained: Aunt Elsa, Aunt Flora, the Princess, Uncle Nessim, my great-grandmother, and us.

■

"Poor Latifa would have laughed," said Aunt Elsa. The much-vaunted apartment in Paris on which Cousin Arnaut had pinned so much hope turned out to be a studio on the fifth floor of an elaborate fin-de-siècle building on Avenue Georges Mandel—a glorified maid's room. There was no elevator in the building, and the stairway got narrower and steeper with each floor, the marble steps turning to stone after the fourth, and from stone to squeaking, sunken wood planks after the sixth. Here, I had come from America one Christmas morning in the early seventies to visit my grandmother and Aunt Elsa. We ate lunch in a makeshift dining room separated from what was to be my cot for the night by a fuchsia Art Deco folding screen.

A dense gray sky lowered over an empty Paris, presaging more rain. It might even snow, said my aunt. Not a sound along the avenue, the unmistakable silence of Parisian Sunday afternoons settling everywhere upon the neighborhood. I heard a Peugeot roar to a stop outside. I looked down. A couple stepped out of a taxi carrying wrapped boxes. Long Christmas luncheons, I thought.

After eating, we moved to what they had nicknamed the

petit salon, another part of the same room, separated by a wood partition. Aunt Elsa offered me an English cigarette from a green tin box, then a cup of Turkish coffee, and we crossed our legs as we sat and spoke, mostly about America. "Man is like a bird, one day he's here, another there," said my grandmother, invoking a familiar Turkish parable concerning a certain very lazy sultan who after years spent sitting on one end of his sofa suddenly decides to move to the other end. It meant that despite appearances, people seldom migrate very far, that things hardly change, that life always comes to the same.

We sat awhile after coffee, until they remembered I was jet-lagged. I said it didn't matter. They offered to let me nap on the sofa, saying they had to mend a dress of Aunt Elsa's and that I could use the time to doze off awhile. I leaned back on the sofa, and they began to whisper, and I thought I heard someone remove my ashtray and my cup of coffee, and soon I made out the discreet and ever-distant patter of a hand-cranked sewing machine smuggling hurried stitches in between long pauses followed by querulous little-old-lady whispers in a language I had not heard in years and whose hushed, spiteful hisses, punctuated by the sputtering old Singer, took me back to the winter of 1956, when all the women in the household, fearing they might have to leave Egypt on a day's notice, massed around the only sewing machine at Sporting, taking grudging turns to make or mend clothes for their families.

When I awoke it was almost evening. We went for a walk on Avenue Henri Martin, past Lamartine's fountain, reaching the edge of the Bois de Boulogne. Did I want to cross the street into the Bois, lovely toward sunset, asked my aunt as she scanned the gray, sodden landscape whose bare trees made me think of cold Corot winters in La Ville d'Avray. Maybe on our next walk, I answered. I had never seen Paris so empty. Christmas, they explained.

When we reached the corner of the street, on a whim, I

touched the outstretched hand of Rodin's statue of Victor Hugo. "Never loved Hugo," said Aunt Elsa, looking at the bearded poet. Then she started to talk of old Signor Ugo, who had become an Egyptian citizen in the hope of spending his remaining years in Egypt. "Even became a Moslem, calls himself Hag Gabalzahri," said Aunt Elsa. "He teaches yoga to officers of the Egyptian army." "But what a survivor." "Not a survivor, a chameleon." "An opportunist." "A madman," they agreed.

As it got dark, we walked back by way of Avenue Victor Hugo and stopped in a café. It was mostly empty, and as soon as they saw the old ladies they brought us tea. My grandmother ordered an almond pastry, which she insisted was for me. "You used to like these so much," she said. I replied I would eat only half, but as we talked, I ended up eating the whole thing. There was something warm and snug about the empty café on Christmas Day, and, looking at the two old women, who had finally managed to take off their thick wool coats without my help, I wanted to hold their hands and promise them many, many things.

Soon, the place began to fill and more voices could be heard around us, many speaking Spanish or Portuguese—servants in the Seizième Arrondissement.

Across the street, families were already standing in line outside the Cinéma Victor Hugo. A group came and sat next to our table and ordered Ricards.

"Do you want to go to the movies tonight?" suggested Aunt Elsa.

I shook my head. They said they went once a week, *pour se dégourdir*, to brighten up a bit.

When it was time to pay, Aunt Elsa said she would pay for her share—roughly a third of the check. Outraged, my grandmother told her she didn't need her third, or her fourth, or her sixteenth! She would pay for the whole thing herself. Aunt Elsa would have none of it, and opened her purse, seizing coins of various sizes, which she counted awkwardly with wrinkled, arthritic fingers.

"I don't want your centimes, keep them for your heirs," barked my grandmother to her sister, who had never had children.

As each struggled furiously to put on her coat and be the first to leave the establishment, the venom between the two nonagenarians reached such a peak that my grandmother lost her patience and told her sister she could no longer live with her. She was tired of eating as though they might starve the next day—especially since they had so very few days left in the first place. "Speak for yourself," snapped Elsa, reminding her sister that she was fully aware I had brought her a dozen Oral B toothbrushes from America and not one of them had she offered to give her. "You may say you're going to die soon, but when it comes to giving me a toothbrush, you act as though you're going to outlive ten sets of dentures."

So saying, Aunt Elsa crossed the empty street and began walking home on the opposite sidewalk of Rue Longchamps. I shuttled between them, but they refused to make up, each saying it was up to the other to apologize. When I delivered the negative report from one sister to the other, each had only one thing to add: "Let her croak."

We returned home in time for their television show. They made up when Aunt Elsa tripped against the foot of a chair. "She's almost blind," whispered my grandmother. "You ask why I won't leave her. She's got no one." We had yogurt, jam, and cheese, *à l'américaine*—that is, in front of the television.

I looked out the window and followed a long, revolving beam traveling above the city and lighting up a smokey, pinkish trail in the sky. "The Eiffel Tower," said Aunt Elsa who had come up to the window and was leaning against me. "She's beginning to forget," she whispered. "She thinks I haven't noticed. She's got no one, either."

Later that evening, both sisters made me promise not to do anything lavish or elaborate *when the time came*. Feeling awkward, I smiled and promised and was trying to brush off the subject until I realized that what they meant was centennials. "Those days are long gone. Small visits are all we ask."

■

When I returned twenty years later, with my wife, the city had hardly changed. I still remembered the station names; the café on Avenue Victor Hugo was the same; and the shop on the Faubourg Saint Honoré where my grandmother had bought me a tie was still there, except much bigger and filled with Japanese tourists. The Victor Hugo movie theater had disappeared. In the old café around the corner, we ordered a *café crème* and a ham sandwich each.

Avenue Georges Mandel was quiet in the early evening. As we neared the corner where Aunt Elsa had lived, her building suddenly came into view.

I pointed upstairs and showed my wife the window from which Aunt Elsa had thrown her husband's pipe on New Year's Eve to make a wish. I showed her the building nearby where Maria Callas had lived. They had spoken in Greek to her, corrected her Greek once.

We took pictures. Of the building. Of me standing in front of the building. Of her taking pictures of me standing in front of the building. She asked again which floor they had lived on. The fifth, I said. We looked up. The windows of Aunt Elsa's studio were unlit and the shutters drawn. Of course they're unlit, no one's home, I thought to myself. They've been dead for twenty years! But then, the apartment couldn't have stayed empty for so many years; surely it belonged to someone else. I seemed to recall that Vili himself had sold it. Still, what if it had never changed hands in all these years, if nothing had changed, if no one had even picked up the fork or touched the cardigan Aunt Elsa let fall before being rushed to the hospital on the night she died? What if her furniture and her china and her clothes and everything she hoarded throughout her life kept vigil for her and remained forever and only hers by dint of the life she had spun around them?

And for a moment I thought that this might also be true of the apartment on Rue Thèbes, that after sixty years with us it could never belong to anyone else and would be forever ours. I wanted to think that it, too, remained exactly the way we left it, that no one cried or quarreled there, that dust collected in the corners, that children were never allowed to scream as they sprinted past the junk room where Flora loved, Vili wept, and Latifa died.

I looked up again. The windows next to Aunt Elsa's dark studio were aglow. I could see a shadow move from the kitchen to what must have been the dining area. It turned to the window, looked out for a moment, and then turned back. The neighbor who had once complained I wasted too much water when bathing was still alive, then.

But I was wrong. After so many years, I had mistaken the windows. The old stingy neighbor lived behind the dark shutters; the windows that were lit were Aunt Elsa's after all. So she is home, I started, almost allowing myself to rejoice at the thought.

"Didn't you ever want to go upstairs to visit?" asked my wife.

I could almost imagine them looking down from the fifth-floor landing, waiting for us at the end of the stairwell, and in typical Sephardi fashion speaking their joy by complaining first: "Is it now that you finally deign to visit us?" "Twenty years, that's forever." "An offering, a prayer, something for us to go on. Instead, nothing!" "That's what comes of living in New York." "Enough, Elsa. The important thing is he's here now."

I pictured them fretting about the kitchen to improvise a makeshift dinner despite my protestations that we had just eaten. "You should have warned us." "But we're not hungry." "How could you not be hungry?"—my wife tapping me on the arm, saying "Let them," almost amused at these distant relatives, dusted off from an ancient find.

Then, realizing it was all hopeless anyhow, that there was no use pretending, "You're too late," they say, with old age straining their voices. "And we're terribly sorry," they add in good socialite French, as if we had come at the wrong hour and had just missed late-afternoon tea.

5

The Lotus-Eaters

It had taken my parents three years to find their jewel in Cleopatra. Life at Smouha after the 1956 war had become too unsafe, and so unsavory, they said—too many vagrants, too much dust, so few Europeans. And late at night, Smouha could turn quite eerie, especially when you heard the drone of ongoing rallies with loudspeakers squawking the latest propaganda. What my parents looked for, and eventually found, was an apartment near Sporting facing the sea on one side and the vast banana plantations of Smouha on the other.

My father was delighted with the study, my mother with the balcony; Om Ramadan was ecstatic about the laundry room; there was even a small room for my new Greek governess, Madame Marie. "What a fabulous home," said the Princess when she came to visit and managed to get lost in the corridor. "How did you ever find it?" My mother said it was the simplest thing in the world: the Venturas, longtime friends of her parents, had finally decided to leave Egypt and were desperate to sell their apartment.

One evening, shortly after we moved in, our dining room was littered with large sheets of sturdy cobalt-blue paper which Abdou had brought from my great-grandmother's house. "They never throw away anything over there," my mother had said. Madame Marie, my mother, and Aziza were busily cutting the large blue sheets in four to cover all of my books and notebooks as school regulations required. Someone had telephoned from school complaining that I did not keep my notebooks in good order. Two weeks later the same teacher called again saying that the issue was not just one of neatness—as Abdou, who had taken the call the first time, had erroneously reported to my mother—but one of conformity, of having each book and notebook bound like everyone else's in class.

A label bearing my full name, properly capitalized, was to be glued to the front of each notebook to indicate the subject, year, class, and volume. The blue paper, moreover, had to be tucked in—tightly—not glued with gummed paper. My mother had no patience with these British-school niceties and wanted to stick the label on the top right-hand corner, as was done in French schools. I insisted that the label had to be placed in the middle of the cover. Would beige paper do? she had first asked. No, it had to be blue, everyone used blue. This was when Abdou remembered the blue paper at Rue Thèbes. He took off his apron, walked to Sporting, and was back in an hour.

"I can't believe you waited over a month to tell us about this," said my father, joining the women after work and helping them cover my books while Madame Marie cut the paper. "How could you forget?"

I hadn't forgotten.

"Then why are we doing it at the last minute?" he asked.

I didn't know why. Maybe because I thought we'd soon be leaving Egypt and so none of this mattered.

My father, however, did not want to leave, and to prove the point had added another floor to his factory, invested in several apartments, commissioned new furniture, and, to cap his list of fantasies, had enrolled me, when I turned nine, in what throughout his early years in Egypt had always seemed an exclusive institution incarnating the very peak of British splendor: Victoria College.

Victoria College—renamed Victory College after the "victory" of the Egyptian forces over Britain, France, and Israel in 1956—was once the pride of the British Empire's educational system. Like other famous British public schools, it was a huge compound boasting large, well-trimmed playing fields and an imposing quadrangle, and was governed by a code of discipline that would have left Matthew Arnold's father, the stout, snub-nosed headmaster of Browning College, thrilled with depraved ecstasy.

English writers, philosophers, and mathematicians had once flocked to teach at VC. Wealthy Britons used to send their sons there, and Alexandria's elite consistently favored VC over the Lycée Français. Everything at VC was marked by spare, Victorian elegance, from the dark interiors that recalled the brooding opulence of its founders, down to the mournful, petty faces of its teachers, who couldn't wait to do to children what had probably been done to them for too many years.

Aside from that, however, the British legacy had been reduced to a handful of meaningless features: atrocious food; a reluctance to adopt anything too visibly modern; a ban on chewing gum and ballpoint pens; a gray uniform with navy piping around the edges of the blazer; an obstinate resistance to all types of Americanisms, especially soft drinks; compulsory gymnastics; corporal punishment; and, above all, awe before any form of authority, including the janitor's. My father, who had never set foot in a British school, and who in typical

The Lotus-Eaters

Sephardi fashion would have given anything to live his life all over again provided it started in an English public school, revered this caricature of Victorian austerity for its enviable aversion to all types of sissy comforts. It made gentlemen out of bullies, and men out of frail, pale-faced boys. It made England England. To his mind, VC was peopled by fair-haired, blue-eyed boys who would one day go to Cambridge and Oxford and rise to the helm of all the great banks and all the great nations that ruled the world. What he failed to notice during our tour of the prestigious institution, one summer day when the school was totally empty, was that VC had essentially become an Arab school wearing the tattered relics of British garb.

After its renaming, VC had fallen on sad days. With the departure of most British nationals, it had become a boarding school for rich Palestinians, Kuwaitis, and Saudis. The rising Egyptian middle class sent all of its firstborn sons there, as did rustic landowners from the Nile Valley and prosperous town mayors. Though VC was still regarded as an English-speaking school, outside of class no one spoke English. One language was favored: Arabic. In class, when a teacher was unable to explain $2\pi r$ in English, his speech, which was mostly pidgin to start with, would invariably revert to Arabic. Europeans, Armenians, and Christian Syrians—there were six of us in my class—usually spoke French among themselves. Charlie Atkinson, who didn't know French, was the last remaining English boy in the entire school. I was the last Jew.

Although by 1960 the study of Arabic had become mandatory for all foreign residents, explanations in Arabic did not much help European boys. Very few of us understood a word of classical or formal spoken Arabic. All we knew was street Egyptian, a sort of diluted, makeshift lingua franca that Egyptians spoke with Europeans. When Mohammed, our servant, telephoned early one morning from the hospital asking to be given the day off because his son had been run over by a truck, he told me, "*Al bambino bita Mohammed getu morto*," meaning, "The son belonging to Mohammed has become dead," adding, "*Bokra lazem congé alashan lazem cimetière*," meaning, "Tomorrow he needed holiday because cemetery was needed." This was not even spoken Egyptian, but in its garbled mixture of French, Italian, and Arabic, it allowed Europeans who never cared to learn Arabic to communicate with the local population.

The little Arabic I knew I had learned at our service-entrance door, which stood wide open on those warm Ramadan evenings in the spring when cooks and servants from up and down our building at Cleopatra would gather around our kitchen, idling away the minutes as they waited for the loud cannon shot from the harbor announcing the time for devout Moslems to eat after the long day's fast. They would not speak our lingua franca among themselves, but in my presence their conversation would automatically devolve into what could only have seemed a form of baby talk, though it was peppered with light, bawdy notes hovering over their speech like an impudent, spirited sneer.

Om Ramadan would come in and sit in the kitchen with Abdou and Aziza. Fawziah, our next-door neighbor's maid, would also step out of her kitchen and come into ours, and sometimes all three would sit in the early evening as Abdou sorted the rice or shelled peas amidst the yell of delivery boys running up and down the stairwell and the clatter of plates and cooking utensils. I loved their gossip—pure, malevolent, petty gossip—their complaints, complaints about one another behind one another's back, about their bosses, my mother, her screaming, complaints about their sons who had turned to crime, about health, disease, death, scandal, housing, poverty, and aching bones. *Rumatizm*, rheumatism—or, as Fawziah would say, *maratizm*, which sent everyone laughing each time, because, corrupted into *maraftizu*, it meant something obscene having to do with women and buttocks.

Sometimes with Abdou, Hisham, and Fawziah, I would sit on a fourth stool, while Abdou clipped away at his large toenails with giant chicken shears, and Fawziah, sitting with the open kitchen door swinging between her knees, drummed elaborate rhythms on both sides of it, tapping away with such speed that it drove our one-armed Hisham to stand up and imitate the vibrant hip twirls of a third-rate belly dancer. Everyone laughed, including Hisham, and we begged him to dance again, the three of us coaxing him with renewed drumming on the kitchen table. To practice that rhythm, I had once tapped it on our dining table, a sound my grandmother found totally revolting and which confirmed all the more the sentiment that I should no longer be allowed to grow up in Egypt. "We must send him to a boarding school in England," she said.

Everyone seemed to agree, including my parents and Aunt Flora.

"He doesn't know how to say two words without mumbling, he has no table manners to speak of, and, to be perfectly candid, Henri," continued Uncle Nessim that same evening, "his English is unacceptable."

"I don't see how I can write Vili and ask him to host the boy for a summer," added Aunt Elsa. "He's simply not fit to go."

Miffed by her sister's rebuke, my grandmother reminded everyone that *I*, at least, attended the famed Victoria College —but without failing to add that, of course, she, too, disapproved of these kitchen-sink *fréquentations* with Arab servants. And turning to Madame Marie—her spy, as my mother called her—she would beg her to wean me away from *these people*. Madame Marie, who held Arabs in the utmost contempt, except when she ventured into the service stairway to ask one of them for a cigarette, couldn't agree more. "Even dogs bark at Arabs," she would say.

In turn, everyone in the stairwell never stopped making fun of her. To irritate her further, one of the servants in the building kept repeating a short rhyming couplet ridiculing the Greeks of Egypt. The first line was in Greek, the second in Arabic:

> *Ti kanis? Ti kanis?*
> *Bayaa makanis.*

> [*How are you? How are you?*
> *You seller of broomsticks.*]

Unruffled by my new Arab *fréquentations*, however, my father claimed they were as good a way as any to learn Arabic. "He knows every cook and servant in our building," he told our guests, the way he would brag that I knew the name of every Greek god and goddess—a revelation that brought no end of sorrow to both Aunt Elsa and Uncle Nessim when they found out that I knew all about Ares and Aphrodite but had never heard of Cain and Abel.

"He doesn't even know the story of Abraham and Isaac, let alone the crossing of the Red Sea," Elsa reported incredulously during our first seder at Cleopatra.

"What are we, then, pagans?" interjected Uncle Nessim.

"Madame Marie, you must promise to do something to save this child. Will you promise us that?" said my grandmother.

Madame Marie, who was so happy to have finally been spoken to in the course of the meal, beamed with pleasure, and promised that everyone could count on her. "*Si fidi di me, signora*, trust me," she said in Italian, seemingly forgetting that my mother did not know a word of Italian.

"Bless you, my dear," said my grandmother.

"*Salud y berakhá*," echoed my great-grandmother.

At which Uncle Nessim, who had picked up his Haggadah, began leafing through its pages and resumed his recitation. At a sign given by Aunt Elsa, everyone stood up, including Madame Marie, who had been invited to the seder because my grandmother thought it was too rude to send her home or make her stay in her room during dinner like a servant. Madame Marie, a devout Greek Orthodox from Smyrna, stood up and sat down, dipped her foods in all the requisite dishes and sauces, ate everything she saw us eat, and repeated "Amen" after everyone else, though with the guarded look of a missionary forced to down a tribal brew. Her biggest fear in working for a Jewish family was to be inadvertently converted to Judaism.

"We say 'Amen' too," she said, attempting to be cordial.

"All religions say 'Amen,' " replied my father.

My father enjoyed teasing Madame Marie by saying that distinctions among religions were entirely superfluous, since we were all brothers under God, Jewish, Moslem, Greek Orthodox, no difference at all—particularly this year, as Passover, Easter, and Ramadan came within days of each other.

"Indeed," my father would say, "there is hardly any difference between Easter and Passover, seeing that the Greek word for Easter is *paska*, which in Italian is *pasqua*, which itself comes from the Hebrew word *pesah*. What do you think the Last Supper was, Madame Marie?"

"It was Christ's last meal."

"Yes, but what were the disciples doing when they gathered for the Last Supper?"

"Eating, of course."

"Leave her alone," said Aunt Elsa, who had read my father's drift and rushed to Madame Marie's defense. "What else were they to do but eat? Besides," she added, fearful that I, the youngest and most susceptible, might turn into another free-thinker, "Easter is one thing, Passover another." Her curt, peremptory air was meant to rescue Madame Marie from my father as well as to put him in his place for linking the two religions.

"I give up," said my father, probably forgetting that everyone had already had the same conversation about the Last Supper that Easter. This time, however, Madame Marie was not about to let him repeat those scurrilous lies about Jesus being Jewish.

"All I know," she explained, "is what my mother taught me when I was a little girl. If Jesus and his disciples were doing anything else during the Last Supper, I don't want to hear it."

A fervent believer, Madame Marie was so moved by the Passion of Christ that she wept all through Easter, often speaking of the nails that had gone through the hands of young Jesus and of the crown of thorns he wore as he hobbled up *via crucis* with this terrible weight on his shoulders and no one there to help him. She cried when she would shut herself in our dark living room early every afternoon and listen to the Greek Orthodox program on the radio, humming along with the liturgy as she began to weep, and weep, and weep some more, her tears spilling over our Grundig, which she would dab with her kerchief, as if the radio itself were an equally devout companion whose tears she understood fully and wished to comfort. She had even cried during the Greek news broadcast and the "Greek Children's Hour."

Madame Marie was also a staunch churchgoer and frequently took me along to cry some more and light votive tapers in memory of her brother, Petro, who, *now that he was there* (which she would say pointing an index finger to the flaky ceiling of the church), perhaps might intercede on her behalf and help persuade her landlord to allow her to install a much larger pigeon coop on the terrace. When you lit the taper you were not to think of the pigeon coop. Sometimes she lit many candles, not because it reinforced her wish but because she had caught herself thinking each time of the pigeon coop, which automatically invalidated her wish. So she would try again. Each taper cost a piaster, the equivalent of half a penny. Sometimes, satisfied with her prayers, she was on the verge of getting ready to leave the church when I would whisper timidly in her ear, "Madame Marie, light another one. I thought of the pigeon coop."

She loved pigeons, and nothing could distress her more than to think of Abdou cooking stuffed dove—an Egyptian delicacy and another source of chafing between them.

"But they are so gentle, and they have no bile," she would protest.

He would say nothing and go on with the slaughter of the birds, which he performed the Jewish way: by slitting the dove's neck—once, twice—with a very sharp knife. Then, releasing the bird, he would laugh as it flew and flounced about our kitchen, slamming into walls and kitchen cabinets, spattering blood everywhere. "It's only a dove."

To bait her, Abdou, like my father, was in the habit of saying that all peoples, Christians, Moslems, Arabs, Greeks, Jews were the same to Allah. This would infuriate Madame Marie, who would refute Abdou's claim with a dismissive gesture that reduced Islam to paltry business. And to prove that God was always on the side of Christians, she would tell everyone on the stairway that after the Turks had conquered Constantinople and turned the Hagia Sophia into a mosque, at night all the Greek religious murals which the Turks had painted over would seep through the infidel's green dye and comfort the few Greeks who had bravely sneaked into the church. When the sultan heard of this he had all the Christians butchered and the icons scraped off the wall until nothing remained.

Abdou shrugged away this tale with a nonchalant *"Mush mumkin,* not possible."

"And what about Saint George?" she rebutted, almost losing her temper, "Saint George who stopped my husband's car in the middle of the desert road and warned him about his flat tire?" Madame Marie believed in miracles. She had seen *al-Afreet,* the devil himself, once, and had even spoken with him when he came in the shape of Madame Longo's parrot and had tried to mount her pigeons.

"Kalam, kalam, words, words," replied Abdou, knowing he was taunting the Greek fanatic by denigrating the two things she cherished most: her faith and her pigeons.

Sometimes, unable to control herself, Madame Marie would explode and remind him that everyone would become Christian in the end. "Even Uncle Nessim, even Abdou, and Om Ramadan too," she said, glorying in the final victory of Christ.

"Rubbish," Abdou would jeer.

"Huh!" she exclaimed. "Pagans, all of you. First there was Noah, then Abraham, then Jacob, then Mohammed, and then came Christ." She was getting all worked up and, extending her index finger and making a sweeping circular motion with her right arm, declaimed: *"Wu baaden al-Messih getu kulu al-Chrétiens."*

At this, the servants on the stairwell broke up laughing, as did Abdou, Fawziah, and I. It was never clear what she intended to say, for her sentence meant either "After Christ, all the Christians came," or "After Christ, everyone will become Christian." But it was that supercilious circular motion of her arm, signifying the universe, that made us laugh each time we mimicked it. Within minutes that gesture had made its way into the annals of the courtyards of Cleopatra.

When she caught me doing it, Madame Marie immediately threatened to tell my teachers.

■

This was no laughing matter, for at VC, anything, even the loss of an insignificant personal item that had nothing to do with school, could be construed as an infraction, and for all infractions the penalty was invariably corporal punishment. There were gradations of corporal punishment, ranked by the severity of the crime or the whim of the teacher: first there was the teacher's palm, with blows striking wherever they fell; then there was the ruler; then the stick; then the cane, the frightful *kharazanah*. Within each category there were refinements and variations worthy of the great Marquis himself: for example, one could be hit with the flat end of a ruler or with its metal edge; on one's flattened palm or on the fingers; on one's arms or one's thighs; with a ridged cane or a flat cane; a wet or dry cane; and so on.

I was hit on my very first day at VC. I was slapped in arithmetic for not multiplying 6 times 8 correctly and got five strikes with a ruler in Arabic class for misreading five words in a five-word sentence. Everyone had laughed. Then I was punished for not finishing my rice and not knowing how to peel a fresh date with a knife and fork. I was made to stand next to the table while everyone else continued eating in the large dining hall. I wanted to take my grandfather's Pelikan pen and thrust it into the forehead of Miss Sharif, my Arabic teacher, who sat at the head of the table. At the end of my first day at school, when the school bus deposited me at our entrance at Cleopatra, I vomited the little I had eaten. I was immediately washed and put in bed. I said I had met five boys. All were

European, all but one spoke French, all had warned me against speaking French.

After being hit on the hands, students at VC would puff feverishly into their hollowed fists. I had done likewise. There was something soothing in the gesture. I had seen some puff even before being hit. That seemed to help too.

In the first week, I was hit for saying I had a cold when all I wanted was to avoid undressing in front of the others before swimming class. I was the only circumcised European and I knew, without even being told by my father, that it was better not to let anyone know I was Jewish.

I was hit for daydreaming, for talking in class, for ink stains left by my Pelikan. I was hit for trying to erase these stains. I was hit for failing to erase them. I spent more time rubbing out a misspelled word than I did trying to write a coherent sentence. I would wet the tip of an eraser with a touch of spit and then, by dint of persistent, delicate rubbing, would either end up making a hole in my notebook paper or dilute the ink until it left an even larger smudge. Permanent damage to your notebook meant you could be hit more than once for the same infraction, since Miss Sharif often forgot she had already punished you for a specific smudge or hole. Tearing the page out did not resolve matters at all; Miss Sharif counted the pages in everyone's notebooks. Notebooks had thirty-two pages.

Her arrival at a student's desk would always signal danger. Unable to see more than a few inches beyond her nose, she would pick up your notebook and hold it up to her eyes, covering her face completely as she stood there, reading awhile, and then, all of a sudden, throw it back at you, hurling one insult after another, as slaps followed the notebook, and kicks the slaps. She threw everything at her pupils' faces: books, chalk, blackboard erasers, pencil boxes, magazines, shrieking, "Oh, my sister!" before propelling her missiles. She even threw her handbag at me once. Then, of course, came the ruler—though, with me, Miss Sharif had decided that a larger instrument of pain had become necessary, which is why she used a double-decker wooden pencil box whenever she struck my hands.

I was also hit for having dirty shoes. Shoes had to be shiny at VC, and our spontaneous morning soccer game in the fields left them dirty and caked with mud. As I soon learned, the easiest way to give them a semblance of polish during the headmistress's inspection was to rub them furtively up and down my socks while standing at attention.

Miss Badawi, the headmistress, would insist on inspecting our nails, our lockers, our pockets, our hair. Whenever I reported to my mother that someone at school had looked through my hair, she would immediately begin searching me for lice, for she suspected that schools never check students' hair unless a lice epidemic was already under way. I remember how we had to hold our heads down as Miss Badawi or Miss Sharif or Miss Gilbertson, my English teacher, searched with their fingers and nails, raking our scalps, roughly. Aside from humiliating you in front of the whole class by announcing that you were a carrier of lice, they would immediately dispatch you to the school barber, who would shave your head so that every scar on your scalp showed. One day they shaved Charlie Atkinson, a lank, blond boy with wavy Rupert Brooke hair and the mildest of manners. He had walked out of the class with hair that caught the sun's glare. When he returned, everyone burst into laughter. No one could have guessed how small Charlie's head really was. The next day his father, a corpulent man in his sixties who had lost everything in Egypt but who had never wished to leave the country, stepped out of an immense old Cadillac and, holding his bald son by the hand, walked to Miss Badawi's office.

Everyone knew he had come to complain of the injustice committed against his son, and while Miss Gilbertson was busy teaching us grammar, we kept our ears wide open, our hearts pounding so loud that we could not even speak in full sentences when called upon. We heard nothing. Everyone thought the worst. Ten minutes later, there was a knock at the door. Miss Gilbertson, who hated having her class interrupted, barked, "Come in." It was Charlie. He apologized for being late and tiptoed over to his desk. He sat down quietly and seemed about to open his book to the page being studied in class when, to everyone's total amazement, he committed the ultimate sin: he lifted wide the cover of his desk. With mischievous relish, Miss Gilbertson was already going over to administer a hiding with her ruler when a voice at the door halted her. It was Miss Badawi. Next to her stood Atkinson Senior. In our excitement, we had failed see them.

Meanwhile, Charlie emptied his desk as fast as he could, stuffing his books, pencil box, and notebooks into his gym bag. Quietly, as if he had rehearsed his steps so often that he no longer had to give them a second thought, he went over to his locker at the back of the room and opened it with his key, emptying its contents into his bag and pockets. Then, taking out his invincible padded Ping-Pong paddles, the likes of which were no longer available in Egypt, he shouted in an exhilarated, shrill voice, "Who wants these?" Mass hysteria suddenly broke out, and everyone, without thinking of who was or wasn't watching, shouted a frenzied "I do!" Charlie threw one paddle and then the other into the center of the room. A mad rush ensued, with everyone falling on Amr, whose desk happened to be in the middle of the room, and who didn't understand what was happening because he didn't know a word of English.

Then Charlie Atkinson walked out. He was last seen standing with his father waiting for their chauffeur to drive around the quadrangle and pick them up.

A month later they shaved Daniel Biagi's head.

Then came Osama al-Basha's turn. Though his father was Egyptian, Osama's mother couldn't have been more British. Osama himself looked typically English, spoke with a perfect accent, and, for fun sometimes, would raise his voice to the pitch of Laurence Olivier, whom he also resembled. He could hardly say a sentence in Arabic. He too was pulled out of Victory College after his haircut.

I knew my turn would come.

■

One day I handed my father a note from my Arabic teacher that I had been carrying in my briefcase for over a week. Father looked at the date on the neatly handwritten French note and asked me if I had been concealing it from him. I said I had forgotten all about it. Predictably, the note complained that I never did my homework, that I never paid attention in class, and that I was bound to repeat the entire grade.

My father took me into the living room and asked me why I never did my Arabic homework.

I didn't know why I never did my Arabic homework.

"You don't know?" he asked.

I didn't know.

"Have you *ever* done Arabic homework?" he asked, as though out of casual curiosity. I thought about the matter for a moment and suddenly realized that indeed I had never done Arabic homework at VC.

"Not once?" he asked sarcastically.

"Not once," I repeated, failing to see that his sarcasm was aimed at me, not at the idea of having to do homework in Arabic.

My father called in Madame Marie. After shutting the glass door, he began to berate her for not making certain I did my homework. She let him scream, but when he called her an ignorant fool, she slumped into a chair and urged him not to say such things in front of the child. Not even her mother had called her names, and it wasn't likely that at forty she was going to allow anyone to do so.

"Madame Marie—" By now my father had lost his patience altogether, explaining that my failure to study Arabic could easily be construed as a seditious act against the present regime. Everyone had to study Arabic.

"But none of the other European boys studies Arabic," I interjected.

"Well, those who are leaving may not have to worry about Arabic. But since we're not planning to leave," he continued, "let us at least pretend that Arabic is important to us. Now let me see the latest assignment."

I opened my briefcase and produced an Arabic book whose pages had not even been cut yet. I told him I had to learn a poem by heart.

"Where is it?" he asked.

I tried finding the page in question but because the pages had not been separated, I wasn't able. "It's on page 42," I finally remembered.

"The class is on page 42 already and you've not done any homework yet?" he asked as he helped me separate the pages with a penknife.

The poem was accompanied by an illustration of a young Egyptian soldier waving a scimitar at three old men clothed in three tattered flags. The first was wearing the Union Jack, the second the *bleu-blanc-rouge*, and the third, a bald, short man with wiry sideburns, a large hooked nose, and a pointed beard, was shabbily draped in the Star of David.

I looked at the twenty-line poem and found myself sweating as I stared at words that were literally swimming on the page.

"My eyes are burning," I said.

Madame Marie inched her way closer to me and looked at the poem over my shoulder. It was her way of avoiding my father's glare.

"I can't read," I said.

"You can't read?" he started. "Let me understand. You not only don't know the poem but you aren't even able to read it?"

I nodded.

"So how do you plan to learn it by heart if you can't even read it?"

"I don't know," I answered, continuing to look down at my book only to realize that I had begun to tremble. I wanted to conceal the shaking by staring more intently at the picture, but my breathing was too shallow, and my chin shook as though it were held by loose wires. I caught myself slurring a few words. I knew there was no turning back, I was almost certainly going to cry.

"What's the matter now?"

"Nothing," I sobbed.

My father saw the picture.

"I don't care how you do it," he said, "but by tomorrow morning you'll have to know this poem by heart."

"How is he going to learn it if neither you nor I can even read Arabic?" asked Madame Marie.

"We'll get Abdou to help him."

My father yelled out Abdou's name. Seconds later, a knock was heard on the living room door. Abdou was carrying a saucer on which wobbled a glass of water. The water was for me; he had heard me crying.

"I want you to help him learn a poem by heart."

"But I can't read."

"Does anyone know how to read Arabic here?"

"There is my son Ahmed," said Abdou. "Do you want me to call him?"

"Call him, call him," yelled my father. Then, turning to me, he added: "Go have dinner now, and we'll see what happens once Ahmed arrives."

"All the same, children should not be taught such ugly things," whispered Madame Marie to my father, referring to the picture.

"Ugly or not ugly, he'll do what everyone else does."

Half an hour later, visitors arrived. Our downstairs neighbor, Madame Nicole, who was Belgian, came with her Egyptian Coptic husband. Our other neighbor, Sarina Salama, who was Jewish, showed up with her daughter Mimi, and their friend Monsieur Pharès, the painter. Drinks were offered. Mohammed was sent out to buy salted peanuts. Everyone had gathered to decide which film to see that evening. The choice was between *Sayonara* and *Gunfight at the OK Corral*. My mother, Madame Salama, and Mimi refused to see a western. *Sayonara* sounded wonderful, but gunfights and gunshots— out of the question! My mother asked whether Abdel Hamid, Madame Salama's millionaire Egyptian lover, would want to join. "He'll come, but only after the theater lights are out. I have to buy him a ticket—*me* buy *him* a ticket!—and leave it at the ticket booth in the name of *Monsieur César*." "But isn't Marlon Brando Jewish?" interrupted Mimi, referring to the government's policy of not showing films with Jewish actors —which is why *Cleopatra* never opened in Egypt. Edward G. Robinson's films were banned as well, as was anything starring Paul Newman, thought to be Jewish. *Ben Hur, The Ten Commandments*, and *Exodus* also were never shown in Alexandria; they portrayed Jewish themes. Kirk Douglas, however, was

so prototypically American that it would never have occurred
to the censor, nor to anyone else in Egypt, including us, that
his real name was Issur Daniilovich. Monsieur Pharès snickered at Mimi's comment, adding that it was just like Jews to
think all famous people were secretly their brothers.

My mother leaned over to my father and softly asked whether
they could take me to the movies with them. "Who's ever heard
of a boy his age going to the movies in the middle of a school
week?" came his raised voice.

We heard a gentle tap on the door. It was Abdou. "My son
is here," he announced. I caught Ahmed's face peeking in from
behind the door.

"Good," said my father, standing up and shaking Ahmed's
hand. He ordered Abdou to give his son something to eat,
knowing he had been fasting all day. My father put his hand
into his pocket and took out a one-pound note, which he gave
the young man. Ahmed stepped back and refused the bill,
saying he had not come for the money. My father insisted,
saying he was very grateful that he had come during Ramadan
and that he would be hurt if the young man refused him.
Abdou's son said, "*Mush lazem*, it's not necessary," while my
father almost pleaded with him, "*Lazem, lazem*," until Ahmed
relented.

Ahmed hardly had time to eat a morsel before he was rushed
through the corridor and into my bedroom, where his father
indicated a chair next to my desk. The young man removed
his jacket, let it drop on my bed, then, changing his mind,
picked it up and placed it neatly around the back of his chair.
He sat down, bringing the chair closer to my desk, smiled,
and blushed uncomfortably, his thin, olive-hued hand shaking
as he flipped through the book in search of page 42. Seeing
that the rest of the pages in the book had not been separated,
without the slightest comment, he stretched back, put his hand

deep into his pocket, and took out a small penknife, and with deft, decisive motions of the wrist, proceeded to separate the pages with his blade as he had learned from a local sheikh who had taught him to read and write. After cutting the pages, Ahmed held the book opened flat on my desk and pressed his hand up and down along the binding without hurting the spine, until the book yielded and stayed open on page 42.

He blushed again, perhaps because our reversed roles made him feel awkward, but also perhaps because he suddenly realized that he would have to teach a Jew a poem vilifying Jews.

He read the poem once to himself. Then, as my Arabic teacher would do in class, he spoke out the first few words, repeated them, and then waited for me to say them back to him. He did not explain the poem; no one ever explained the poems. They were always about poison, Jews, vengeance, and motherland. But he said the words with a slow, deliberate air about him, never correcting my mistakes save by repeating the words the right way, and always smiling each time I said something, as if I were doing him a special favor merely by mouthing unfathomable words in classical Arabic.

In the space of an hour I had learned the poem by heart. "Read it to yourself before you go to bed and as soon as you wake up," he said, as though prescribing medicine, for this was how he had learned almost all the Koran by heart. I told him that I did not know how to read very well. "Do you want me to teach you?" he asked, as if it were the most natural thing in the world. "It's very easy," he added.

We spent the next hour learning how to spell the words in the poem. Then, before leaving, he made me recite the poem again. "See how easy it was—and you were so scared," he said as Madame Marie walked us to the kitchen. I thought I had concealed my fear quite deftly.

In bed, I began leafing through the book before turning to

the poem, staring at illustrations of brawny Arab youths lunging toward the liberation of Palestine with their spiky bayonets, while a thousand jittery Jewish noses took aim at the intrepid victors, who were trampling the flag of Israel. Dead bodies lay strewn upon the sand. Every page with a poem on it was accompanied by a similar drawing, except for the Mother's Day poem, where the artist had sketched a sort of languid, middle-aged Egyptian mother lavishing her love upon seven children, the eldest of whom brandished the giant flag of Egypt in one hand, and the portrait of President Nasser in the other. He was wearing a cross between a cadet's uniform and school apparel, with shirt sleeves rolled up to his shoulders.

Suddenly I was seized with panic, the thought cramping my chest. What if I forgot the poem I had learned that night? I immediately repeated the first few words to myself. No, they were all in place, nothing forgotten.

Later that night, I was awakened by the light patter of rain on my windowpane. With intense joy and gratitude, I listened to the peaceful springtime showers on the streets of Cleopatra, realizing, from the sound of the rain, that the water was not dribbling down the slats of my shutters and pooling along the windowsill, but tapping directly against the panes themselves. To please me, Abdou had gone against my mother's orders and left the shutters wide open so that light might stream in at dawn and fill the room and remind me of summer mornings at our beach house at Mandara. I wondered why she was always set against leaving the shutters open, especially when you could see lights from nearby buildings reflected on the ceiling at night.

I turned on my shortwave radio and listened to a French song.

Hours later, I heard Mother tiptoe into my bedroom. I judged from the rustle of her clothes that she had rushed to see me while still wearing her coat. They had danced—I knew she liked dancing—and when she bent down to kiss me, I made out the scent of wine on her breath. I was happy for them.

■

As soon as I awoke the next morning, I scanned my mind to see if it still bore traces of the poem. To my utter surprise, I found that the poem hadn't budged.

When I walked into the dining room, I saw my father eating a soft-boiled egg. He was wearing a bathrobe and had just come out of the shower. Next to him was seated Monsieur Politi, also eating a soft-boiled egg. Abdou was standing behind my father, pouring tea from the teapot, obviously eager to hear his son complimented.

My father asked about my late-night tutorial. I told him I had learned the poem by heart. He asked me to recite it. I shook my head. Then, turning to Abdou, he asked, "Does Ahmed want to give him private lessons?" Abdou said he could have asked for nothing better, except that his son was soon to be inducted into the army and would not be free for another two years. "Pity. We'll have to find another tutor."

Never would Arabic be as easy as it was that evening with Ahmed.

During a short recess that day in school, I made fun of Amr, who, like many Arabic-speakers, had never learned to distinguish between *b* and *p* in English pronunciation. That morning Miss Gilbertson had tried to teach him the difference. From her mean and benighted point of view, it must have seemed that Amr was refusing to learn out of spite. She called him up to the front of the class, took out a piece of paper which she tore into very tiny confetti, and put five or six of these pieces into her palm. She then brought her hand close to her mouth and uttered a loud *b*. Nothing happened. "Now see the difference," she warned, and produced a *p* sound, at which the confetti went flying from her palm. "Here, you try it." She placed little pieces of torn paper in Amr's palm. "Say *buh*," she said. "*Buh*," he repeated. Nothing happened. "Now say *puh*." Whereupon Amr said, "*Buh*." "No, *puh*," she insisted. "*Buh*," he repeated. "No, you fool, it's *puh, puh, puh*." She began raising her voice, blowing all the confetti out of both their palms. "*Buh, buh, buh*," he repeated, trying very hard to please her, and then, seeing she was upset, produced a last, defeated, hopeless—"*Buh*."

By then the class was beside itself, some of us falling from our seats with laughter. Even Miss Gilbertson, who never laughed and who had a malignant stare permanently riveted to her face, was smiling broadly, first giggling at each of Amr's failed attempts, and finally bursting out laughing herself, which gave the class license to break into an uproar, while Amr stood befuddled and crestfallen until it occurred to him that there was no reason why he shouldn't laugh with the others, which he did.

At recess, I ran into Amr and jokingly asked him to "Blease bass de bebber." He knew I was making fun of him and called me "*Kalb al Arab*, dog of the Arabs." This was too offensive, and I lunged at him, both of us tussling on the playing field until the headmistress, Miss Badawi, hurried over and separated us. "You should not be fighting," she yelled. "But he insulted me," I argued. "He called me 'dog of the Arabs.'" She did not give me time to finish my complaint. "But you are the dog of the Arabs," she replied in Arabic, smiling, as if it were the most obvious thing in the world.

Stunned, I was almost sure I had misconstrued her words. I was even about to protest again. But I said nothing and went to the bathroom, where Michel Cordahi, a native French-speaker who came from one of Egypt's wealthiest Christian families, helped run water over my scraped knee. I cleaned myself as best I could and arrived in Arabic class with my legs still red from the fall.

Before the recitation was to start, Miss Sharif briefly went over the poem and had the class name all of the Arab nations in the world. The poem itself was a long, high-minded, patriotic ode dedicated to the unity of the Arab world. It calumnized almost all the nations of Europe and, in its *envoi*, stirred all Arab boys and girls to free the last two Arab countries from the yoke of foreign dominion: Algeria and Palestine. France was suitably anathematized, as was England. Finally, by way of perorating her little speech, Miss Sharif inveighed against the *Yahud*, the Jews, throwing her fist in the air in an imitation salute, and sending the adrenaline rushing through my body each time she mentioned the word. The students responded to Miss Sharif's battle cries, asking questions and voicing their agreement, which only intensified the vehemence of their outrage. Handwritten posters in colored ink, which the students had brought in, hung along the walls of the classroom, decrying imperialism, Zionism, and the perfidy of the Jews.

Something ugly and dangerous prevailed in class whenever the *Yahud* were mentioned. All I could do was stiffen helplessly and wish that some unknown force might come and take me away, that the ceiling might fall on Miss Sharif, that a terrible beast might squirm its way out of the sea and yawn at our classroom door. Without budging from my seat, I would try to make myself scarce, stare into the void, and drift away.

While Miss Sharif was speaking to the class about Nasser's vision of a united, Pan-Arab nation, I waited for the inevitable. She had warned I'd be the first to recite the poem that day, and I already knew that at the end of her prefatory remarks she would go to her desk, search for her glasses in her handbag, open her book, and, turning her gaze to the window, as if her thoughts had wandered a bit and were still hovering on VC's giant, green cricket field, would suddenly call my name. I waited to hear it any moment now. Quietly I tore out a very tiny corner of my notebook and drew a Star of David on it. It might bring me good luck. Not knowing what to do with the star, and not wishing to leave it lying about in my desk or in my pockets—which were always subject to summary inspection before the entire class—I put it in my mouth, moved it around a bit, and then let it stick to my palate, where it rested, untouched by my tongue or by my teeth, as Michel Cordahi had told me he did with the Host.

Once again I searched through my mind for the words of the first verse. They were still there, all of them, like children who haven't shifted a limb since being put to bed hours earlier. I contemplated them almost lovingly.

Then Miss Sharif called my name. A shot of adrenaline coursed through me, along with a cold, numbing spasm.

I went to the front of the class, cleared my throat, cleared it again. I would try to deliver the poem fast and be done with it. I spoke out the title, recited the first verse, which merely restated the title, and, rather pleased with myself, was already searching hard for the third line, when all of a sudden the poem disappeared.

I recognized some of the phrases the boys in the front row kept whispering to me, but I was unable to put them together. Besides, knowing that Miss Sharif must also have heard their taunts and whispers, I didn't know whether to acknowledge them with a passing smile or merely stare into space, pretending I hadn't heard them.

"This is an important poem, the most important poem in the book," she said. "Why didn't you study it?" I did not know why I hadn't studied it. "I don't know what to do with you any longer," she said, working herself into a temper. "I don't know, I just don't know—oh, my sister!" She exploded in a rage, ready to strike me any moment now. "Oh, my sister!" she yelled again, letting fly all the colored chalk with which she had drawn a map of the Arab world. "We shall have to go to see Miss Badawi."

It was only on our way to Miss Badawi's office that it finally dawned on me, on this nippy, sunny morning, that she would almost certainly resort to the stick, maybe even the cane.

Much, much worse, however, was the fear that my father would come to know of my crime and be furious that evening. Once again he would tell me that in failing to remember the poem I was probably showing government informants that in my parents' home no one took Arab education very seriously. This was almost sure to ruin my parents.

To my surprise, I did not get the stick; instead, Miss Badawi called home and announced that I was suspended from school for the day. My mother and Madame Marie hopped into a cab and were there to pick me up in less than half an hour. With Madame Marie as her interpreter, my mother apologized to Miss Badawi and promised that from now on I would have an Arabic tutor every day.

Outside school grounds, when she asked me why I had not studied the poem, I broke down and cried.

"We're taking the tramway home," she said.

We boarded the second-class car at the Victoria terminal and headed directly to the upper deck, all three of us crammed into a tiny space in the open-air porch to the right of the spiral staircase. Before boarding, my mother, a born and bred Alexandrian, remembered to buy heated peanuts for the ride. It was windy, and light gray patches hovered over what was sure to remain a bright, sunny day. From where we perched, I could see the stuccoed school turret rising above the dining hall where, at this time, my classmates were queuing up for lunch. I thought of the food, always the same cheap, nauseating, doughy rice laced with bits of meat. Someone in school had composed a little rhyme in Arabic, which, unlike every other Arabic poem I ever heard, I shall never forget:

> *Captain Toz,*
> *akal al-lahma,*
> *wu sab al roz.*
>
> [*Captain Phooey*
> *gobbled the meat*
> *and left the rice.*]

I almost laughed out loud as I thought of these words. I told my mother the words, for she had seen me smile and wanted to know why. She also remembered bad food from her boarding days at Madame Tsotsou's and said she knew how cruel teachers could be. She laughed about Captain Toz, wondering how he managed to avoid the dread rice. At VC we had to eat everything on our plate. "Or else?" she asked. "They hit you very hard." "We'll see," she said, dipping her fingers into the paper cone of peanuts.

The tram began to rumble and squeak. Soon it cleared the curve at Victoria and began to pick up speed to the next station.

"We won't go home," she said on impulse. "We'll go downtown."

This was a miracle. We were going to travel from one end of the city to the other, and eventually, after lunch, would have forgotten all about Miss Sharif and Miss Badawi and the paean to Arab unity. "Stop worrying so much!" said my mother when I kept asking about what she thought Miss Badawi might tell my father. She turned to her right and named the first station after Victoria, wearing that blithe, high-spirited, girlish smile that could infuriate my father when he was reporting gloomy news; then he'd call her the most irresponsible, selfish optimist he knew, because she refused to put on his frown and worry.

"This is Laurens," she said, pointing to the next station, whose platform at that hour was silent and deserted. And before I knew it, she named all of the stations on the Victoria line, a litany of French, Greek, German, Arabic, and English names that are forever braided in my mind with the image of my mother riding up on the *impériale*, wearing sunglasses, her colored scarf and dark hair flying about her face against the backdrop of the sea, smoking a cigarette and trying as hard as she could to divert my mind from my worries at school. I would never forget their names: Sarwat, San Stefano, Zizinia, Mazloum, Glymenopoulo, Saba Pasha, Bulkley, Rouchdy, Moustafa Pasha, Sidi Gaber, Cleopatra, Sporting, Ibrahimieh, Camp de César, Chatby, Mazarita, Ramleh.

Nearing Rouchdy, I saw row upon row of ancient villas with large trees and gardens, some even with fountains. As the tram swerved and tilted to the left, I suddenly knew I had spotted the Montefeltro home. It, too, like so many others, had been converted into an Arab public school. Loud girls wearing khaki smocks swarmed about the garden. When I mentioned Signor Ugo to my mother, she said he had become a history teacher at the Lycée Saint Marc.

"We'll go to the movies," she said.

■

After Ramadan that year, my father decided to hire an Arabic tutor: Sheikh Abdel Naguib. All I remember was his extraordinarily smelly feet and his calloused hand resting on my thigh when he corrected my pronunciation of the Koran. He taught nothing but the Koran, and all he did each time was have me memorize one or two sections, or suras, though without ever bothering to explain them to me. My assignment was to copy suras many, many times every day.

Compared to Arabic class, nothing could have been more soothing than spending hours at my desk copying the same sura ten, twenty, thirty times while the April sun lingered on my notebook and cast a silent, peaceful spell in my room, gracing the wall, the books, my desk, my hand, and my copy of the Koran like a premonition of intense summer midday light, warm sea weather, and beach-house fellowship.

An old Matisse reproduction in my room beamed and beckoned in the morning light, and between the balusters lining the artist's balcony in Nice were patches of blue—as always, the sea.

From Abdou's kitchen came the scent of lime, melons, and overripe cucumber. Any day now, they'd pack everything, throw bedsheets over all the furniture, and off we'd go to our beach house at Mandara. "*Lazem bahr*," Abdou had said, "we need the beach." Ramadan always started one thinking of summer.

I worked away quietly, studiously, filled with the vacuous bliss of medieval scribes who put in a long day's work at their desk without ever reading or understanding a word of what they've copied all day.

But Sheikh Abdel Naguib was not pleased at all. I had missed an entire verse each of the thirty times I had copied the same sura. "But couldn't you tell the sura made no sense if you omitted this verse?" he asked, raising his voice, to which I would quietly, and respectfully, admit that I couldn't, because, as was clear to everyone who knew me, I was totally incapable of understanding anything I was reading in Arabic unless it was explained to me first.

Sheikh Abdel Naguib doubled my homework during summer vacation at Mandara by having me copy each sura sixty times. On average, this would take an hour, especially if I calculated the number of lines needed for each sura and began copying the first word sixty times, then next to it the second word sixty times, then the third word sixty times, and so on. Madame Marie, who didn't know whether my method for recopying the same sura was particularly edifying, would once in a while come into my room and observe my progress, and almost worry, "You're working very, very hard."

In the distance, I could make out the drone of the old Bedouin bagpipe player who would appear at around three as he trundled barefoot on the burning sandy roads of Mandara. Everyone referred to him as "the poor devil," because he continued to wear the shredded remnants of his old British band uniform. After him came the beggar-and-baboon show. And after that, the garbagewoman, *al zabbalah*—or, in pidgin French, *la zibalière*—carrying a huge, stinking burlap bag filled with food that had been rotting for days in the heat, knocking at our door every afternoon asking for a glass of water as she stood outside, almost panting from the heat, saying, "*Allah yisallimak, ya Abdou*, may God save you, Abdou."

After her knock came the call of the bread-and-biscuit vendor, and the ice cream vendor after him, and then noises made by neighborhood boys who would start to gather not far from our house, saying things I did not quite catch, until, roused from my stupor and straining an ear again, I would realize they were my friends about to head into the sandy hinterland to engage in yet another kite fight. They were tying used razor blades onto the kite's head and tail.

The Greeks of Mandara had by far the best kites and always won. These were boys from a local Greek orphanage whose two giant kites, named the *Paralus* and the *Salaminia*, reigned over the skies each summer. As our kite bore toward them, the *Paralus* and *Salaminia* would at first refuse to engage, hissing it away like lazy cobras, ordering it back with a graceful, peremptory swerve and nod of their heads. But once it got close, without warning, first one and then the other came swooping down, tearing through it in two successive strikes without even getting tangled, until our stunned and helpless kite lurched awhile and then came plummeting down in a straight descent, crashing onto the sand as everyone scattered for fear of the blades. Two older Greeks would monitor the events from afar, yelling instructions as the fighting got rougher, while their boys chanted and clapped their hands, watching the *Paralus* and the *Salaminia* close in on their next target, this time without provocation.

In the back of my mind all through my scribal exercises were images of the *Salaminia* plunging from above as soon as it caught sight of our poor, unnamed victim and gashing it to pieces with its pointed rostrum. My mind would drift to other things as I kept copying, word after word after word. Then, all of a sudden, in the distance, I made out the victorious chant of the Greek orphans. The *Salaminia* had won again.

The boys were waiting on the dunes for me to finish copying my suras. Momo (Maurice-Shlomo) Carmona was crying. "They cheated," he cursed. Someone was holding the skeletal remains of our fallen Icarus: scraps of sliced bamboo cane and torn white canvas made in my father's factory. Even our parents were sorry for us. "You are wasting too much time," said my father.

·

The next year at VC was no better than the first. By the second month it became obvious I was failing every subject, including art.

One morning Madame Marie warned me that my father had received a telephone call from Miss Gilbertson expressing renewed concern over my work. My father wanted to speak to me, she said. I could hear his vigorous puffing as Monsieur Politi counted indefatigable one-and-two's in his thickly accented Judeo-Arab French. My mother had awakened earlier than usual and was wearing a green bathrobe; her jet-black hair, still wet from the shower, was hastily combed back. She was cutting my croissant into little slices, and was particularly solicitous of me during breakfast.

Abdou looked at me almost ruefully. "*Shid haylak*," he whispered as my father walked into the room. "Courage."

"Well?" asked my father.

I said nothing. I hated vague preambles to what was clearly going to escalate into a bitter scolding. Mother sat with her arms crossed, looking down, as though she herself was about to be chided. I stared at her, almost imploring her to smile, or at least return my gaze.

"Leave us," said my father to Madame Marie. "You too," he told my mother after Madame Marie stood up. Madame Marie waited at the door for my mother to join her.

"No, I'll stay," she insisted, trying to contain her anger while dismissing Madame Marie.

"Always, always meddling," he started. "It's between him and me, him and me."

"And I'm his mother. And that shit of an Englishwoman could just as easily have called *me* instead of you, *me* instead of you!"

"And spoken through whom? Abdou?" asked my father, ironically. "And don't call her a shit in front of the boy."

"Just get on with what you have to say to him. Can't you see you're upsetting him by keeping him waiting?"

"Then let me tell you what I've decided," he said, turning

to me. "I've already spoken about it to Miss Gilbertson," he continued, meaning to emphasize this fait accompli, "and she agrees it would be an excellent idea for you to move into her home and live with her as a boarder for a while."

It came as the most terrifying threat in my life. I could think of nothing else for the rest of the day, for the rest of the week, the rest of the school year. The prospect haunted me like an evil spirit, insinuating itself everywhere, undoing every joy.

"I'm sorry, but this is crazy!" exclaimed my mother.

"Crazy yourself!"

"And you're a monster."

At some point during breakfast, once my father had collected himself, he managed to explain his plan with kindness and something verging on apology in his voice. My study habits, my command of English, my work in Arabic, my discipline, even my bearing—everything had degenerated. Something drastic was needed. Since going to a boarding school in England was precluded—Jews were allowed neither to send money abroad nor come back to Egypt once they had exited the country—the choice was either to hire a tutor or to send me to a local boarding school. We had already tried the first. As for boarding school, my father had his doubts; he imagined such places as being full of merrymaking pranksters and nighttime pillow fights, places where no one did any studying at all.

For a fee, however, I could live with Miss Gilbertson. After all, she was not so terrible. She would teach me what all English boys my age knew. She would civilize me out of Abdou's kitchen and out of my mother's tempestuous reach.

All I could think of when I imagined Miss Gilbertson's home was a small, dark bedroom, a pair of striped pajamas, my toothbrush standing next to hers in the bathroom, and old brown furniture in an old brown apartment where all one did was read alone, eat alone, or sit alone at a long brown table in the evening under the scowling vigilance of old Britain. Miss Gilbertson would pry into my secret world and monitor my dreams, my most secret, shameful thoughts with the castigating gaze of a corrections officer and director of conscience. My mother said she would never let it happen, that I needn't worry. But my grandmother supported the project. Aunt Elsa thought, 'Why not?' Madame Salama snickered and guaranteed it never hurt a boy my age to be left alone with a depraved spinster. Her lover, Abdel Hamid, opined that it might have the opposite effect, and Madame Nicole concluded that whatever parents did for their children always proved wrong in the end. Besides, she added, parents had the most deleterious influence on children, so why not separate them, since they were bound to be at war?

Then my father did what he always did in times of stress: he stalled. The idea itself was never abolished; it was simply remanded, suspended, and, like Dreyfus, I was never officially absolved. Even when it became clear that my father himself questioned the wisdom of his project and had more or less given it up, no one dared remind him that he had abandoned it, for fear of encouraging him to think about a matter which had been unofficially dismissed precisely because he believed it was still being thought about. Perhaps, in the end, my father simply tired of the idea.

■

Monsieur al-Malek, my new tutor, was the next best solution. An Arab Jew, Monsieur al-Malek spoke English, French, and Arabic fluently and was the current headmaster of the École de la Communauté Israélite. He would ring our bell every weekday evening at five, greet everyone in English, including Abdou, whose language he knew better than Abdou himself, and would ask me whether I could kindly show him to my room. There he would open my briefcase, rummage for evidence of mischief or deceit on my part, invariably find it, upbraid me, and proceed to go over my Arabic and arithmetic assignments. "I won't tell your father," he would say at some point in every tutorial, "but these hours are almost wasted. You're not applying yourself," he would add, and, closing his book, would explain by means of examples taken from the lives of his two sons what applying oneself meant.

During tutorial it often happened that I would make out the happy signs that the living room was crowded with guests who had come for tea and drinks. Nothing was more welcome than the muted sound of the doorbell, followed by the rehearsed startled ecstasy of Abdou's exclamations as he opened the door to Mr. or Mrs. So-and-so and the tap of shoes on the hard wooden floor leading into the living room.

One evening, Monsieur al-Malek dawdled a bit longer than usual before leaving the foyer, and it was there that he ran into my mother who, more out of courtesy than inclination, asked him to join the guests for tea. He resisted, but on being urged once more, consented, and then took off his coat, which he had just put on, gave Aziza his hat, and stood at the entrance to the living room, rubbing his hands as though he had just walked in from the cold. There he was hailed by my father, who liked him even less than my mother did but had a lot of respect for a man who everyone said was a very learned teacher.

My father poured scotch into his glass, threw in a large ice cube, and then asked him whether he wanted it plain or with Vichy water. "Vichy, Vichy," said Monsieur al-Malek as though he always drank scotch with Vichy water. He sipped it once and said it was excellent. "Johnnie Walker, naturally!" he added. "I can't stand this man," whispered Aunt Flora, who was also there among the guests that evening and whose voice was totally drowned out by the sound of traffic rising from the avenue. Mother had kept the balcony windows open that night, and scented drafts from the Smouha plantations and from the jasmine someone had brought blended in with the intimate, stale smell of cigarettes, giving our living room a sensual, luxuriant air.

Suddenly, there was a ring at the door. Abdou was heard shutting the kitchen door leading to the main entrance, and before he had time to proclaim his pleasure, a loud voice thundered, with Abdou finally appearing at the living room door holding a gentleman's wide-brimmed hat in his hand. Behind him was the gentleman himself, trailed by his wife. "But it's Ughetto!" shouted my grandmother.

"And Ugo it is," he said storming into our living room with strides that screamed "Make way." "For you, for you, and for you. More I couldn't get," he said as he distributed presents from his most recent trip abroad. He had brought ten prized Tobler chocolate bars, which the company—including Monsieur al-Malek, my grandmother, Madame Marie, and Abdou—devoured on the spot. Signor Ugo had also brought my mother an immense bottle of Crêpe de Chine, for me a child's *Plutarch's Lives*, for my father the latest edition of the Larousse dictionary—things one could no longer buy in Egypt. Our last Larousse dated back six years.

"Ugo, you're an angel," said my grandmother as she unpacked and stared at the hand blender he had brought her from France. "This is a miracle." Everyone sat and admired the small device with its tiny helical blades. They had never seen anything like it. "How does it work?" asked Madame Salama. "I'll show you right now," said Signor Ugo's wife. Almost the entire living room marched to the kitchen to watch my grandmother whip up one-minute mayonnaise. A whir was heard in the kitchen, and sixty seconds later my grandmother, followed by a retinue of exultant ladies, returned victorious, brandishing a large glass containing a yellowish paste which she held out in her right hand as the Statue of Liberty holds out her beacon. Everyone wanted to try.

As they filtered back into the living room, Signor Ugo called out to my grandmother in Italian. "Sit next to me, you old witch," he said, "I want to feel young again." Everyone started to laugh, including my grandmother, who had been very quiet that evening, because earlier on, while waiting downstairs for Abdou to help her into the elevator, she had run into Madame Sarpi, who had accidentally knocked her onto the marble floor, and then, to make matters worse, fallen on top of her. "Ugo, be quiet, my legs are killing me."

"Amputate, darling, amputate!" Which inspired him to tell a bawdy joke about a very well-endowed idiot who, in order to sneak his way into a harem disguised as a eunuch, had said, "Amputate, amigo, amputate."

His wife implored him not to tell the joke, but tell it he did, and with gusto, especially when the moment came for the punchline. "Ugo, you're disgusting," she said, slapping him on the shoulder. "I burn for you, darling," he replied, "*Ardo, ardo*," he added, preparing to bite her.

"Ugo, wherever you go you bring joy," said my grandmother. "Now tell us what to do. We're so worried about the boy. His Arabic teachers hit him all the time, and now he won't study for school at all."

I pretended not to listen and continued speaking with Aunt Flora.

My mother was quiet. Abdel Hamid, Madame Salama's lover, immediately jumped in, insisting that discipline was all that a child should know. "Everyone exaggerates the feelings of children—but parents, too, have feelings," he added. "Besides, teachers don't hit without a reason, you know."

"He never studies," chimed in Madame Marie.

"That's not the point, one must understand why," interjected Monsieur al-Malek, who till then had remained silent to survey the situation before risking a comment. Monsieur Pharès, the painter, brought a bent index finger right next to his nose and, with repeated curved motions, meant to suggest a parrot's beak, made fun of my hooked nose. "No, that's not the reason, either," added Monsieur al-Malek, passing a platter of cakes to Abdel Hamid. Abdel Hamid, who was diabetic, kept staring at the cakes, and then passed them on to Madame Nicole. "The problem is that we never try to get inside a child's head," insisted Monsieur al-Malek. "One needs patience. And plenty of psychology."

"Patience and psychology are very nice words, but it's gone too far, to say nothing of what *they'll* think"—my father meant government informers—"when they see that in this house we totally disparage everything to do with Arabic culture. *They* already know everything that goes on in this house," he went on, "so can't we try to be a bit more inconspicuous and be like everyone else for a change?"

"*They* are the last people you should worry about," said Aunt Flora, turning to my father. "It's *him* you should think of. They shouldn't hit him."

My mother nodded. She said she found the practice barbaric.

"In your place, Henri," said Monsieur Pharès, "I wouldn't let anyone hit my son."

My father said that if what they did to me was called hitting, then what should we call the treatment he had received from the Jesuits when he was a boy.

"What do they hit you with?" asked Abdel Hamid.

"A ruler," I said.

"A ruler! Fancy that, a ruler!" chuckled Abdel Hamid. "In my time they used a bamboo cane and a whip. Remember the bamboo cane?" he said, turning to my father with almost nostalgic recollection. "We also had Monsieur de Pontchartrain's walking stick, and Père Antoun's *khartoum*—literally a garden hose. You never forgot that!"

Aunt Flora insisted that children stop learning the moment they are threatened with corporal punishment. My father said he was not sure, but that he liked to defer to the judgment of professional pedagogues. My grandmother said that an Arab pedagogue was a contradiction in terms. Madame Nicole suspected they *jouissaient* each time they spanked little boys.

Still, Madame Salama, Monsieur Pharès, and Madame Sarpi held on to the belief that I should stay at VC and make a special effort to apply myself. Monsieur al-Malek agreed, but advised that I be taken out of the Christian religion class and put in Islam class. What difference would it make which religion I studied, since I was neither a Christian nor a Moslem. In Islam class, at least, I would have the advantage of hearing five more hours of Arabic each week, and hearing the best-written Arabic might help a great deal.

"Could be a wonderful idea," mused my father.

I was reluctant. I did not want to study the Koran, nor did I want to be the only European in a class of Moslems; certainly I didn't want to have to take off my shoes during religion class, which is what devout Arabs did.

Meanwhile, my grandmother and Montefeltro were debating opposing views. Signor Ugo reminded my father that since we were Italians, it only made sense that I go to the Don Bosco Italian School of Alexandria. All Italians would eventually have to leave Egypt and settle in Italy—so why not learn the language of Italy? My grandmother thought differently. Perhaps we should hire an Italian tutor twice a week.

"A capital idea too," said my father.

At this point Monsieur al-Malek plunged into the fray as

though he held the definitive key to the riddle. "How long do you plan to stay in Egypt?" he asked my father.

"For as long as they'll let me. What a question!" replied my father.

"Then the boy needs to know Arabic. It's that simple!"

But my mother disagreed. "Sooner or later we'll have to leave. And when we leave, all these years devoted to Arabic will have been wasted. Can't you see? Let him fail Arabic— and let him fail it every year—but meanwhile let him learn things that matter instead of devoting so much time to these disgusting poems where all they teach him is to hate Jews."

Signor Ugo looked grave. He had started to tell my father how he had seen Dr. Katz at the Muhafza—the municipal headquarters—only a few months earlier. Everyone had read about the famed doctor's imprisonment on spying charges; his name was brought up at least once a day in class. "It's worse than in '58. They can arrest anyone now. They throw you in jail on the most trumped-up charges. They picked me up at my tailor, took me to the Muhafza, stripped me naked, and before I knew it, they had brought in this huge Doberman drooling right in front of my thing there and began questioning me. He can tell when you lie, they warned, tugging at the leash. I was terrified. Things are very bad," he said, his face clouding the more he spoke.

"They tortured Katz," said his wife. "Ugo was lucky."

"Didn't they know you were Jewish too, though?" asked my father.

"But—but don't you know, then?" asked Signora da Montefeltro.

"Don't know what?" asked my father.

"They don't know!" she said, turning to her husband. "You've got to tell them, Ugo."

"It's nothing. It's just that last month we got baptized. Supposedly a precautionary measure, which will end up making no difference in the end, but it was my friend Father Papanastasiou's idea, and he insisted."

"And what did you convert to?"

"Father Papanastasiou is Greek Orthodox, so we converted to Greek Orthodoxy. What am I going to do, choose between one form of Christianity and another?"

Our jaws must have dropped.

"Come, come, you Sephardi are no strangers to this, so don't look so shocked."

"It's not that I'm shocked, it's that your Greek is so awful," said my grandmother. "You could at least have chosen a more plausible religion."

"Please! I've had enough headaches about it already. If you want a word of advice, I'll arrange for you to speak to Father Papanastasiou yourself. He'll make Christians of everyone here—you, Monsieur Abdel Hamid, Henri, Abdou the cook."

Madame Nicole couldn't help laughing. My father, sitting next to her, leaned over and smiled something under his breath. She tried to suppress her laughter.

Mimi, who had been sitting almost too quietly next to her mother, wearing her mother's tight clothes so as to look older and more flashy, suddenly got up, put a handkerchief to her face, and rushed out of the room, breaking into loud sobs in the kitchen. Her mother got up and rushed after her.

"What happened? What's the matter with her?" asked my grandmother.

"*Mimi è una civetta,*" sang Signor Ugo—"Mimi is a flirt."

"She's crying. That's what's the matter," retorted Madame Sarpi, who was a close friend of Madame Salama.

"But why?" asked Abdel Hamid.

"Because she's crying," answered Madame Salama, who had just overheard Abdel Hamid's question and was returning to the living room. "Mimi's gone home," she said indicating the kitchen door. A moment of silence followed. "She calls me at the office, you know," said my father. "I know," answered the mother, "just be patient with her, it's all I ask. It'll pass."

My mother turned to Madame Salama. "What's the matter with Mimi?" she asked.

"The usual," answered her neighbor.

"Still?"

Madame Salama nodded.

There was another ring and Abdou announced that Kassem and Hassan were at the door.

Kassem and Hassan were mechanics at my father's factory. They were wearing what looked like gray Sunday suits, not their usual overalls. They were in obvious distress.

Kassem, the younger of the two, was holding a clear plastic box tied with a red ribbon. When he saw my mother step out of the living room, he walked up, greeted her, and gave her the box. "From the two of us." Hassan, who had stayed back a few steps, was smiling at her. To their thinking, this was a very European gift, and my mother later said they must have spent a lot on it.

She was immediately delighted when she opened the box and produced a silver rose made of gleaming silk. She thanked them and, just to show them, pinned it to her dress right then and there. Abdou brought out two uncapped bottles of Coca-Cola for the visitors. They exchanged news about the barracks. Abdou's son and Hassan's brother were in the same regiment.

My father greeted the two mechanics heartily and invited them into the living room. Awkwardly, they entered the room with their bottles in their hands and, not knowing where to sit, proceeded directly to an empty sofa next to the balcony where they sat side by side. Kassem, encouraged by my father, handed Hassan his bottle and began to unroll a very large sheet of tracing paper on which was drawn the model of a strange engine. My father took it to the light, studied it attentively, and declared that this time he liked it.

"You'll never guess what these gentlemen here have done," he told everyone in the room. "They've taken the boiler of a sunken World War Two German freighter, reinforced it, and installed it at my factory."

"Why, is your factory sailing away?" joked Signor Ugo, who knew that his joke was a thorny one, for it was common knowledge that the Egyptian government planned to nationalize more businesses and factories that year.

The two Egyptians spoke no French but understood that my father had just complimented them. He then offered them a drink. They were very reluctant and pointed to the Coca-Cola bottles, but yielded in the end. Kassem accepted a cigarette from Madame Salama and held it, Egyptian style, between his pinky and ring finger. They were discussing the famous Egyptian singer Om Kalthum, whom both idolized. Madama Salama offered Hassan a cigarette too, but he declined with the uncomfortable look of people who turn down a dish not because they do not want it, but because they are embarrassed to eat it in front of strangers. "I apologize but I can't stay," Kassem then said. No sooner had Kassem spoken than Hassan took his cue and stood up as well. "My wife is expecting me," explained the older of the mechanics. "Wives!" joked Madame Salama in Arabic. "And yet, without wives where would you men be?" My father walked them to the foyer. "Mark my words, you will be rich one day." "May God hear you!" replied Kassem.

Only then did I realize who Kassem was. Latifa's son.

A short while later, Madame Nicole suddenly remembered she had to leave. "Already?" asked my grandmother. "Unfortunately, yes." "And where to at this hour?" asked Madame

Salama. "My seamstress." "I see. Your seamstress," echoed her upstairs neighbor. "My seamstress," smiled Madame Nicole with something of a sigh in her voice, as though to imply that we all had our crosses to bear, and hers was passion. "Ach, Madame Nicole—" said my grandmother. "*Bonsoir tous*," said Madame Nicole curtly, picking up her keys and cigarette case from the tea table. "She's right, the poor woman," added my grandmother once Madame Nicole had left the room. "Beautiful as she is, and with a husband like hers—"

My grandmother had once heard Madame Nicole trying to escape her husband's blows, screaming, "*Arrête, arrête, salaud*," while he yelled, "*Bint al-sharmuta*, you whore's daughter," both of them going at each other on the metal staircase like a pot banging at a frying pan. "But she hits him too, don't you worry," my grandmother went on.

My father walked Madame Nicole to the door. Then, as soon as she was gone, he said he would have to leave to meet a client.

"At this hour of the night?" asked my mother.

"I'll be back in no time."

"And leave me alone with all of these people whom I hardly understand? Can't it wait until tomorrow?"

"It can't." Another heavy silence.

"Look, I don't have the time to argue, but if you want, come with me and see for yourself."

Defeated, my mother said she would stay home.

"Where is he going?" asked Signor Ugo as soon as he saw my father put on his raincoat.

"I don't know," said my mother. I heard Madame Salama say something about patience and fortitude. My mother said she would rather throw herself from the window than go on living like this.

Whenever Mother threatened to throw herself from the window, I always made certain to watch each time she came near one. In bed at night, I would strain an ear and follow her movements around the house. Sometimes I would get out of bed, tiptoe across the corridor, and, from behind the curtain, spy on her as she read a novel on the sofa, or had coffee by herself on the veranda overlooking the smoky fields of Smouha, or sat next to a salesman—a jeweler, or one of the various antiques dealers who came to display their wares in the evening. Sometimes, coming out of bed at night, I would catch her dialing the telephone in secret, alone in the living room, holding the handset in one hand, cupping the mouthpiece with the other, not uttering a sound. I knew she was trying to find my father. But then, sometimes, I heard nothing at all—and I knew then that she had either thrown herself off the living room balcony or gone to visit Madame Salama next door through the service entrance. On this night all the windows in our apartment were neatly closed. Mother had scrupulously placed her leather bookmark in her novel and turned off all the lights except for those in the pantry, for her late-night return from Madame Salama's. Her bedroom light was on, as always—to let government spies think everyone was at home.

■

Months later we took Signor Ugo up on his offer and, early one Friday morning, my father and I put on suits and went to pick him up at his pension on Rue Djabarti. He was late, so we got out and waited downstairs on the empty sidewalk. It was one of those translucently quiet early spring mornings in Alexandria when the shops were still closed and the city patiently, almost lazily, awaited morning prayers. A smell of *ful*, the national bean breakfast, permeated the air. Both of us were hungry. Signor Ugo would probably be outraged if he caught us eating such a poor man's meal. "And it's always so messy," said my father as we decided to give up the thought. Through the pension's open door came another smell: of coffee and *loucoumades*, fried dough steeped in honey. "We'll have to eat something along the way," said my father.

Signor Ugo was wearing a shimmering silk tie such as he alone seemed to possess; my father later said that only wealthy men of a certain age wore such ties. He also wore a Borsalino hat, a scrupulously pressed tweed jacket, and sparkling gold-buckled shoes. "Aha, so you're here already," he said by way of greeting us. "Paulette cannot come. This weather always gives her headaches. Typical Alexandrian: loves the sun, but loves it in the shade."

"It's off the Corniche, not far behind Mandara," said Signor Ugo as he sat down in the front seat and pulled out a pack of Elmas. He tapped his cigarette very lightly on the back of the white pack where, as usual, something had already been scribbled in royal-blue ink.

The Corniche at eight o'clock on this cloudless Friday morning was empty of traffic, and we raced past familiar sights on our way to Mandara, a cool wind fanning through Signor Ugo's rolled-down window. We passed Sidi Bishr, the largest beach before Mandara, where no signs of summer life had sprung up yet. The beaches were deserted, the billboards along the coast road bore last year's posters, and none of the small summer shops and stalls that cropped up everywhere during the season were anywhere in sight along the shuttered, un-painted rows of cabins lining the beachfront. Restaurants had not removed last year's *hassiras*—bamboo thatches that pro-tected patrons and beachgoers when tables were put out on the sidewalk. Some of the *hassiras* had mildewed and fallen to the ground and lay flat in the middle of the streets; others hung from wooden rafters, with their ends sweeping the sidewalk, flapping against the wind like trapped kites at the end of summer.

As we neared Mandara, the unpaved road lay covered with

caked and hardened sand. A recent *hamsin* had left sweeps of sand everywhere. Even al-Nunu's Coca-Cola shack lay almost buried, the sand filling the grooves of the corrugated tin sheets that made up the four walls of his summer home. Another shack, not far from his, had caved in under the weight of the sand.

Signor Ugo told my father to make a right turn, and then another that led up a very steep hill. A turbaned Bedouin with two daughters wearing nose rings emerged from a small hut to watch our car spin its way up the sandy path. "You can see the monastery across the tracks." In front of us was a rather large and dilapidated villa whose surrounding walls were lined with spikes and barbed wire. As we pulled up, another Bedouin opened a large gate and my father continued uphill until we reached a level pebbled roadway leading through a meticulously well-kept arbor flanked by manicured fields and flower beds. We finally stopped before what looked like an old, run-down chapel. As soon as we got out, the smell was unmistakable: we were in the middle of the desert, and yet, from this cold promontory, we could see the familiar beaches of Mandara and Montaza extending for dark-blue miles toward the deep, with short white lines streaking the immediate shoreline.

"*Vré pezevenk!*" shouted a tall, bearded man as soon as he saw Signor Ugo getting out of the car—"You pederast!" He had been supervising a gardener working a plot of flowers. He began to walk toward us with a pair of hedge shears and a broad smile, rubbing the dirt from his fingers with a rag. "*Pezevenk kai essi!*" Signor Ugo retorted in half-Turkish, half-Greek—"Pederast yourself!" They shook hands heartily, as the tall, bearded Greek brought the shears close to Signor Ugo's groin and pretended to make small cutting motions. Then, turning to my father and me, "What, more *conversos*?" he said jokingly, greeting us with his broad smile well before

Signor Ugo introduced us. "*Conversos* of my stamp, if you understand," he added. "I understand, I understand," said Father Papanastasiou. "Communion on Sundays, but Fridays the *Shema*. In other words, an *alborayco*, a halfbreed. A *pezevenk*," said the Greek priest. "Precisely!" snickered Signor Ugo. "With you Jews nothing is ever clear," the Greek continued. "Come, have some lemonade." Then, turning to my father, he explained that their friendship went a long way back, "since before the war." I didn't ask which one. He explained that *alborayco* came from al-Burak, Mohammed's steed, which was neither horse, nor mule, male nor female. "Poor Jews, you're citizens nowhere and traitors everywhere, even to yourselves. And don't make that face, Ugo, your own prophets said it, not me."

The first thing Father Papanastasiou said once we moved into his study was, "I am not like the others." My father nodded as though to confirm that this had been obvious from the very start. "And do you know why?" A long pause followed, almost as if he expected an answer from us. "I will tell you why. They are priests first, and men last. But do you know what I am?" Again a long pause. Should one say yes or no? I looked at the room, cluttered with what must have been hundreds of icons and old books. A rancid odor of incense filled the air. It was even on my hands and in the glass of lemonade he had offered me. "I will tell you what I am: I am a man first," he said, raising his thumb, which he jiggled a bit, "then I'm a soldier," raising his index finger as well, "and then a priest," raising his middle finger. "Ask anyone. Him too. These hands," he said, producing a pair of colossal fists that would have intimidated Peter the Great, Rasputin, and Ivan the Terrible, and could easily have crushed the keyboard of the old Royal typewriter sitting on his desk, "these hands have touched everything and they have done everything—do you know what I mean?" he said, turning to me and staring with such intensity that I whispered, "Yes, I do." "No, you don't," he snapped, "and, God willing, you never shall or you'll have me to answer to. And frankly I don't know which is worse, God or me."

"Vassily, stop your confounded nonsense, and let's get on with it," interrupted Signor Ugo.

"But I was just chatting," he protested.

"You've got the boy trembling all over as if he saw Satan himself—you call that chatting?"

"Chatting. What else?"

"Vassily, sometimes you speak and act no better than a Greek shepherd from Anatolia. And do you know what?" said Signor Ugo, turning to my father and pointing to the typewriter. "This fellow here is a world authority on Fayum."

My father immediately concluded that the burly priest must be a specialist in disease control, especially since Fayum was known for its contaminated waters. He started to say he had heard that many peasants were dying of something uncannily reminiscent of cholera. Did Father Papanastasiou think cholera might soon strike in Egypt then?

"And if it did, would I care?" growled the latter.

"Not the Fayum of today," Signor Ugo broke in. "He's a specialist in the early Christian portraiture from Fayum. He looks at these portraits and in a second can tell you whether they're authentic or not. He teaches the poor orphans here how to paint nothing else."

"Speaking of orphans," said my father, "I have brought something in my car for the boys. Can someone give me a hand unloading it?"

"A hand? And what do you call these?" said the priest raising his voice, displaying two outstretched palms, each as big as the Peloponnese.

We stepped out of the study and my father held open the

trunk while Father Papanastasiou unloaded three cardboard boxes. Two young Greeks wearing blue jeans came to get more boxes from the backseat. "What are they?" asked Father Papanastasiou. "Knitted summer shirts for the boys. Mercerized cotton—here, feel," said Signor Ugo, handing over one of the shirts to the priest. The priest unfolded and examined it. "But this costs a fortune," he said, almost protesting as he crinkled part of the shirt in his fist, the better to appreciate its velvety sheen. "Vassily, say thank you," said Signor Ugo. "Thank you." My father said it was nothing. "When the boys come back this afternoon, we will give them the new shirts. They need Easter presents, the poor bastards." As they heaped the cardboard boxes in the entrance, I thought it strange that my father had never given me a shirt like that. "I can get you hundreds of them," he said later in the car, after we had dropped off Signor Ugo at his pension.

"We need to discuss a few things," my father said to me while staring at the priest. "Do you want to wait in the car?"

I said I would stay in the garden. The three men walked back into the study.

I stood by myself, realizing I was the only one present on the church grounds. The two young men who had helped unload the boxes could be seen making their hasty way downhill, sliding and skipping in the sand, their shoes almost sinking with each step, finally disappearing behind a stretch of palm trees. Then, not a sound, not even the wind, nor the ravens. It was as quiet as it gets in the desert—the silence of the ancient Greek necropolis in Alexandria, or the clear, beach-day silence of early Sunday mornings in the city.

I looked around and couldn't understand why anyone would bother maintaining such a beautiful garden when the buildings were so utterly run-down. The monastery had probably been a private estate donated to the poor by a wealthy Greek family.

The Lotus-Eaters

I walked to the edge of the grounds, where a broken-down pergola overlooking the sea created what might once have been a snug little corner for reading or contemplating the water that stretched out to the farthest reaches of Sidi Bishr. To the left, a shanty, mud-hut Arab hamlet hid quietly behind rows of drying laundry. Large birds, hawks probably, descended to feed on a rock nearby.

I looked through one of the windows into the chapel and thought I saw a classroom. There were maps against the wall, children's drawings, icons, and a picture of Pericles. I walked through a narrow corridor leading into what must have been a very old stable that had long ago been converted into a workshop. Beyond the workshop was another plot of land, this one totally fenced in by giant sunflowers which turned their ghoulish eyes on me and watched my every step as I moved about cautiously. All of a sudden I was seized by the uncomfortable feeling that someone was gazing at me from behind. I instantly turned around.

And then I saw them. Leaning against the stable wall, like two giant overturned umbrellas, with their ribbing exposed and their supple bamboo keels glistening yellow, twice my height and taller still than I could ever have imagined them —because no matter how close I got to them in the past I had always watched them from afar—were the *Paralus* and the *Salaminia*, each with its giant tail coiled many times over on the workshop floor like a huge intestine crammed into a tiny abdomen. The kites looked totally stripped, like unfinished rowboats, vulnerable to my searching gaze. The builders had discarded last year's cellophane cover sheets and were about to glue new ones. I moved closer to feel the ribs, but with caution, remembering that bamboo cuts worse than glass. Only then did I discover the ramming spikes that could tear other kites to pieces. Unlike ours, these were not discarded razor blades attached to the body of the kite; instead they were sharpened bamboo extensions of the kite's very skeleton—the difference, as Momo explained to me later, between an old lady wearing dentures and the bite of a strong male wolf.

Momo would never forgive me. All I would have had to do was take out my penknife and cut the bamboo. We would rule the skies that summer. For a moment, I felt like a Phoenician spy sneaking into an empty Greek shipyard, determined to wreak as much damage to the enemy as possible, only to lose his nerve upon beholding the *Paralus* and the *Salaminia*, the pride of the Athenian fleet, sitting majestically on opposite docks awaiting minor repairs.

I walked out of the building and heard my father calling me.

Throughout the silent ride back home, one thought kept galling me: Madame Marie would become so unbearably vain when she found out that we were planning to convert to her religion. Signor Ugo said he had to go to church almost every Sunday. Madame Marie would love nothing more.

But that evening, after depositing Signor Ugo, my father stopped the car in front of our building at Cleopatra, looked at me awhile before letting me out, and said, "Don't worry, I don't think we'll be doing anything with our Greek priest. I couldn't stand facing him every week. Still, I want to think about all this some more," he added, as though he planned to do so as soon as we had said goodbye. Then, almost as an afterthought, he said it might be easier to convert to Protestantism. "At any rate, there's no real rush," he added, as I shut the door and watched him drive away, knowing I wouldn't see him before breakfast.

■

As in previous years, Easter and Passover coincided with Ramadan. But this year the atmosphere was grim, and there were no arguments between Abdou and Madame Marie, and no one complained about my manners. My great-grandmother had had an accident after our small family seder at Sporting. She had woken in the middle of the night and reached for her ginger cookies in the drawer of her bedside table, only to find them missing. Aunt Elsa had removed them, knowing that her mother would not want to eat leavened biscuits during Passover. But the old woman had forgotten about matzoh, and, not finding her favorite snack in its usual place, got out of bed, and on her way to the kitchen tripped on an old stool. She immediately started to bleed from the head, and Uncle Nessim, Aunt Elsa, and my grandmother made several attempts to staunch the flow. One of them put ground coffee on the wound. Dr. Zakour, the new family doctor, was called, and he did what he could, but the old woman never regained consciousness. They had not even called an ambulance.

Later that morning, with everyone milling outside her bedroom, Uncle Nessim finally opened the glass door and closed it behind him, saying, "She's left us." Soon after, they covered her up in a shroud, and in a matter of hours she was gone. Madame Marie complained that this wasn't how it was done among Christians, that Christians doted on you awhile before taking you away. Then she remembered she owed the *aguzah*, the old one, three pounds. To ward off misfortune, she immediately went downstairs, purchased three loaves of sugared bread, and on her way from the bakery gave them to the first three beggars she found.

We spent a rainy afternoon in the smaller living room. No one cried, no one even said they remembered this or that about her. Abdou came in to ask for the afternoon off, and then someone suggested that the best thing for us was to go to the movies, which we did, all seven of us, including Madame Marie.

Three days afterward, Madame Marie was taken to the hospital to have her gallbladder removed. When she returned weeks later, she had lost a lot of weight, looked old, and complained of eczema on both hands. She watched me eat lunch, asked how I was faring at school, and said she was disappointed to hear that, instead of studying *normal* religion, I was now in Islam class, as Monsieur al-Malek had recommended. "Have you become Moslem?" she asked. I shook my head. "But what did you tell them when they asked why you wanted to study the Koran?" I said that I had told them my family was thinking of converting to Islam. When I finished my lunch, Madame Marie did not stand up to clear my dishes, as was her habit. Nor did she say anything about washing my hands. Nor did she urge me to begin doing my homework or avoid going into the kitchen to speak to the other servants. She promised to take me to St. Katherine's one day. Then she drank her coffee, thanked Abdou, and left.

■

A week later, after Madame Marie called to apologize, saying she had found less strenuous, part-time work in a Greek home for the elderly, my parents decided to hire a governess named Roxane, a Persian girl who had studied dance in Spain and who, through a series of misadventures, had landed in Alexandria living with a British journalist who wrote for one of the domestic English-language newspapers. She was young, sprightly, dark-haired, extraordinarily beautiful, and, unlike Madame Marie, who sat in the shade with other nannies while I went bathing in the sea, would hop in and swim faster than anyone. When she came out of the water, she would run to our umbrella and almost bury herself in her towel, with only part of her face and goose-pimpled legs showing. Then she combed her long hennaed hair and lit a cigarette. Her skin beamed in the sunlight, and in the evening at Mandara she would sit on the veranda with my parents, wearing a dark-blue summer frock with white polka dots, the odor of suntan lotion still on her skin as she waited for Joey to come pick her up in his Anglia. She took few things seriously, and everything she said or heard you say seemed to have an unintended edge which never failed to amuse her and which often made me think that I was far more clever than I had ever imagined—which, in my own heady way, was exactly what I needed in order to be frank with someone who seemed to understand not only who I was but who I always wanted to be.

Roxane broke all bounds, came late, took off, and yet offended no one, and with her unflagging mirth and good cheer managed to make me do things and eat things I would never have thought possible. When she was at home I no longer hung out in the kitchen, and when she told me that her brother was called Darius and her father Cambyses, I knew that life could rise above the ordinary and become legendary. In the morning she greeted me with a wily smile, which always made it seem we had said things we were agreed never to repeat to anyone. In the evening we would read Plutarch together. And at night she insisted on reading me a few verses by Hafiz, to ensure a good day on the morrow. She would read the verses in Persian first, translate the meaning, give an interpretation that was invariably farfetched but happy, and then kiss me good night.

The one who fell for her hardest was Signor Dall'Abaco, my Italian tutor, a former aspiring diplomat who had escaped his native Siena during Mussolini's regime and whom Signor Ugo had dug up for us from the Alexandrian private-lessons circuit, saying the Sienese gentleman spoke the best Italian there was. Signor Dall'Abaco had read every book as well as every magazine. He would borrow magazines from the main Italian bookstore in the city and return them in perfect condition after having read them up and down the tramway line on his way to his various private pupils. Like Monsieur al-Malek, whose displeasure he did not wish to incur and around whose hours he was compelled to work his schedule, he enjoyed tea and cocktails after tutorial, always managing to have himself invited into the living room, because he loved company and because his lonely bachelor's life gave him so little opportunity to talk about the two things he loved most: literature and opera. He arrived that April and remained my tutor for five years.

When Signor Dall'Abaco began teaching me Dante, he was particularly gratified when my father knocked at the dining room door to ask if he might sit at the end of the table and listen in. Uninvited, Roxane would do the same. Her presence when he spoke about Farinata, Count Ugolino, and Ser Brunetto, or when he told the story of Paolo and Francesca, must have sent his old Sienese blue blood coursing through his veins, for the Persian girl, who could speak Italian only by corrupting her Spanish, seemed to understand the exiled Guelf and the displaced Sienese gentleman as well as she understood Hafiz, Joey, me, and all the men in the world. She understood what it meant to have lost everything and eat salted bread when all your life you'd had the unsalted Tuscan kind. And she understood what it was to rely on others for income, small income.

> *Tu proverai sì come sa di sale*
> *lo pane altrui, e come è duro calle*
> *lo scendere e'l salir per l'altrui scale.*

> [*You will know how salty is the taste*
> *of another's bread, and how hard the path*
> *to descend and come up another man's stairs.*]

The Lotus-Eaters

Signor Dall'Abaco was speaking to her, to me, to himself, to Dante.

"If you learn a canto a day," he would say, "within three months, from now until August, you will know the entire *Commedia* by heart." But he may have been speaking to Roxane.

He went on to tell her that when the British had interned all Italian males living in Egypt, he had spent his prison term like Silvio Pellico, the nineteenth-century Italian patriot, memorizing a canto a day. "You, in prison, Signor Dall'Abaco! I cannot picture you behind bars." The Sienese was moved.

She had said this as we sat in the car on our way to Mandara one Friday morning in early June. Signor Dall'Abaco had come for the day and would later be driven back to the Sidi Bishr station, from where he would take the tram to the city.

As we drove, all of us crammed together with the windows open, Signor Dall'Abaco explained *Tosca*, and after going over some of the more obvious harmonies, began to sing Cavaradossi's last aria, and repeated it several times, asking me to sing it, then my friend Cordahi, who had come to stay the night, then—distracted man that he was—my mother, and finally Roxane. Everyone giggled, including Hassan the driver who, to prove he was no fool, sang a few bars himself, unintentionally Arabizing the aria as he sang. Signor Dall'Abaco liked this Middle Eastern touch, and after teaching us the famous choral air from *Nabucco*, asked Hassan how he would go about singing it. The driver obliged, and there was great mirth in the car, with Roxane mimicking the Egyptian's treatment of Verdi. Signor Dall'Abaco explained to us the history of the Mohammed Ali Theater in Alexandria and of the big opera house in Cairo, for which the Egyptian khedive had commissioned *Aïda*. "Verdi came to Egypt?" I exclaimed in total disbelief. "In Egypt and how," he replied, sounding as patriotic as Miss Sharif.

On our way to Mandara, we came upon my father's carter, Abou Ali, driving the factory's carriage on its lopsided wheels. He was headed for Mandara as well, lugging all of our belongings—summer gear, equipment, utensils, toys, even a new ice box, and the giant Grundig that had weathered all of Madame Marie's sorrows and which my father had replaced with a newer model but never had the heart to part with. Everything was sloppily piled together and swathed in old carter's cord; the carriage with its cannibalized British tank wheels and its tottering horse, who could hardly canter, looked more like a Gypsy van escaping famine and invaders than a vacation load on its way to a summer home. Hassan waved at the old *arbaghi*, and Abou Ali waved back with his whip.

Joey was driving his car behind ours, carrying as passengers my grandmother, Aunt Flora, and Uncle Nessim. Aunt Elsa, who was mourning for her mother, had consented to come at the last minute so as not to be left alone at home. But she sulked throughout the trip, thinking, as she never ceased to remind us, that our speeding to Mandara during a period of mourning made us look like avid peasants who had never seen the beach before.

To prove her right, as soon as we arrived, my friend Cordahi and I, along with Roxane and my mother, immediately changed into our bathing suits and were already hastening to go swimming, while Signor Dall'Abaco made himself comfortable on the veranda overlooking the sea, explaining that he had not brought his bathing suit. Perhaps he deliberately tried to look comfortable to discourage us from insisting he go to the beach with us. Or perhaps he felt he had sufficiently overcome his natural shyness by accepting my mother's lemonade on the veranda and did not wish to pass another test of endurance by complying with complicated beach rituals that were totally foreign to him.

I, however, was only too pleased to practice these rituals—

picking up beach paddles exactly where I had left them in September; balancing the weight of the umbrella on my shoulders; finding the same folded beach blanket, sun-tan lotion, or old tennis balls that never seemed to die; remembering to take a second bathing suit in case I wished to change; and packing the old bottle of benzine—and the cotton that went with it— to wipe off the tar which inevitably washed up on the beach and blackened our feet.

The house itself was in full bustle as the servants busily unloaded the cars. Some had arrived the previous evening and had already set up much of the place.

Signor Dall'Abaco's quiet corner on the veranda seemed the ideal place for a man who was born to stay out of everyone's way.

I sympathized with his reluctance to go swimming, not just because I had experienced it myself at VC, but because I had seen many of our guests at Mandara, particularly my father's employees, pretend an irrational fear of the beach when all they were afraid of was us and of getting in our way. Some chose to stay behind while everyone else went swimming simply because they didn't dare ask us for towels. "Did you have a good swim?" they would ask when we came back from the beach.

My mother told Signor Dall'Abaco he could borrow a bathing suit from a closet filled with suits of all sizes. But he continued to dawdle about the house, whose stuffy and musty air betrayed the closed-up winter months. He even showed an interest in the Spanish furniture and asked whether we ever used the house in the winter. "Sometimes at Christmas," said my mother.

"Hurry," Roxane shouted when she caught sight of Joey's car on the driveway. "We're going to the beach."

"You go, I'll join you later," he shouted back.

"*Allora*, Signor Dall'Abaco, are you going to change, yes or no?" asked Roxane.

"All right, but I'm not sure I'll swim."

She affected impatience, as though he had been put under her charge as well. Signor Dall'Abaco looked at Joey, who was helping the servants take down the new *hassira* from the roof rack. He envied the young reporter, probably hated him, and would have given everything to be in his place.

"Maybe the water's not warm yet—" he had begun to say.

"You must put on a bathing suit," she insisted, ushering him into one of the bedrooms. The tentative man entered meekly. He waited for me and Cordahi to leave the room and then closed the door behind him, slowly, almost reluctantly, and softly turned the key. We waited almost five minutes. When Roxane knocked at the door urging him to hurry, his nervous voice was heard apologizing, saying that of all the bathing suits he had tried inside, none seemed to fit someone as skinny as he.

When he finally came out he was wearing a suit whose original owner no one remembered but who must have been much thicker and taller than the Italian tutor, for he had rolled the top of the bathing suit several times down his tummy.

Signor Dall'Abaco turned out to be all bones, and his spindly legs didn't have a speck of hair on them. But what made Roxane burst out laughing was his two big toes, which, without shoes, stood permanently erect. Even my mother noticed them, and, turning to Roxane in front of Signor Dall'Abaco, asked why did he keep his big toes up like that? "I don't know," he replied with typical self-derision. "I don't do it on purpose." "But don't you run the risk of falling?" He looked down as though his toes were distant cousins he had always wanted to disclaim. "They don't bother me," he said.

We walked to the beach by way of the usual chalky shortcut,

and as soon as we crossed the sand we could not wait to jump into the water. Signor Dall'Abaco stood along the shoreline, with his feet in the water and a benign look on his face as he watched us scamper about and dive into the surf. "I told you he wouldn't swim," said my mother to Roxane.

And indeed, though he said he loved Mandara, and though he would come two or three times a week in the summer to teach me Dante and De Amicis' *Cuore*, spending the rest of the day with us, courting Roxane one year, then Aunt Flora, then my mother, I never saw him swim. In the evening, just after drinks on the veranda with my father and guests from neighboring villas, he would excuse himself and say he had to go back to the city. As usual, someone would drop him off at the Sidi Bishr tramway station, where he caught the night tram to Ramleh, riding second class with his borrowed magazine neatly folded in the left pocket of his imported Italian sport jacket.

After dinner that first evening at Mandara, everyone sat around the dining table with two kerosene lamps lighting the area as we played cards. Aunt Elsa opened a jar of *marrons glacés*—a rare treat in Alexandria. My grandmother, fearing not enough would be left for the guests, divided one with me; then, seeing there were plenty to go around, divided another, and after that another still. Elsa scolded her, saying that she should either take a whole *marron* or none at all, but that this habit of cutting things into halves only to eat the same amount in the end was thoroughly distasteful. Uncle Nessim told her to calm herself. Signor Dall'Abaco did not like sweet things. Joey did. He asked Signor Dall'Abaco for his *marron* and then reached for the jar to stab the last one with his fork. "By all means, *ne vous gênez pas*, don't be bashful," said Aunt Elsa, puckering her lips. Her prized possession was gone in less than five minutes. Joey, who had hung his tweed jacket on the back of his chair, turned around and looked into his pockets, producing two sealed packages of cigarettes: Greys and Craven A's. "This indeed is a treat," said my father, who never dared buy anything on the black market. "May I too?" asked Signor Dall'Abaco. "But of course, Signor Dall'Abaco." "Mario," corrected Signor Dall'Abaco. "Mario," repeated the amused Englishman as he downed more scotch. Almost everyone was smoking. Joey offered a cigarette to Abdou, who accepted reluctantly, saying he would smoke it later.

The inevitable subject of school was touched on momentarily. Joey had a colleague, a poet of sorts, whose Greek wife taught at an American school—the best school in the city—and with almost no debate it was agreed that I should go there the following year, VC being no longer viable, especially after what happened the last week of Ramadan.

"As long as there aren't any repercussions, what your wife did that day was very brave," said Aunt Flora.

"As long as there aren't any repercussions," repeated my father.

"We did worse in our day," said Aunt Flora, whose years at the conservatory were filled with infractions of all sorts.

"And I was a downright terror," said Joey, the old pupil from Eton, looking up as he chased an eddy of smoke with his breath. "And, God knows, I've done much worse than change into my gym clothes during another class."

"But this was Islam class," interrupted my father.

What had happened during Islam class on that particularly warm day in May was that I had secretly taken off my gray trousers and put on white shorts. Then I removed my shirt, without removing my tie. My undershirt. My socks. My watch. Other students had followed suit and were changing as well, except that, out of respect for their religion, they had refrained from putting on their tennis shoes. It was young

Tarek who, more out of piety than malice, had alerted Miss Sharif to what had happened. Lifting her eyes from her copy of the Koran, she saw to her amazement a class almost entirely dressed in white. "He's made them change into their gym clothes," said Tarek. "Oh, my sister!" she exclaimed, racing toward me and slapping me hard on the head with the book. "Oh, my sister!" she shrieked.

I was summarily hauled off to Miss Badawi's office.

That evening, when I returned from a soccer game, Roxane noticed bluish stains on the backs of my thighs. Otherwise I would never have told. She tried to brush them off with her palm, then, horrified, ran out and told my mother, who immediately came into my room, asking for an explanation. Roxane's perturbed face and my tears as I narrated the events of the morning must have moved her to quell her horror, and once I was in the bathtub, she got down on her knees next to Roxane and both women joined in bathing me, so watchful and solicitous with the washcloth that I felt like a soldier having his wounds dressed by two young nuns.

My father was distressed, and all through dinner was trying to decide whether to be furious with the school or with me.

"This time they've gone too far," said my mother.

"No, this time *he's* gone too far. He's insulted their religion, and when he insults their religion *we* insult their religion, and when we insult their religion, we get arrested, we go to jail, we lose everything and get expelled from Egypt. I don't need to have my name popping up all the time at the Muhafza. Do you understand now?"

"I don't want to understand."

The next morning, as my father was bathing after his exercises, my mother told Monsieur Politi to put on his jacket in a hurry, instructed Abdou to tell the bus driver that I would not be going to school that day, and rushed all of us downstairs, where she ordered Hassan, my father's driver, to take us to VC. We got there twenty minutes before any of the school buses; the boarders were probably still finishing breakfast. Mother told me to get out of the car. The dumbfounded Politi, his athlete's chest bulging out of his jacket and looking very much like a gangster's bodyguard who had forgotten to put on a tie, followed close by.

She led us directly to Miss Badawi's office, which she remembered from her previous visit. She asked Politi to wait outside. We knocked, were told to wait, and when Miss Badawi finally opened the door, were told by way of greeting that we were not entirely unexpected. Her measured smile conveyed no apology but rather a sense of collected, bureaucratic compassion for the parents of unruly children who are punished for their own good.

My mother, who spoke no English, asked me to tell Miss Badawi that she wished to know what had happened. "You mean yesterday?" she asked. I nodded. Miss Badawi gave a long speech detailing school rules, pacing her explanation to give me time to translate for my mother, all the while staring at me intensely as I tried to convey her version of my guilt to my mother. My mother nodded at each sentence, though I knew I was speaking far too incoherently for her to understand much. As often happened between us, we were going through the motions of communication for the benefit of third parties. At one point, my mother interrupted me, saying, "I know, I understand, tell her I understand," and then, before I knew what she was doing, she had turned me around and was pointing to the eggplant-colored weals on the back of my legs, touching each one, saying, "Look at this, and this one, and this one here," with the disparaging manner she would use when unfolding a dress and asking her tailor to take a good look at this blemish, that imperfection, and that stain left behind by his sloppy assistant. Miss Badawi arched her eyebrows like a shopkeeper refusing to take back defective merchandise, alleging that all sales are final.

I had been staring at it for almost five minutes without realizing. It was Miss Badawi's cane, leaning against a corner behind her chair. So this was the weapon, these the ridges that hurt the most, they looked so harmless. "Yes, but tell your mother we cannot guarantee we will never use the cane on you again. Tell her." I told my mother they could not guarantee they would never use the cane on me again. I watched Mother nod. Would she back down now? I continued to translate the headmistress's reiteration of school policies, and then my mother's subsequent question, until I feared that she would yield.

Suddenly there was a terrible yell. Mother had shrieked at the top of her lungs the way she shrieked at shopowners, servants, and itinerant vendors. The school janitor and gardener had gathered outside on the patio. I watched their faces looking in through the windows. My mother pointed at the cane and said, "Tell her—doesn't she know this hurts?" I said: "She asked me to ask don't you know this hurts." "Of course it hurts," replied Miss Badawi, slightly put off by my mother's screams yet wearing the same smile she had when she first opened the door. "We can talk all you want," her expression said, "but the school won't apologize."

It was the smile—the eerie, insolent, pernicious grin with which she once called me "dog of the Arabs" and which had flitted across her face when she asked me whether I wanted the cane wearing my school uniform or my gym clothes—it was this smile that persuaded my mother there was absolutely no hope, that her visit was a lost cause.

Her decision was so sudden that Miss Badawi was still smiling after it happened. "You don't smile like this with me, not with me," shouted my mother so loudly that all of VC must have heard her voice that day. More startled than upset, the headmistress brought her palm to her cheek, either in disbelief or to cover the red handprint that was now beginning to blossom there. "But what is this, what is this?" she said in Arabic. My mother picked up the bag she had left on Miss Badawi's desk and, turning to me, said, "Let's go." One of Miss Badawi's hairpins lay on the floor in front of her door. I pushed it gently with my foot. "I'm reporting you to the Muhafza," said my mother.

Miss Sharif was standing outside with Miss Gilbertson when we came out of Miss Badawi's office. As soon as my mother saw Miss Gilbertson, she looked at her directly and said, "*Sale putain*," and spit on the ground.

I told her I did not wish to go to my desk or empty my locker. We headed straight to our car, which was waiting for us on the other side of the quadrangle. I never returned to VC again.

We were home in less than twenty minutes, still very shaken by the events of the morning. My father was beside himself when he heard the news. He called my mother names, cursed Hassan and Monsieur Politi, and warned them never to take orders from my mother again. "Anyway, what difference does it make, we're finished here," he added.

A few weeks later my father reduced Monsieur al-Malek's hours. "Children need to rest during the summer," he explained. However, by equalizing Monsieur al-Malek's and Signor Dall'Abaco's hours, he conceded for the first time that Arabic might not be all-important, that we might not stay in Egypt forever.

We never heard from VC about the incident. My report card was disastrous and my grade for Egyptian National Studies, a course taught entirely in Arabic, was—predictably enough —*zero*. My father, unable to understand how I could have done so poorly, decided to punish me. No movies for the week. Then he forgot and broke his resolution when it rained one evening and there wasn't anything else to do but head to the movies.

■

As soon as you awoke at Mandara, the first thing you did was run to the window and see what sort of water you would have that day. Even in bed sometimes you heard the waves from a distance and from their sound already knew the weather. Sometimes the shouting of children from the beaches told you they were catching waves and that therefore the sea was rough that day. But then there were times when you did not hear a sound, not of boys, not of waves, not of vendors, nothing, everything was at a standstill, as though something in the air smothered every sound. And then you knew the water was *as smooth as an oil slick*—Aunt Flora's words—not even a ripple.

The house smelled of ground coffee. Roxane was already in the kitchen brewing a small pot, smoking a cigarette. She was wearing her bathing suit. Joey, she said, was still sleeping, everyone was sleeping, none of the servants had arrived. Softly, we opened the door to the veranda, knowing that the view awaiting us, once we lifted the loosely woven curtain, would be nothing short of miraculous. No one was in sight, only a few parked cars with their hoods sparkling in the early morning light, and beyond them—past the sand dunes, and the aged palm trees, and all the villas basking in Sunday silence—the pale-blue sea, glaring in the morning light.

"What a day!" said Roxane. She was walking slowly, careful not to spill any of the coffee in her cup, heading for my grandfather's small, heavy steel table, which, because of the rust, was painted a different enamel color every summer. When the paint chipped at the corners, you could count the layers like tree rings and see how many years it had been in our family —it too, like so many things here, was far older than I was.

We were about to sit down by the row of balusters overlooking the sea when we suddenly noticed Signor Dall'Abaco on a wicker chair in the corner, with his spindly legs resting on top of the balustrade, tilting back somewhat. "When did you wake up?" asked Roxane. "Hours ago," he answered, "I came to watch the dawn."

I had never seen dawn.

"Did you sleep well?" he asked.

"Mmmmmm. Fabulously," she replied. "Fabulously." She yawned, stretching her arms.

"I haven't seen a morning like this in so long I can't remember the last time."

Roxane looked out to the sea.

"Is anyone else awake?" she asked.

"No," answered Signor Dall'Abaco.

She was drinking her coffee very slowly, with her feet resting on the balustrade. "Did you want me to make you a cup of coffee?"

He said he would wait for the others.

We heard a door open. I was dismayed. Others would undoubtedly ruin the spell of the moment.

But the sound had come from the garden. Someone must have opened the gate and was heard crossing the gravel path leading to the veranda. And then I realized who it was. I had totally forgotten the small miracle of mornings here in Mandara: the fig vendor. He was always the first to come; then the iceman; then the vegetable vendor; finally, fruits at about ten.

Roxane picked out two dozen figs and asked him to weigh them. She gave one to each of us. "One," she said, with an implicit "no more until breakfast."

But breakfast was an hour or two away. I suggested we go

and buy *ful*. At this time of the morning the *ful* was bound to be excellent. "Do you know where to buy it?" asked Roxane, who had never been at Mandara before. I nodded. The *ful* vendor would stop his van on the corner of Rue Mordo by the side of the sand dunes, and people would come with their large pots. Signor Dall'Abaco said he had never tried Mandara's *ful*. Then he confessed he had never had *ful* before. "But you've been living here for thirty years, Mario," she said. "*E pazienza*," he replied, meaning, "And what can I do about that now!" We would have to hurry, I said, because the vendor did not wait long at the same corner. The worst thing was following him around his stops and missing him each time.

But I was hasty for another reason. I wanted no one to join us or prevent us from going on our expedition that morning. Signor Dall'Abaco said he had to change first, but I assured him shorts were perfectly respectable, there was no one around at this hour. Roxane put on a shirt whose tails she tied around her waist. She was carrying a cigarette in one hand, and in the other a large empty pot.

I led them to the back garden and into the driveway, where the bees were so loud that the entire arbor sounded like a distant cataract or a big steam engine churning away. Signor Dall'Abaco said he was afraid of bees. I told him they never stung. All one had to do was walk steadily and avoid sudden movements. Both of them believed me.

Signor Dall'Abaco held open the old door to our garden. We seldom used it, though it was said that this had been the only gate to the villa several decades ago. It, too, like so many other gates in Alexandria that no one used any longer, bore an eroded family crest, a doorbell that failed to chime when you swung the door open, and an old Colonial knocker.

Signor Dall'Abaco said these old knockers would be very valuable one day. "One day, when nineteenth-century antiques will be impossible to find in Europe, people will come here from all over the world to buy this knocker," said Signor Dall'Abaco.

"But it's worthless," said Roxane.

"Mark my words. Come back in twenty years, and it'll be worth its weight in gold."

"Where is your *ful* vendor?" Roxane cut in.

"Where is the *ful* vendor indeed," echoed Signor Dall'Abaco, who was probably the best disposed person in the world and never minded being interrupted.

We passed by Momo Carmona's house. It was still boarded up for winter. Had they moved to Europe or were they just late this year? My father said their uncle had lost everything. Perhaps they had too. I remembered Momo would not go to the beach on the day they had nationalized his uncle, nor had he come to the kite fight that afternoon. Hisham had been reading aloud from a newspaper the names of individuals whose assets or businesses had been nationalized that day. Pleased that my father's name was not on the list, yet not willing to rejoice quite yet, I asked whether he had read all the names in the newspaper. "Wait, there are many more here," he said, smiling, as he turned a page filled with columns of nationalized assets: Madame Salama's lover's, Aunt Flora's, Uncle Nessim's, and nearly everyone's. My father decided it wouldn't be prudent to dismiss him now.

I pointed out Uncle Vili's old house at Mandara to Roxane and Signor Dall'Abaco. But it did not seem to interest them. Then came the Russian countess's villa. Whoever lived there now, I wondered. That didn't interest them either.

We crossed an unpaved road until we hit on a garden hedged by a *hassira*. Then came the dunes. The dunes led to one of the beaches of Mandara and, at the other end, to the Greek monastery. Beyond that was the desert.

The Lotus-Eaters

Our feet sank in the sand, but the sand wasn't hot yet, and our only source of discomfort was the shavings of dry bamboo working their way into our sandals. We expelled them by shaking our feet.

Ahead of us I made out the shape of the *ful* vendor's van. We waved and shouted for him to wait for us. He waved back. When we finally reached his van, Roxane handed him the pot. He filled it and wished us a holy Sunday. We stared at him with a puzzled look: Why would a Moslem ever want to wish us a holy Sunday? He must have read our surprise, for, after looking around furtively, he pulled up his sleeve, displaying the inside of his wrist on which a large cross was tattooed. "I'm a Copt." The current regime was not sympathetic to Copts.

Though Signor Dall'Abaco was an atheist, Roxane a Zoroastrian, and I a Jew, all three of us wished him a holy Sunday in return. Signor Dall'Abaco insisted on paying. It was his way of thanking us for hosting him for the weekend. I tried to tell him to please let Roxane pay, but he said absolutely not, that he would pay, especially since he had brought nothing, not even a bathing suit. Roxane argued. Then he pleaded. We let him pay.

To change the subject on the way back, Signor Dall'Abaco said the tattooed sign of the cross had reminded him of Ulysses' scar which Eurikleia, his maid, recognizes when her master returns to Ithaca after twenty years' absence.

Roxane did not know who Ulysses was but she was saddened by the years of exile logged by the old soldier. "Twenty years," she kept repeating. "Twenty years, that's something," she said, as though Ulysses were a contemporary whose unresolved fate was still a source of concern.

"Twenty years is nothing," replied the Sienese gentleman, who had not returned to Italy since the late thirties. "When I left Italy, you weren't even born, Roxane," he said, as though that was how he now measured time.

"And I think you're a bit in love with me, Signor Dall'Abaco."

"And I think so too," he said. Both of them burst out laughing, and the more they laughed, the more she spilled the *ful*, and the more we all laughed together. "How stupid of me," she said, "to have brought the pot but not the cover."

I looked up into the morning's crystal glare. The air smelled fresh, new, as though unbreathed by humans, the way it always smells at the beginning of a summer day that is bound to turn unbearably hot. Even the dunes felt clean, soaking up the glare, so that after looking up at the sky we had to look down, to be soothed by the color of sand around us, unable even to look at the villas ahead. I had only to lift up my eyes, and there would be the sea.

"The sun burst on the flawless brimming sea into a sky all brazen."

It was Signor Dall'Abaco quoting Homer in Greek and then translating into Italian. This, I suddenly realized, must be the sunlight of ancient Greece, of translucent Aegean mornings where glinting quartz extends for miles until it touches the sea, and the sea touches the early-summer sky, and the sky touches every tree and every hill and every house beyond the hills. Today, too, all I need is the presence of water nearby, a clear sky, and intense glare forcing me to look down, and suddenly, wherever I am in the world, my mind will inevitably drift to the most sunlit author of antiquity, only to remember how I encountered him for the first time at Mandara that morning when we trundled back, spilling *ful* along the sand dunes. Signor Dall'Abaco told us how Ulysses' companions, after eating of the forbidden lotus, had lost all desire to go back to Ithaca and refused to wander more. After twenty years, he said, Ulysses was the only one who made it back alive.

The Lotus-Eaters

"Again with your Ulysses!" exclaimed Roxane.

"Or so they say," continued Signor Dall'Abaco. "Dante teaches that, after returning to Ithaca, he went on to explore other lands. Many agree. But I think it is Cavafy, the Alexandrian, who is right. He says that Ulysses wavered, unable to decide between going back to his wife or living as an immortal with the goddess Calypso on her island. In the end, he opted for immortality and he never went back. As the goddess pleads," and Signor Dall'Abaco began to recite,

Why spurn my home when exile is your home?
The Ithaca you want you'll have in not having.
You'll walk her shores yet long to tread those very grounds,
kiss Penelope yet wish you held your wife instead,
touch her flesh yet yearn for mine.
Your home's in the rubblehouse of time now,
and you're made thus, to yearn for what you lose.

The story of a man who chose his mistress and immortality over wife, child, and home infuriated Roxane. Signor Dall'Abaco simply arched his eyebrows and shrugged his shoulders, as if to say who was he to argue with poets. I asked him to recite more verses by Homer. He did.

For the first time in my life I knew exactly what I wanted to do this summer, and every other summer after that. I asked Signor Dall'Abaco if he would be willing to teach me Greek. Delighted, he said, but only after Italian class—and still, it might take years. "But then, who knows," he said with a smile, as we opened the old gate to our garden.

Signor Dall'Abaco taught me Greek for five years, slowly, sedulously, the way an impoverished Sicilian schoolteacher in Siena had taught it to him years before. After we left Egypt, he continued my Greek lessons by correspondence, selecting passages that I would always translate a bit hastily and with a sense of guilt and obligation. Ten days later, sometimes a little more, I would receive his dishearteningly elaborate and messy comments around my sheet of paper, which now reeked of cigarette smoke from his favorite café, where he liked to scribble—*scribacchiare*. He would place numerals above most of my words in Greek, the way Aunt Flora put numerals on her students' score sheets, to indicate the preferred order of the words. When he could not decide which word was best, he would list every Greek synonym that crossed his mind. Reading his letters in my room in Massachusetts years later, I conjured the aging Signor Dall'Abaco writing his eight-page bulletins in small script as he sat and smoked at a small table at Athinéos, overlooking the old harbor, known as Portus Eunostus, the port of good return. There he would translate Greek texts into Italian for me to translate back into Greek, though he knew that I knew that my Greek was growing progressively worse and that these exercises in translation had become nothing but an elaborate pretext for staying in touch. He would describe the city, the sea, the slovenly Cairenes who came up each summer, Roxane, and her husband, Joey, who had grown so fat and bald one wouldn't know him, ending each of his letters with his immutable formula, "Now I must write," meaning his other letters, those sent to his lawyers in Italy for a long-standing suit against the Italian government for the return of assets seized by the Fascists before the war. He would have settled for a pension, he used to say. In reply, I described my studies, women, the stuffy hot spells, the cucumber-and-feta-cheese sandwiches a fellow Italian and I ate on Oxford Street as we awaited a beach season that never really came. *Lazem bahr*, I reminded him.

"You have crossed the Pillars of Hercules," he wrote back, "all is possible now!" I was the only human he knew who had gone to America. "But, *ahimé!*—never become a teacher, for then you'll eat others' bread and tread others' stairwells."

I stopped hearing from him. At first I thought it was just like Signor Dall'Abaco to decide it was time to stop pestering me with these fatuous exercises. But then he did not answer my second letter. Or my third. Or my Christmas greetings—of that year or the next. Then I too stopped writing. Perhaps I knew but didn't want to know. I could have telephoned but I never did. Or perhaps I half-expected I would eventually receive a profusely apologetic letter signed by a man who for almost ten years had ended his letters with the same two words: *Lazem scribacchiare.*

Years later, I received a small parcel wrapped in sturdy, recognizable Third World paper. It had come by ship and the string that held the package together was riddled with knots and little lead seals. I did not know the handwriting. I opened it and found a small, cheaply bound book wrapped in wax paper. *Alexandrians*, edited by Mario Dall'Abaco: an anthology of Alexandrian writers from antiquity to modern times. Some of the poems I had never seen before; others were familiar; the one on Ulysses was Signor Dall'Abaco's, not Cavafy's. Not knowing whom to thank, I sent the printer a check.

A few months later I received another, slightly larger package wrapped in the same cobalt-blue paper, which I had failed to place the first time. Palming my way through the crumpled newspaper in the box, I expected to find more volumes of *Alexandrians*. Instead I touched something cold, like a palm waiting to touch my own. It was an old bronze knocker. "When we heard they were rebuilding Mandara, we immediately rushed to the villa and it was Mario himself who took it down. He used it as a paperweight. He would have wanted you to have it. He went peacefully a year ago. Remember me, your loving Roxy." The knocker has never left me. It sits on my desk today.

6

The Last Seder

When my father put down the receiver, he looked at us in the dining room and said, "It's started." No one needed to be told what he meant. It was common knowledge that *these* telephone calls came at all hours of the night—threatening, obscene, abusive calls in which an unidentified voice claiming to represent a government office asked all sorts of questions about our whereabouts, our guests, our habits, reminded us that we were nothing, that we had no rights and would soon be driven out, like the French and the British before us.

Until then, we had been spared these calls. Now, in the fall of 1964, they started. The voice seemed to know all about us. Indeed, it knew all our relatives abroad, read all our mail, named many of my friends and teachers at the American School, which I had been attending since leaving VC four years earlier. It knew everything. It even knew about the incident of the stone that day. "And I bet you're enjoying quail tonight," it said. *"Bon appétit."* "A bad omen," said my grandmother.

Aunt Elsa said she hated Wednesdays. Bad things always came on Wednesdays.

My father said he too had had premonitions, but what had the voice meant about the incident of the stone?

At which point Aunt Flora decided to tell him. Earlier that day we had joined the crowd that lined the Corniche, waiting to get a look at President Nasser, standing for hours in the sun, cheering and waving each time anything resembling a motorcade came around the bend of Montaza Palace. Then we saw him, perched in his Cadillac, waving with a flat, open palm, looking exactly as he did in the pictures. People began to cheer, men and women jumping and clapping, waving small paper flags. A girl in a wheelchair, perched at the edge of the sidewalk almost touching the curb, had been holding a rolled-up sheet of paper tied with a green ribbon. Now the president had passed and she was still holding it, looking disheartened and crying. She had failed to drop her written message into his car. Abdou, who had come with us, had noticed her earlier and said she probably wanted the Raïs to pay for an operation or a new wheelchair. Her older brother, equally distraught—and probably blaming himself for failing to maneuver her close enough to the motorcade—was busy telling her it didn't matter, they would try the next time. "I don't want to live like this," she wailed, covering her face with shame as he wheeled her away toward a part of Mandara we did not know.

On our way home a stone hit Aunt Flora on the leg. "Foreigners out!" someone yelled in Arabic. We never saw precisely who had thrown it, but as soon as she shouted, a group of youths immediately began to disperse. The stone had hit her on the ankle, but it didn't break the skin, there wasn't any blood. "As long as I can walk—" she kept saying, rubbing her shin with her hand. Then, remembering the bottle of cologne in her bag, she applied some liberally over the bruise, occasionally massaging her leg as she limped along.

No sooner had we reached home that afternoon than we came upon another commotion, this time in our garden, where everyone was screaming, including al-Nunu who, on hearing the sudden noise, had come out of his hut armed with his machete. Al-Nunu was yelling the most, followed by Mohammed and my mother, everyone racing about in the garden, even my grandmother, who was now yelling at the top of her lungs. I asked Gomaa, al-Nunu's helper and catamite, what was the matter. Out of breath, Gomaa shouted, *"Kwalia!"*

Quail!

Every autumn, quail would descend on Egypt from as far away as Siberia and, as soon as they caught sight of land, would literally drop from the sky, exhausted. That afternoon a bird had fallen in our garden right next to where my grandmother was having tea with Arlette Joanides and her daughter, who were leaving Egypt and had come to say farewell. Instinctively my grandmother had taken the elaborate needlepoint canvas on which she had been working for over a year and thrown it over the exhausted quail. The bird, though it was faster than the old woman, was too tired to fly away. It kept hopping about our garden until it was joined by two more birds that must have fallen earlier, unbeknownst to my grandmother. This was far better than anything she could have dreamed of, and the old woman began to yell. Everyone came rushing to her rescue until they saw the birds, and then they joined the trapping party.

From adjoining gardens as far back as Rue Mordo we could hear similar screams as everyone at home or on the street dropped whatever they were doing to catch this exquisite manna that tumbled from the heavens each year.

And yet, despite the great joy they brought that day—to Abdou, although he would have to start dinner all over again; to Aunt Flora, who had almost forgotten her wound and was resolved to keep it from my father; and to my grandmother, for whom quail season coincided with the making of fruit preserves—still, the sight of this peerless Egyptian delicacy struggling for life as it tried to elude our frenetic grasp never failed to announce the arrival of autumn and the end of our summer in Mandara.

No one stayed on in Mandara after quail season. By early October, the streets were deserted, with only a few Egyptians, mostly Bedouins, remaining where they lived all year round. Packs of stray dogs—some young enough to have been adopted by summer residents who then left them behind at the end of the season—would come out from everywhere, scrounging for food, sometimes landing at our door, always barking, especially at night. By then, the beaches were completely empty, the Coca-Cola shacks were all closed, and, at night when we drove back from the movies, ours was the only light on our street, a faint, forty-watt flare beckoning from our kitchen, where Abdou would wait up for us, listening to Arab songs on the radio. Sometimes, though, he would have gone back to the city at night, and then there was no light awaiting our return, and Mandara would become a ghost town, and all one heard when my father turned off the car radio, and then the engine, was the sound of our movements in the car, the sound of our steps along the pebble path leading to our door, and, behind the house, down by the bend near al-Nunu's shack, the sound of waves.

Once in the house, my first impulse was always to turn on the lights in the entry and rush down the oppressive corridor and light up one room after the other—the veranda, the kitchen, the living room, even the radio in my bedroom, hoping to liven the entire house and give myself and my parents the illusion that there were still summer guests in the house who would presently come out of their rooms. One could even nurse the illusion of guests to come.

At midnight our anonymous caller asked whether we had been to the theater. My father told him the name of the film we saw.

We stayed at Mandara very late into the fall that year. We always stayed too long. It was my mother's way of refusing to admit summer was over. But there was another reason for delaying this year. After Mandara, we had decided not to return to Cleopatra but to move instead to Sporting, so that everyone in the family might be together. My mother was put in charge of selling all the furniture at Cleopatra.

I saw the apartment at Cleopatra for the last time a few weeks later, when my mother asked me to go up with her to set aside clothes for Abdou and Aziza. All of our furniture was now covered in sheets, and the window shutters were closed tight, lending our apartment, usually so sunny in October, a gloomy, sepulchral air, while the old sheets, which I could remember Abdou hastily throwing over sofas and armchairs at the very last minute before leaving for Mandara early that June, looked like tired, old, deflated phantoms. "All of it will be sold," said my mother with a pert, busy air that could easily be mistaken for anger but which was her way of showing enthusiasm. She loved novelty and change and was as excited now as she had been on moving here five years earlier.

I never met the man who bought all of our furniture, nor did I witness the transaction nor the actual lining up of our bedroom and dining room furniture on our sidewalk at Cleopatra. Aziza said Abdou was the only one who wept. I came back one day after school to find the place empty. "Maybe we shouldn't have moved," said my father. His voice sounded different now that the rugs and the furniture were gone.

I asked him if he was going to throw away all those books on the floor. No, he replied. We would take them to Sporting. Meanwhile, he was leafing through what looked like twenty to thirty thick green notebooks, tearing out occasional sheets that he intended to save. I asked him what he was doing. "These are notebooks I kept when I was a young man." Was he going to throw them away? "Not all, but there are things here I would rather disappeared." "Did you write anything against the government back then?" I asked. "No, nothing political. Other things," he said, unable to conceal a tenuous smile. "Some day you'll understand." I tried to tell him I was old enough to understand. But I knew what he'd say: "You think you are." He said he could still remember witnessing his parents' emptied home thirty years before on the day they had left Constantinople. As had his father seen his own father's home. And our ancestors before that as well. And so would I, too, one day, though he didn't wish it on me—"But everything repeats itself." I tried to protest, saying I hated this sort of fatalism, that I was free from Sephardi superstitions. "You think you are," he said.

I looked at the apartment, incredulous at how much larger it was without furniture.

I tried to remember the first time I had seen it, five years earlier. My grandmother and I had gotten lost in it, mistaking our way through doors and corridors, watching the workers sanding the floors and putting up a wall to create an additional room for someone called Madame Marie. I remembered the kitchen talk in the month of Ramadan, the smell of fresh paint and of newly restained furniture and of Mother's jasmine, and the window she threatened to throw herself from each time she thought she'd lose my father. I remembered Mimi and Madame Salama. They had moved to Israel. Monsieur Pharès lived in Florida; Abdel Hamid was paralyzed from the waist down; and Madame Nicole's husband had converted to Islam and finally repudiated her for behavior unbecoming a wife. Fawziah worked for an Egyptian family who treated her poorly. Monsieur al-Malek was now a second-tier schoolteacher in Marseilles waiting for a pension. And Abdou's son, Ahmed, so full of kindness, was shipped back from Yemen after a guerrilla patrol had captured and beheaded him.

Then, without warning, Aunt Flora, too, received a telephone call. In her case, the voice informed her that she had two weeks to leave Egypt. She left, as did other family friends, in the fall of that year, just a few days after we moved to Sporting. We knew our turn would come.

■

Aunt Elsa used to say that when bad things happen they come in threes. If you broke two plates, no one was really surprised when a third fell from your hands. If you cut yourself twice, you knew that a third cut was already hovering, waiting for the perfect alignment of sharp object and skin. If you got scolded twice, if you failed two tests, or lost two bets, you simply cowered for a few days and tried not to look too dismayed when the third blow came. When it did come, however, you would never say it was the last of the three. You had to pretend that a fourth might follow or that perhaps you had counted wrong or that this millennial rule had just been changed to confound you. That was called tact. It meant you were not presumptuous and would never dare trifle with the inscrutable machinations of fate.

Of course, we always sensed that our midnight caller knew exactly how we thought about these things. He would call twice and then not call again that night, knowing we would not go to bed until his third call came. Or he would call three times, let us sigh in relief and then, just as everyone was getting ready to retire, call again. "Is he there?" the voice would ask, meaning my father. "No, we don't want to speak with him. Just checking." "Who were your guests tonight?" "What did you buy today?" "Where did you go?" And so on.

Harassment calls began to punctuate all our evenings—by

their absence as much as by their presence—reminding us that what were agreeable family evenings could easily deteriorate into bitter feuds as soon as grandmother hung up the telephone. "But why did you have to answer. Didn't I tell you not to?" my father would complain. "And why couldn't you tell him where I was?" he would add. "Because I don't think it's his business," his mother would reply. "But why do you persist in being rude to them? Why provoke them?" he would shout back at her. "Because this is what I felt like doing. Next time you answer."

Part of the late-night caller's ploy lay in calling when he knew my father was not home. Then, sometimes, thinking it was my father or even a friend calling late in the evening, I would pick up the receiver, and the stranger's voice, seemingly so harmless, even obsequious, would begin saying things I knew I should know nothing about. At other times, it was a rough street vendor's voice barking questions whose purpose I couldn't fathom, much less know how to answer. He would always end with the same words: "Tell him we'll call again tomorrow."

A day would pass. Then another. Sometimes three. Then two phone calls in succession. No one would pick up. "Maybe it's your father," my grandmother would say. It wasn't. Then no calls for another week.

Perhaps, the law of *jamais deux sans trois* didn't hold after all. But then, just when you were on the verge of giving up on it, it showed signs of renewed regularity—just long enough, that is, to trick you again.

Now, it so happened that Aunt Elsa had had strange forebodings the week before the Egyptian government nationalized all of my father's assets. *Une étrange angoisse*, a strange anxiety, right here, she kept repeating, pointing to her chest. "Here, and here, sometimes even here," she would say, hesitantly, as though her inability to locate the peculiar sensation in her chest made it more credible. "Something always happens when I have these feelings." She had had them on the eve of President Kennedy's assassination. And back in 1914. And of course in 1939. Madame Ephrikian, warned by Aunt Elsa to leave Smyrna in 1922, still called her *une voyante*, a seer. "Seer my eye!" exclaimed my grandmother behind her back.

"She's swallowed a cheap barometer, and it rattles inside her old rib cage. Whatever is itching her there, you can be sure it's just her conscience."

My grandmother was alluding to a quarrel the sisters had had over who would get Uncle Vili's prized nineteenth-century barometer following his sudden escape from Egypt. Uncle Vili liked to hunt duck, so, naturally, the sisters quarreled over who would inherit his rifles as well. One day, the rifles, the barometer, and his golf clubs disappeared. "*Les domestiques*," alleged Aunt Elsa. "*Les domestiques* my eye!" replied my grandmother. "She swallowed them, just as she'll swallow everything we own one day." "We don't have to worry about that now," interjected my father, "the Egyptian government has already thought of it."

The news that my father had lost everything arrived at dawn one Saturday in early spring 1965. The bearer was Kassem, now the factory's night foreman. He rang our bell, and it was my father who opened the door. Seeing his boss look so crushed on guessing the reason for his untimely visit, the young foreman immediately burst into a fit of hysterical crying. "Did they take her, then?" asked my father, meaning the factory. "They took her." "When?" "Last night. They wouldn't let me call you, so I had to come." Both men stood quietly in the vestibule and then moved into the kitchen while my father tried to improvise something by way of tea. They sat at the kitchen table, urging one another not to lose heart, until both men broke down and began sobbing in each other's arms. "I found them crying like little children," was Aunt Elsa's refrain that day. "Like little children."

The crying had also awakened my grandmother, who, despite protestations that she never slept at night on account of the "troubles," was a very sound sleeper. She shuffled all the way into the kitchen to find that Abdou, who had just come in through the service entrance, had also joined in the tears. "This is no good," she snapped, "you'll wake Nessim. What's happened now?" "They took her." "Took whom?" "But the factory, signora, what else?" he said using the pidgin word for factory, *al-fabbrica.*

My grandmother never sobbed. She got angry, stamped, kicked, and grew flushed. Aunt Elsa was right when she claimed that her sister cried out of rage—like Bismarck, the Iron Chancellor—and not out of sorrow. Her eyelids would swell and grow red, and with the corner of her handkerchief she would blot away her tears with flustered and persistent poking motions, as though, in her fury, she was determined to inflict more pain on herself. This was the ninth time she had seen the men in her life lose everything; first her grandfather, then her father, her husband, five brothers, and now her son.

A moment of silence elapsed. "Here," she said, mixing sugar in a glass of water and handing it to my father. It was reputed to calm one's nerves. "I'm having tea, thank you," he said. But Abdou, who was still sobbing, said he could use it. Meanwhile, Aunt Elsa kept repeating, "See? I knew it, I knew it. Didn't I tell you? Didn't I?" "Do you want to shut up!" shouted her sister, suddenly shoving a large bowl containing last night's homemade yogurt along the kitchen countertop with such force that it exploded against the wall. "Who cares?" she shouted, anticipating her sister's reproach. "Who cares at a time like this, who?" She began to pick up the shards while Abdou, still sobbing, begged her not to bother, he would pick them up himself.

It was the noise of this quarrel that finally woke me that Saturday morning. I could tell something was amiss. As happened each time someone died, everyone's instinct was always to keep the bad news from me. Either the names of the deceased were scrupulously withheld from everyday conversation, or, when the names were mentioned, those present would heave a sigh signifying something nebulous and clearly beyond my scope, adding the adjectival *pauvre*, poor, to the name of the afflicted like a ceremonial epithet conferred on the occasion of one's death. *Pauvre* was used for the departed, the defeated, and the betrayed. "*Pauvre* Albert," my deceased grandfather; "*pauvre* Lotte," my deceased aunt; "*pauvre* Angleterre," who had lost all of her colonies; "*pauvres nous*," said everyone! "*Pauvre moi*," said my mother about my father. "*Pauvre fabrique*" was on everyone's lips that day. The last time they had used that expression was when the factory's main boiler exploded, severely damaging the building and almost ruining my father.

I found my father sitting in the living room with Kassem and Hassan, whispering instructions to them. When he saw me, he nodded somewhat absentmindedly, a sign that he did not want to be disturbed. I picked up the newspaper—a grown-up habit I was trying to acquire—and sat by myself in the dining room. I had heard at the American School that all young men in America read the newspaper first thing in the morning with their coffee. Coffee too was on my list. One sipped and thought of things to do that day and then remembered to go on reading one's newspaper. No yogurt this morning. Instead, the smell of eggs and bacon and of butter melting on toast wafted from the kitchen. I had seen American breakfasts in movies and at school and had instructed Abdou I wanted eggs with bacon every Saturday.

The early-spring sun beamed on the brown table in the dining room, spilling sweeps of light down the backs of the chairs and onto the faded red rug. My grandmother was like me; we liked bright rooms whose shutters were kept open all night and day, liked the clean, wholesome smell of sun-dried sheets or of sun-washed rooms and balconies on windy summer days; liked the insidious, stubborn eloquence of sunlight flooding under the door of a shuttered room on unbearable summer days; even the slight migraines that came from too much sun we liked. Through the window, as always on clear Saturday mornings, sat patches of unstirring turquoise in the distance, rousing the thirst for seawater which all schoolboys in Alexandria knew, and which seduced you into thinking of long hot hours on the summer beaches. Two more months, I thought.

When my grandmother walked into the dining room, she tried to hide that she had been crying. "Nothing," she replied to my unasked question. "Nothing at all. Here is your orange juice." She shuffled toward me on her ever-grieving bunions, kissing me on the back of the head, and then pinching my nape. "*Mon pauvre*," she said, passing her fingers through my hair. "Couldn't this have waited a while longer, couldn't it?" she kept muttering, nodding to herself. Then, sensing I was about to renew my question, she said, "Nothing, nothing," and drifted out of the dining room. I ate my eggs in silence. Then my mother walked in and sat across from me. She, too, looked upset. Nobody was eating. So they had quarreled. But I hadn't heard her shouting.

"Look," she said, "they took everything."

It was like hearing that someone had died, a sinking feeling in my diaphragm and a tickling at the back of my ears. I pushed my plate away. My mother, whom I had not seen get up, was stirring sugar into a glass of water, saying, "Drink it all up now." It meant I had had my nerves shaken. I was a man, then.

■

Even so, I did not fully understand what was so frightful about losing one's fortune. A few of those we knew who had lost theirs went about living normal, everyday lives, with the same number of houses, cars, and servants. Their sons and daughters went to the same restaurants, saw the same number of movies, and spent as much money as they always had. On them, however, loomed the stigma—even the shame—of the fallen, the ousted, and it came with a strange odor that infallibly gave them away: it was the smell of leather. "Did you smell the abattoir," was my father's word for it, whispered maliciously after visiting friends about to leave the country. Every family that had lost everything knew it was destined to leave Egypt sooner or later, and, in one room, usually locked and hidden from guests, sat thirty to forty leather suitcases in which mothers and aunts kept packing their family's belongings at a slow, meticulous pace, always hoping that things might right themselves in the end. Until the very end, they hoped—and each of their husbands always swore he knew someone in high places who could be bribed when the time came. My father began to boast of the same contacts.

And then it dawned on me. When people came to visit us, they too would sniff out that funny leather smell and whisper *abattoir* behind our backs as they nosed about our home, wondering where on earth we had tucked all of our suitcases. The *abattoir* phase was bound to start soon, and with it an accelerated dose of family squabbles. Which store sold which suitcases cheaper? The question would tear our family apart. What articles should we buy for Europe? Gloves, socks, blankets, shoes? No, raincoats. No, hats. More fights. What would we leave behind? Aunt Elsa wanted to take everything. It figures, said my grandmother, who wanted to leave it all behind. Should we tell anyone? No. Yes. Why? More screaming. And finally, the one question bound to send everyone flying into a rage: Where would we settle? "But we don't even know the language they speak over there." "Why, did you know Arabic before coming here?" "No." "So?" "But it's so cold there." "And here it was too hot. You've said so yourself."

Meanwhile, we were given a reprieve, and like a baffled prisoner whose sentence has been temporarily commuted, or a stranded traveler whose return trip is inexplicably delayed, we were allowed to move about freely and do as we pleased, our lives suspended, taken over by unreal pursuits. It was well known that the fallen spent more and worried less. Some even started to enjoy Egypt, especially now that they could splurge, knowing they couldn't take abroad what the government was determined to seize from them. Others took advantage of the respite and did nothing all day save roam about aimlessly and hang around cafés, affecting, they thought, the unruffled dignity of condemned aristocrats.

When finally I spoke with my father that morning, he said it had come as no surprise. He had gone to bed knowing what awaited him in the morning and had told no one, not even Mother. Then I mustered the courage and asked what would happen now. They still needed him at the factory, he said. But that would pass, and then the inevitable would arrive. What? They would ask us to leave. Everything would have to be left behind. Meanwhile, there were some savings tucked away here and there, though technically we owned nothing. They might let us sell the furniture. But the cars were no longer ours. My father would recall old debts. Bound to be ugly, that. I wanted to know who owed him money. He told me their names. I was surprised. Their son was always having new shoes made. "How long, do you think?" I finally asked, like a patient imploring his doctor to say things aren't so hopeless after all. He shrugged his shoulders. "A few weeks, maybe a month." Then, pausing, he added, "At any rate, for us it's finished."

It meant our everyday lives, an era, the first uncertain visit to Egypt in 1905 by a young man named Isaac, our friends, the beaches, everything I had known, Om Ramadan, Roxane, Abdou, guavas, the loud tap of backgammon chips slapped vindictively upon the bar, fried eggplants on late-summer mornings, the voice of Radio Israel on rainy weekday evenings, and the languor of Alexandrian Sundays when all you did was go from movie to movie, picking up more and more friends along the way until a gang was formed and, from wandering the streets, someone would always suggest hopping on the tram and riding upstairs in second class all the way past San Stefano to Victoria and back. Now *it* all seemed unreal and transitory, as if we had lived a lie and suddenly had been found out.

"What should I do in the meantime?" I asked, emphasizing distress in my voice, because I could not see pretending that life would go on as usual. "Do? Do whatever you want—" my father started to say, letting me already savor the thought of dropping out of school and spending every day that spring going to the museum in the morning and then wandering through the bustling streets of downtown Alexandria, stalking my every whim. But my grandmother interrupted: "Never, no," she said with growing agitation. "He has to go to school. I won't accept it." "We'll see," said my father, "we'll see." She was about to go on, when he said, "Don't raise your voice, now of all times, not now." As she walked out of the room, I heard the tail end of her sentence, "—telling his son to become a degenerate, of all things. Who's ever seen such a thing? Who? Who? Who?"

At that point a click was heard at the front door and Uncle

Nessim walked in. He had recently abandoned his habit of leaving the house at the crack of dawn and taking long walks along the Corniche, and seeing him now, everyone was dumbstruck. All morning we had been whispering because we were sure he was sleeping in his room. We had never even discussed whether to keep the bad news from him.

The truth is that, at the age of ninety-two, Uncle Nessim was dying of stomach cancer. He would spend hours in bed, crouched in a semifetal position which he said was the least painful—and thus, folded in two, hugging himself, he would sometimes fall asleep. Only once had I caught him in that position. They were tidying his room, and as I passed by his open door, I spied him lying in bed, wearing striped pajamas, holding his chest as if it were the dearest thing he owned. He looked sallow and small. The previous Friday evening, while reading the Sabbath prayers, he seemed absent and exhausted. He did not smile when my father said, as he always did before prayers, "*Falla breve*, Nessim, make it short." He ate nothing. His sisters had prepared a special pinkish jelly pudding for him, and it stood staring at him in a glass goblet while he kept reading. He cut the prayer short. But when it was time to eat, he dipped his spoon into the wobbly pudding, played with it, tasted it, and then, sensing we were all staring at him, said he couldn't. It was then I realized that beneath his dark smoking jacket and the glistening purple ascot peeped the faded, blue-striped outline of his pajamas. He wanted to go to bed. There was no one to take over the prayer. Neither my father nor I knew Hebrew, and both of us refused to have anything to do with prayers, even in French. "This is very sad," said Aunt Elsa. "There was a time when this room was full of people, full of candles too. The table didn't even have enough leaves to seat everyone. The house is too big now. And Nessim is not well."

I remembered the room on those crowded *taffi al-nur* evenings, generations piled together, the oldest and the youngest separated by a century—so many of us. Now no one was left. They had stowed away the good china and gaudy silverware; dinner was served in one course; someone was always listening to the radio during the meal; and, because Aunt Elsa was put in charge of family expenses, even the wattage of the dining room lamp had been dimmed, so that a weak, pale-orange glow was cast over our faces and our meals, the shade of our last year in Egypt. My mother compared the once-resplendent dining room chandelier to a dying man's night-light.

The old furniture looked older, drabber, and there were entire sections of the apartment that had probably never been touched since the Isotta-Fraschini days. The service stairway had become so dirty that I never ventured near it. Almost all the furniture was in disrepair, much of it patched together or put aside, waiting for a heaven-sent visitor who, with the patience, know-how, and devotion of a carpenter's son, might finally remove the gummed paper that held so many caned chairs together in our dining room and perform the long-awaited miracle. "Sand always wins in the end," Aunt Elsa said, quoting her brother Vili as she ran her finger through the dust that had accumulated on the brown furniture after a particularly fierce *hamsin* that year. No one cleaned much of anything any longer. The apartment smelled of cloves, not just because they used it in cakes all the time, but because the three remaining siblings used it on their aching teeth.

Nessim was scheduled for surgery two weeks before Passover. As a precautionary measure, he was persuaded to transfer all of his assets to Aunt Elsa. "You watch," said my grandmother, peeved they had considered her unfit to handle the responsibility because she had suffered a mild stroke a few summers before. "Mark my words," she said and proceeded to make gestures mimicking the passage of food from the mouth down the esophagus and into the stomach. "She'll swallow all of it." In fact, Nessim's money was never seen or heard of again.

Strangely, Uncle Nessim had suddenly felt better during the night and had decided to go out for his usual walk at dawn. Everyone was so surprised to see him up and about, that instead of chiding him for taking a walk in his condition they began to pester him with questions. "But nothing's the matter with me," he kept saying, "I feel perfectly fine." "But you could have fallen, or gotten sick. Something might have happened." "Then I would have died and that would have been the end of that." When you get old, he used to tell me, you don't care about death. You aren't even ashamed of dying.

He proceeded to light a cigarette and asked for a cup of coffee. Dazzled by his spectacular recovery, Aunt Elsa kept fretting. "I knew it was a *kapparah*." *Kapparah*, in Jewish lore, was the necessary catastrophe that precedes an unforeseen windfall. You do badly at school, but that same afternoon someone you love narrowly escapes being hit by a car; you loose a precious jewel, but then you run into a very old acquaintance you thought had entirely disappeared. *Kapparah* allowed you to experience bad luck, but with the understanding—and it had to be a vague, uncertain understanding, not a clear-cut *deal*—that for each blow you received, you averted a significantly worse one.

No sooner had my grandmother heard the word than she shot her sister a venomous stare. "Look at her, the pernicious viper that she is," she whispered to me, "look how she's dying to tell him about the factory. She's going to keep dropping hint after hint until he finds out." "Not at all," protested Elsa in whispers. "Can't one be happy without having one's motives questioned every time? Living with you is like being in jail sometimes."

As soon as coffee was brought in, Nessim took his cup and motioned to my father and me to follow him into the living room, then shut the frosted glass door behind him. "They took her, didn't they?" he asked. My father nodded. "How did you know?" "What am I, stupid?" he interjected. "All I had to do was take a look at all your dour faces." Then, smiling, "This *kapparah* is costing you quite a bit, isn't it?" he said. "But don't worry, I'm not really better. I just wanted to see the Corniche for the last time." Then, still smiling, he pointed to the door where the crouched outlines of both sisters could be seen glued to the glass. They moved away as soon as he neared the door.

A week later Nessim died. During the night following his operation, the sutures tore open and blood began to seep into his mattress, soaking the floor beneath. When Aunt Elsa, who was spending the night with him in his hospital room, awoke from a slumber, he was already gone.

"I wonder what the third blow will be," said my grandmother a few days afterwards. "We don't need many hints to guess that," was my father's reply.

On the morning when the news of Nessim's death arrived, I awoke to a strange, persistent, owl-like hooting coming from the other end of the apartment. It had probably been going on for hours. I remembered trying to dispel it in my dreams. Finally, I slipped out of bed to see what it was. There were two nurses in the foyer, and with them Aunt Elsa, sobbing. She was seated on the sofa, still wearing her hat and clasping her handbag. She must have slumped down on the sofa as soon as she entered the apartment. Before her was an empty glass of what had undoubtedly been sugar-water. I tried to comfort her by caressing her arm. She didn't seem to feel it, but when I stopped, she whimpered something inaudible that sounded like a plea. "Stay, stay," she repeated, but I did not know whether she meant me or her brother. Then the hooting started

again and she began saying things in Ladino, always repeating
the same five or six words in a ritual intonation which I could
not understand. Abdou was trying to make her drink some
more; she kept refusing, turning to him and repeating the same
words she had been saying to me. He answered her in Ladino,
saying the señora was right, she was right, of course he had
had plenty of life left in him, but fate willed otherwise, and
who could question Allah. I shot him a quizzical look, wondering what she had been saying, and on our way back to the
kitchen he explained, in Arabic, "She keeps saying he was only
ninety-two, only ninety-two," whereupon both of us burst out
laughing, repeating "only ninety-two" as if it were the funniest
mot de caractère in Molière. The joke spread to Zeinab, across
the service entrance, who passed it on to the servants upstairs,
and downstairs, down to the porter, to the grocer across the
street, and who knew where else.

My grandmother's reaction was no better. Upon seeing her
sister seated half-dazed on the sofa, she immediately threw a
tantrum. The two sisters hugged each other, and Aunt Elsa,
whose tears had subsided by then, once again began to sob.
"See what you've made me do," she kept repeating, "I didn't
want to cry again, I didn't want to cry."

The sight was so moving, that I too would have sobbed
along with them had I not bit my tongue and forced myself
to think of other things, of funny things, anything. But as
though guided by a perverse logic, my thoughts, however
farfetched and bizarre, seemed determined to lead me back to
poor Uncle Nessim, who, until two weeks ago, would sit in
the family room busily refreshing his knowledge of spoken
Hebrew because he wanted to die in Israel. There was nowhere
to turn to forget. I tried to read in my room but could not.
No one wanted to speak. Even the servants were unusually
quiet. I would go to the kitchen and sit with Abdou and try

to squeeze yet one more droplet of humor out of *only ninety-two*. But even that seemed stale now.

Uncle Nessim had lent me a nineteenth-century edition of Lord Chesterfield's letters. He thought I should read them; all young men should, he said. A few days later, Aunt Elsa knocked at my door and asked for the book. It would be put together with his other things, she said. I don't know how she found out I had it. But a few evenings later, when she was not home, I unlocked her bedroom door and rifled through her possessions, determined to rob her. Not only did I take back the Chesterfield, but I relieved her stamp collection of some of its rarest items. Many years later, while visiting her in Paris, I was helping her arrange her stamps in a new album when it finally occurred to her that she was missing her most valuable specimen. "These Arabs fleeced me well," she complained, while I threw a complicit look at my grandmother, who, at the time, had found out about my expedition into her sister's bedroom. This time, however, my grandmother returned an empty gaze. She had forgotten.

■

That evening, I slipped into Uncle Nessim's bedroom. I sat on his bed, looking out the window, catching the flicker of city lights, remembering how he spoke of London and Paris, how he said that all gentlemen, of whom he fancied himself one, would have a glass of scotch whiskey every evening. "It will kill me one day," he prophesied, "but I do love to sit here and watch the city and think about things for a while before dinnertime." And now, I too would do the same, think about *things*, as he put it, think about leaving, and about all the people I would never see again, and about this city, so inseparable from who I was at that very instant, and how it would slip into time and become stranger than dreamland. That too would be like dying. To be dead meant that others could come into your room and sit and think about you. It meant that others could come into your room and never know it had once been yours. Little by little they would remove all traces of you. Even your smell would go. Then they'd even forget you had died.

I opened the window to let in the city noise. It came—though distant and untouched, like the laughter of passersby who don't know someone's ill upstairs. The only way to shake off this lifeless gloom was to go out again, or find a secluded corner somewhere and read Cousin Arnaut's dirty books.

That night we all went to see the late-night showing of the new French film *Thérèse Desqueyroux*. It was the first time I had been to the theater at that hour, and I was immediately dazzled by this unfamiliar adult world, by its glamour and mystery, the whispered undertones during intermission, the spiffed-up young men two to three years older than I sitting with girls in the back rows, and the strange legend of perfume, mink, and cigarettes, that hovered about women like an elusive presage of love and laughter in crowded living rooms where they sat and talked with the men who loved them, as men and women talked in my parents' living room when there was company and I had gone to bed.

Later we went to an expensive restaurant in the city, and when I asked whether we could afford it, my father looked amused and said something like, "Don't worry, it isn't as bad as all that." We were with friends, and my grandmother and Aunt Elsa had come, and no one spoke of Nessim, and we ate with hearty appetites, and afterward, as was sometimes our habit, we drove along the Corniche, no one saying a word as we listened to the French broadcast until we stopped the car and got out to take a good whiff of the sea, listening to the bronchial wheezing of the waves as their advancing lines of spray clashed against the seawall.

That night the midnight caller called. Was everyone home? Yes, everyone was home. Where had we been? We're in mourning, please, leave us alone. Where did you go, he insisted. "May a curse fall on the orifice that spawned you and your mother's religion," said my father and hung up.

∎

The following day, returning from tennis, I was greeted by loud howling from the kitchen. My mother and my grandmother were quarreling at the top of their lungs, and Abdou, who normally took Sunday afternoons off, was busily trying to appease them both.

"Here are your damned prunes," shouted my mother. "Damn yourself, damned ingrate," retorted my grandmother, her voice cracking with emotion. "Who did you think I was trying to cook it for? For me?" The rest was sputtered in random fragments of Turkish, Ladino, and Greek.

Fearing for her sister, and despite her desire to remain impartial, Aunt Elsa tried to calm my grandmother and whispered something in Ladino, which sent my mother flying into a greater rage. "Always whispering, you two, with your cunning, beady, shifty, Jewish eyes, whispering your furtive little Ladino secrets like two ferrets from the ghetto of Constantinople, always siding with each other, the way she"—indicating my grandmother—"sided with you against her husband until she killed him like a dog, like a dog he died, wouldn't even let her visit him in his hospital room when he died." "What do you know, what? You good-for-nothing seamstress from Aleppo," shouted Elsa now, openly joining the fray. "Aren't you ashamed to speak like this while Nessim's body is still warm with life?" "Nessim this, Nessim that," tittered my mother. "He is well rid of you both. If you knew how he loathed you. Turned him into an alcoholic in his own bedroom, you did. Ha, don't make me say any more. You killed him, both of you, just as you killed your husbands. Whose turn is it now? Mine, do you think?"

It was then that I saw my grandmother, who clearly could not tolerate much more of this, do something I had never seen done in our family: she slapped herself on the face. "*This* for allowing my son to marry her. And this"—she slapped her other cheek, harder—"for begging, begging him to remain faithful to her." "Don't do that," shouted my mother, "don't do that." She grabbed both of her arms. A quick look at Abdou signified, "Get her a chair."

Things immediately began to subside. "Do you want to have a stroke, so he'll be able to blame me for the rest of my life? Enough like this!" Meanwhile, my grandmother had slumped on the chair next to the telephone in the corridor, holding her head in her hands. "I can't go on like this, can't go on like this. I don't want to live, let me die." "Die?" exclaimed my mother, "she'll outlive all of us. Sit down. Abdou, bring some water for the signora."

Finally Abdou and I separated the trio, and I discovered how the quarrel had started. Mother and daughter-in-law had disagreed on the recipe for *haroset*, the thick preserve made from fruits and wine that is eaten at Passover. My mother wanted raisins and dates, because *her* mother used raisins and dates, but my grandmother wanted oranges, raisins, and prunes, because this had been her family's recipe for as far back as she could remember. "*Maudite pesah!* Cursed Passover!" cried my grandmother. Sugared water was promptly distributed to all three in their respective rooms. "Your mother should be put away, this is not a life," said Elsa. When I went to see how my mother was doing, I made the mistake of telling her what Aunt Elsa had said, whereupon she got up and stomped into Elsa's room, ready to start another row. "But I didn't mean anything by it," she pleaded, beginning to sob. "Ach, there is no end to this. Poor Nessim, poor Nessim," she lamented, then changing her mind, "lucky Nessim, lucky Nessim."

At that moment the doorbell rang. I was convinced it was one of the neighbors coming to complain about the noise. Instead, standing at our door were two Egyptian gentlemen wearing three-piece suits. "May we come in?" one asked. "Who are you?" "We are from the police." "One moment," I said, "I will have to tell them inside," and, without apologizing, shut the door in their faces. Immediately I rushed inside and told my grandmother, who told Aunt Elsa, who told Abdou to tell the gentlemen to wait outside; she would be with them presently. Aunt Elsa locked her bedroom door, then went to wash her face before walking calmly into the vestibule. "May we come in?" they repeated. "I am a German citizen," she declaimed as if she had been practicing these lines with a third-rate vocalist for many, many months, "and will not allow you into this house." "We want to speak to the head of the household." "He is not here," she replied. "Where is he?" "I do not know." "Who is *he*?" asked one of the two, pointing at me. "He is a child. He doesn't know anything," said Aunt Elsa who, only a few days before, had said I was quite a *jeune petit monsieur*.

Although she had just sprinkled her face after crying, Aunt Elsa's glasses were smeared by a white film, probably dried tears, which made her look tattered and poor and certainly not the *grande dame* she was trying to affect at the moment. "*Cierra la puerta*, shut the door," Aunt Elsa told me in Ladino, referring to the door leading to the rest of the apartment. This was the first time she had ever spoken to me in Ladino, and I pretended not to hear and stood there gaping at the two policemen, while my grandmother, who didn't want to interfere with her sister's handling of the men, kept shuffling up and down the long corridor, peeking furtively into the vestibule, only to turn around and walk back along the corridor, pinching her cheeks—a gesture of anxiety in our family—as she repeated to herself "*Guay de mí, guay de mí*, woe is me, woe is me."

Meanwhile, at the other end of the apartment, my mother, who was not even aware of the policemen's visit, was weeping out loud, and Elsa, who could not understand spoken Arabic very well, kept straining her ears, apologizing for the noise within. "She is crazy," she said to one of the policemen, referring to my mother. "*Toc-toc*," she smiled, rotating her index finger next to her skull, "*toc-toc*." The policemen departed, leaving a warrant for my father. "I made them go away," she said.

Another disaster occurred no more than an hour later. Abdou had left, taking whatever remained of his day off. My mother had gone to wash her face, and, after leaving the bathroom, went directly to her room and slammed the door behind her. My grandmother, who hated sudden noises, winced but said nothing. A while later, on my way to the living room, where I planned to read by myself, I felt something damp about my feet. It was water. Mother, as I immediately realized, had once again forgotten to turn off the faucet and had flooded the bathroom, kitchen, and corridor areas. I rushed to tell her of this latest mishap, and as we were coming out of her room, I saw my grandmother standing in the dark corridor, looking at the ceiling, trying to determine where all this water had come from.

My mother rushed to the kitchen, took as many burlap rags as she could find and immediately threw them on the floor, asking me to help her roll the carpets away from the flood. She then brought a large pail, and kneeling on all fours, was attempting to soak up the water with the rags, wringing and unwringing swatches of cloth that bore the pungent odor of

Abdou's floor wax. "I forgot to turn off the faucet," she lamented, starting to weep again. "Because I am deaf and because I am crazy, deaf and crazy, deaf and crazy," she repeated to the rhythm of her sobs. My grandmother, who was also on all fours by now, was busily wringing old towels into the pail, soiling her forearms with the grayish liquid that kept dribbling from the cloth. "It doesn't matter, you didn't hear the water, it doesn't matter," she kept saying, breaking down as well, finally exclaiming, "*Quel malheur, quel malheur*, what wretchedness," looking up as she wrung the towels, referring to the flood, to Egypt, to deafness, to having to squat on the floor like a little housemaid at the age of ninety because we no longer had servants on Sunday.

Early that evening, the caller rang. "Why were you not at home this afternoon?" asked the voice. "May you rot in sixty hells," replied my father.

■

"I want you to sit down and be a big boy now," said my father that night after reading the warrant. "Listen carefully." I wanted to cry. He noticed, stared at me awhile, and then, holding my hand, said, "Cry." I felt a tremor race through my lower lip, down my chin. I struggled with it, bit my tongue, then shook my head to signal that I wasn't going to cry. "It's not easy, I know. But this is what I want you to do. Since it's clear they'll arrest me tomorrow," he said, "the most important thing is to help your mother sell everything, have everyone pack as much as they can, and purchase tickets for all of us. It's easier than you think. But in case I am detained, I want you to leave anyway. I'll follow later. You must pass one message to Uncle Vili and another to Uncle Isaac in Europe." I said I would remember them. "Yes, but I also want each message encoded, in case you forget. It will take an hour, no more."

He asked me to bring him a book I would want to take to Europe and might read on the ship. There were two: *The Idiot* and Kitto's *The Greeks*. "Bring Kitto," he said, "and we'll pretend to underline all the difficult words, so that if customs officials decide to inspect the book, they will think you've underlined them for vocabulary reasons." He pored over the first page of the book and underlined *Thracian, luxurious, barbaroi, Scythians, Ecclesiastes*. "But I already know what they all mean." "Doesn't matter what *you* know. What's important is what *they* think. *Ecclesiastes* is a good word. Always use the fifth letter of the fifth word you've underlined—in this case, *e*, and discard the rest. It's a code in the Lydian mode, do you see?" That evening he also taught me to forge his signature. Then, as they did in the movies, we burned the page on which I had practiced it.

By two o'clock in the morning, we had written five sentences. Everybody had gone to bed already. Someone had dimmed the lamp in the hallway and turned off all the lights in the house. Father offered me a cigarette. He drew the curtains that had been shut so that no one outside might see what we were doing and flung open the window. Then, after letting a spring breeze heave through the dining room, he stood by the window, facing the night, his chin propped on the palms of his hands, with his elbows resting on the window ledge. "It's a small city, but I hate to lose her," he finally said. "Where else can you see the stars like this?" Then, after a few seconds of silence, "Are you ready for tomorrow?" I nodded. I looked at his face and thought to myself: They might torture him, and I may never see him again. I forced myself to believe it— maybe that would bring him good luck.

"Good night, then." "Good night," I said. I asked him if he was going to go to bed as well. "No, not yet. You go. I'll sit here and think awhile." He had said the same thing years before, when we visited his father's tomb and, silently, he had propped his chin on one hand, his elbow resting on the large marble slab. I had been asking him questions about the cemetery, about death, about what the dead did when we were not thinking of them. Patiently, he had answered each one, saying death was like a quiet sleep, but very long, with long, peaceful dreams. When I began to feel restless and asked whether we could go, he answered, "No, not yet. I'll stand here and think awhile." Before leaving, we both leaned down and kissed the slab.

■

The next morning, I awoke at six. My list of errands was long. First the travel agency, then the consulate, then the telegrams to everyone around the world, then the agent in charge of bribing all the customs people, then a few words with Signor Rosenthal, the jeweler whose brother-in-law lived in Geneva. "Don't worry if he pretends not to understand you," my father had said. After that, I was to see our lawyer and await further instructions.

My father had left the house at dawn, I was told. Mother had been put in charge of buying suitcases. My grandmother took a look at me and grumbled something about my clothes, especially those "long blue trousers with copper snaps all over them." "What snaps?" I asked. "These," she said, pointing to my blue jeans. I barely had time to gulp down her orange juice before rushing out of the house and hopping on the tram, headed downtown—something I had never done before, as the American School was in the opposite direction. Suddenly, I was a grown-up going to work, and the novelty thrilled me.

Alexandria on that spring weekday morning had its customary dappled sky. Brisk and brackish scents blew in from the coast, and the tumult of trade on the main thoroughfares spilled over into narrow side-lanes where throngs and stands and jostling trinket men cluttered the bazaars under awnings striped yellow and green. Then, as always at a certain moment, just before the sunlight began to pound the flagstones, things quieted down for a while, a cool breeze swept through the streets, and something like a distilled, airy light spread over the city, bright but without glare, light you could stare into.

The wait to renew the passports at the consulate was brief: the man at the counter knew my mother. As for the travel agent, he already seemed apprised of our plans. His question was: "Do you want to go to Naples or to Bari? From Bari you can go to Greece; from Naples to Marseilles." The image of an abandoned Greek temple overlooking the Aegean popped into my head. "Naples," I said, "but do not put the date yet." "I understand," he said discreetly. I told him that if he called a certain number, funds would be made available to him. In fact, I had the money in my pocket but had been instructed not to use it unless absolutely necessary.

The telegrams took forever. The telegraph building was old, dark, and dirty, a remnant of colonial grandeur fading into a wizened piece of masonry. The clerk at the booth complained that there were too many telegrams going to too many countries on too many continents. He eyed me suspiciously and told me to go away. I insisted. He threatened to hit me. I mustered the courage and told the clerk we were friends of So-and-so, whose name was in the news. Immediately he extended that inimitably unctuous grace that passes for deference in the Middle East.

By half past ten I was indeed proud of myself. One more errand was left, and then Signor Rosenthal. Franco Molkho, the agent in charge of bribing customs officials, was himself a notorious crook who took advantage of everyone precisely by protesting that he was not cunning enough to do so. "I'm always up front about what I do, madame." He was rude and gruff, and if he saw something in your home that struck his fancy, he would grab and pocket it in front of you. If you took it away from him and placed it back where it belonged—which is what my mother did—then he would steal it later at the customs shed, again before your very eyes. Franco Molkho lived in a kind of disemboweled garage, with a makeshift cot, a tattered sink, and a litter of grimy gear boxes strewn about the floor. He wanted to negotiate. I did not know how to negotiate. I told him my father's instructions. "You Jews," he snickered, "it's impossible to beat you at this game." I blushed. Once outside, I wanted to spit out the tea he had offered me.

Still, I thought of myself as the rescuer of my entire family. Intricate scenarios raced through my mind, scenarios in which I pounded the desk of the chief of police and threatened all sorts of abominable reprisals unless my father was released instantly. "Instantly! Now! Immediately!" I yelled, slapping my palm on the inspector's desk. According to Aunt Elsa, the more you treated such people like your servants, the more they behaved accordingly. "And bring me a glass of water, I'm hot." I was busily scheming all sorts of arcane missions when I heard someone call my name. It was my father.

He was returning from the barber and was ambling at a leisurely pace, headed for his favorite café near the stock exchange building. "Why aren't you in jail?" I asked, scarcely concealing my disappointment. "Jail!" he exclaimed, as if to say, "Whoever gave you such a silly notion?" "All they wanted was to ask me a few questions. Denunciations, always these false denunciations. Did you do everything I told you?" "All except Signor Rosenthal." "Very good. Leave the rest to me. By the way, did Molkho agree?" I told him he did. "Wonderful." Then he remembered. "Do you have the money?" "Yes." "Come, then. I'll buy you coffee. You do drink coffee, don't you? Remember to give it to me under the table." A young woman passed in front of us and father turned. "See? Those are what I call perfect ankles."

At the café, my father introduced me to everyone. They were all businessmen, bankers, and industrialists who would meet at around eleven in the morning. All of them had either lost everything they owned or were about to. "He's even read all of *Plutarch's Lives*," boasted my father. "Wonderful," said one of them, who, by his accent, was Greek. "Then surely you remember Themistocles." "Of course he does," said my father, seeing I was blushing. "Let me explain to you, then, how Themistocles won the battle at Salamis, because, that, my dear, they won't teach you in school." Monsieur Panos took out a Parker pen and proceeded to draw naval formations on the corner of his newspaper. "And do you know who taught me all this?" he asked, with a self-satisfied glint flickering in his glazed eyes, his hand pawing my hair all the while. "Do you know who? Me," he said, "I did, all by myself. Because I wanted to be an admiral in the Greek navy. Then I discovered there was no Greek navy, so I joined the Red Cross at Alamein."

Everyone burst out laughing, and Monsieur Panos, who probably did not understand why, joined them. "I still have the Luger a dying German soldier gave me. It had three bullets left, and now I know who they're for: one for President Nasser. One for my wife, because, God knows, she deserves it. And one for me. *Jamais deux sans trois*." Again a burst of laughter. "Not so loud," the Greek interrupted. But I continued to laugh heartily. While I was wiping my eyes, I caught one of the men nudging my father's arm. I was not supposed to see the gesture, but I watched as my father turned and looked uneasily at a table behind him. It was the woman with the beautiful ankles. "Weren't you going to tell me something?" asked my father, tapping me on the knee under the table. "Only about going to the swimming pool this morning." "By all means," he said, taking the money I was secretly passing to him. "Why don't you go now?"

·

Two days later the third blow fell.

My father telephoned in the morning. "They don't want us anymore," he said in English. I didn't understand him. "They don't want us in Egypt." But we had always known that, I thought. Then he blurted it out: we had been officially expelled and had a week to get our things together. "Abattoir?" I asked. "Abattoir," he replied.

The first thing one did when *abattoir* came was to get vaccinated. No country would allow us across its border without papers certifying we had been properly immunized against a slew of Third World diseases.

My father had asked me to take my grandmother to the government vaccine office. The office was near the harbor. She hated the thought of being vaccinated by an Egyptian orderly—"Not even a doctor," she said. I told her we would stop and have tea and pastries afterward at Athinéos. "Don't hurt me," she told the balding woman who held her arm. "But I'm not hurting you," protested the woman in Arabic. "You're not hurting me? You *are* hurting me!" The woman ordered her to keep still. Then came my turn. She reminded me of Miss Badawi when she scraped my scalp with her fingernails looking for lice. Would they really ask us to undress at the customs desk when the time came and search us to our shame?

After the ordeal, my grandmother was still grumbling as we came down the stairs of the government building, her voice echoing loudly as I tried to hush her. She said she wanted to buy me ties.

The Last Seder

Outside the building, I immediately hailed a hansom, helped my grandmother up, and then heard her give an obscure address on Place Mohammed Ali. As soon as we were seated, she removed a small vial of alcohol and, like her Marrano ancestors who wiped off all traces of baptismal water as soon as they had left the church, she sprinkled the alcohol on the site of the injection—to *kill* the vaccine, she said, and all the germs that came with it!

It was a glorious day, and as we rode along my grandmother suddenly tapped me on the leg as she had done years earlier on our way to Rouchdy and said, "Definitely a beach day." I took off my sweater and began to feel that uncomfortable, palling touch of wool flannel against my thighs. Time for shorts. The mere thought of light cotton made the wool unbearable. We cut through a dark street, then a square, got on the Corniche, and, in less than ten minutes, came face-to-face with the statue of Mohammed Ali, the Albanian founder of Egypt's last ruling dynasty.

We proceeded past a series of old, decrepit stores that looked like improvised warehouses and workshops until we reached one tiny, extremely cluttered shop. "Sidi Daoud," shouted my grandmother. No answer. She took out a coin and used it to knock on the glass door several times. "Sidi Daoud is here," a tired figure finally uttered, emerging from the dark. He recognized her immediately, calling her his "favorite *mazmazelle*."

Sidi Daoud was a one-eyed, portly Egyptian who dressed in traditional garb—a white *galabiya* and on top of it a grossly oversized, gray, double-breasted jacket. My grandmother, speaking to him in Arabic, said she wanted to buy me some good ties. "Ties? I have ties," he said, pointing to a huge old closet whose doors had been completely removed; it was stuffed with paper bags and dirty cardboard boxes. "What sort of ties?" "Show me," she said. "Show me, she says," he muttered as he paced about, "so I'll show her."

He brought a stool, climbed up with a series of groans and cringes, reached up to the top of the closet, and brought down a cardboard box whose corners were reinforced with rusted metal. "These are the best," he said as he took out tie after tie. "You'll never find these for sale anywhere in the city, or in Cairo, or anywhere else in Egypt." He removed a tie from a long sheath. It was dark blue with intricate light-blue and pale-orange patterns. He took it in his hands and brought it close to the entrance of the store that I might see it better in the sunlight, holding it out to me with both hands the way a cook might display a poached fish on a salver before serving it. "Let me see," said my grandmother as though she were about to lift and examine its gills. I recognized the tie immediately: it had the sheen of Signor Ugo's ties.

This was a stupendous piece of work. My grandmother looked at the loop and the brand name on the rear apron and remarked that it was not a bad make. "I'll show you another," he said, not even waiting for me to pass judgment on the first. The second was a light-burgundy, bearing an identical pattern to the first. "Take it to the door," he told me, "I'm too old to come and go all day." This one was lovelier than the first, I thought, as I studied both together. A moment later, my grandmother joined me at the door and held the burgundy one in her hands and examined it, tilting her head left and right, as though looking for concealed blemishes which she was almost sure to catch if she looked hard enough. Then, placing the fabric between thumb and forefinger, she rubbed them together to test the quality of the silk, peeving the salesman. "Show me better." "Better than this?" he replied. "*Mafish*, there isn't!" He showed us other ties, but none compared to the first. I said I was happy with the dark-blue one; it would go with my new blazer. "Don't match your clothes like a pauper," said my grandmother. The Egyptian unsheathed two more ties from a different box. One with a green background, the other light blue. "Do you like them?" she asked. I liked them all, I said. "He likes them all," she repeated with indulgent irony in her voice.

"This is the black market," she said to me as soon as we left the store, the precious package clutched in my hand, as I squinted in the sunlight, scanning the crowded Place Mohammed Ali for another horse-drawn carriage. We had spent half an hour in Sidi Daoud's store and had probably looked at a hundred ties before choosing these four. No shop I ever saw, before or since—not even the shop in the Faubourg Saint Honoré where my grandmother took me years later—had as many ties as Sidi Daoud's little hovel. I spotted an empty hansom and shouted to the driver from across the square. The *arbaghi*, who heard me and immediately stood up in the driver's box, signaled he would have to turn around the square, motioning us to wait for him.

Fifteen minutes later, we arrived at Athinéos. The old Spaniard was gone. Instead, a surly Greek doing a weak impersonation of a well-mannered waiter took our order. We were seated in a very quiet corner, next to a window with thick white linen drapes, and spoke about the French plays due to open in a few days. "Such a pity," she said. "Things are beginning to improve just when we are leaving." The Comédie Française had finally returned to Egypt after an absence of at least ten years. La Scala was also due to come again and open in Cairo's old opera house with a production of *Otello*. Madame Darwish, our seamstress, had told my grandmother of a young actor from the Comédie who had knocked at her door saying this was where he had lived as a boy; she let him in, offered him coffee, and the young man burst out crying, then said goodbye. "Could all this talk of expulsion be mere bluffing?" my grandmother mused aloud, only to respond, "I don't think so."

After a second round of mango ice cream, she said, "And now we'll buy you a good book and then we might stop a while at the museum." By "good book" she meant either difficult to come by or one she approved of. It was to be my fourteenth-birthday present. We left the restaurant and were about to hail another carriage when my grandmother told me to make a quick left turn. "We'll pretend we're going to eat a pastry at Flückiger's." I didn't realize why we were *pretending* until much later in the day when I heard my father yell at my grandmother. "We could all go to jail for what you did, thinking you're so clever!" Indeed, she had succeeded in losing the man who had been tailing us after—and probably before—we entered Athinéos. I knew nothing about it until we were inside the secondhand bookstore. On one of the stacks I had found exactly what I wanted. "Are you sure you're going to read all this?" she asked.

She paid for the books absentmindedly and did not return the salesman's greeting. She had suddenly realized that a second agent might have been following us all along. "Let's leave now," she said, trying to be polite. "Why?" "Because." We hopped in a taxi and told the driver to take us to Ramleh station. On our way we passed a series of familiar shops and restaurants, a stretch of saplings leaning against a sunny wall, and, beyond the buildings, an angular view of the afternoon sea.

As soon as we arrived at Sporting, I told my grandmother I was going straight to the Corniche. "No, you're coming home with me." I was about to argue. "Do as I tell you, please. There could be trouble." Standing on the platform was our familiar tail. As soon as I heard the word *trouble*, I must have frozen on the spot, because she immediately added, "Now don't go about looking so frightened!"

My grandmother, it turned out, had been smuggling money

out of the country for years and had done so on that very day. I will never know whether her contact was Sidi Daoud, or the owner of the secondhand bookstore, or maybe one of the many coachmen we hired that day. When I asked her in Paris many years later, all she volunteered was, "One needed nerves of steel."

■

Despite the frantic packing and last-minute sale of all the furniture, my mother, my grandmother, and Aunt Elsa had decided we should hold a Passover seder on the eve of our departure. For this occasion, two giant candelabra would be brought in from the living room, and it was decided that the old sculptured candles should be used as well. No point in giving them away. Aunt Elsa wanted to clean house, to remove all traces of bread, as Jews traditionally do in preparation for Passover. But with the suitcases all over the place and everything upside down, nobody was eager to undertake such a task, and the idea was abandoned. "Then why have a seder?" she asked with embittered sarcasm. "Be glad we're having one at all," replied my father. I watched her fume. "If that's going to be your attitude, let's *not* have one, see if I care." "Now don't get all worked up over a silly seder, Elsa. Please!"

My mother and my grandmother began pleading with him, and for a good portion of the afternoon, busy embassies shuttled back and forth between Aunt Elsa's room and my father's study. Finally, he said he had to go out but would be back for dinner. That was his way of conceding. Abdou, who knew exactly what to prepare for the seder, needed no further inducements and immediately began boiling the eggs and preparing the cheese-and-potato *buñuelos*.

Meanwhile, Aunt Elsa began imploring me to help read the Haggadah that evening. Each time I refused, she would remind me that it was the last time this dining room would ever see a seder and that I should read in memory of Uncle Nessim. "His seat will stay empty unless somebody reads." Again I refused. "Are you ashamed of being Jewish? Is that it? What kind of Jews are we, then?" she kept asking. "The kind who don't celebrate leaving Egypt when it's the last thing they want to do," I said. "But that's so childish. We've never not had a seder. Your mother will be crushed. Is that what you want?" "What I want is to have no part of it. I don't want to cross the Red Sea. And I don't want to be in Jerusalem next year. As far as I'm concerned, all of this is just worship of repetition and nothing more." And I stormed out of the room, extremely pleased with my *bon mot*. "But it's our last evening in Egypt," she said, as though that would change my mind.

For all my resistance, however, I decided to wear one of my new ties, a blazer, and a newly made pair of pointed black shoes. My mother, who joined me in the living room around half past seven, was wearing a dark-blue dress and her favorite jewelry. In the next room, I could hear the two sisters putting the final touches to the table, stowing away the unused silverware, which Abdou had just polished. Then my grandmother came in, making a face that meant Aunt Elsa was truly impossible. "It's always what she wants, never what others want." She sat down, inspected her skirt absentmindedly, spreading its pleats, then began searching through the bowl of peanuts until she found a roasted almond. We looked outside and in the window caught our own reflections. Three more characters, I thought, and we'll be ready for Pirandello.

Aunt Elsa walked in, dressed in purple lace that dated back at least three generations. She seemed to notice that I had decided to wear a tie. "Much better than those trousers with the snaps on them," she said, throwing her sister a significant glance. We decided to have vermouth, and Aunt Elsa said she would smoke. My mother also smoked. Then, gradually, as always happened during such gatherings, the sisters began to reminisce. Aunt Elsa told us about the little icon shop she had kept in Lourdes before the Second World War. She had sold such large quantities of religious objects to Christian pilgrims that no one would have guessed she was Jewish. But then, at Passover, not knowing where to buy unleavened bread, she had gone to a local baker and inquired about the various qualities of flour he used in his shop, claiming her husband had a terrible ulcer and needed special bread. The man said he did not understand what she wanted, and Elsa, distraught, continued to ask about a very light type of bread, maybe even unleavened bread, if such a thing existed. The man replied that surely there was an epidemic spreading around Lourdes, for many were suffering from similar gastric disorders and had been coming to his shop for the past few days asking the same question. "Many?" she asked. "Many, many," he replied, smiling, then whispered, "*Bonne pâque*, happy Passover," and sold her the unleavened bread.

"*Se non è vero, è ben trovato*, if it isn't true, you've made it up well," said my father, who had just walked in. "So, are we all ready?" "Yes, we were waiting for you," said my mother, "did you want some scotch?" "No, already had some."

Then, as we made toward the dining room, I saw that my father's right cheek was covered with pink, livid streaks, like nail scratches. My grandmother immediately pinched her cheek when she saw his face but said nothing. My mother too cast stealthy glances in his direction but was silent.

"So what exactly is it you want us to do now?" he asked Aunt Elsa, mildly scoffing at the ceremonial air she adopted on these occasions.

"I want you to read," she said, indicating Uncle Nessim's seat. My mother stood up and showed him where to start, pained and shaking her head silently the more she looked at his face. He began to recite in French, without irony, without flourishes, even meekly. But as soon as he began to feel comfortable with the text, he started to fumble, reading the instructions out loud, then correcting himself, or skipping lines unintentionally only to find himself reading the same line twice. At one point, wishing to facilitate his task, my grandmother said, "Skip that portion." He read some more and she interrupted again. "Skip that too."

"No," said Elsa, "either we read everything or nothing at all." An argument was about to erupt. "Where is Nessim now that we need him," said Elsa with that doleful tone in her voice that explained her success at Lourdes. "As far away from you as he can be," muttered my father under his breath, which immediately made me giggle. My mother, catching my attempt to stifle a laugh, began to smile; she knew exactly what my father had said though she had not heard it. My father, too, was infected by the giggling, which he smothered as best as he could, until my grandmother caught sight of him, which sent her laughing uncontrollably. No one had any idea what to do, what to read, or when to stop. "Some Jews we are," said Aunt Elsa, who had also started to laugh and whose eyes were tearing. "Shall we eat, then?" asked my father. "Good idea," I said. "But we've only just begun," protested Aunt Elsa, recovering her composure. "It's the very last time. How could you? We'll never be together again, I can just feel it." She was on the verge of tears, but my grandmother warned her that she, too, would start crying if we kept on like this. "This is the last year," said Elsa, reaching out and touching my hand. "It's just that I can remember so many seders held in this very room, for fifty years, year after year after year. And I'll tell you something," she said, turning to my father. "Had I known fifty years ago that it would end like this, had I known

I'd be among the last in this room, with everyone buried or gone away, it would have been better to die, better to have died back then than to be left alone like this." "Calm yourself, Elsica," said my father, "otherwise we'll all be in mourning here."

At that point, Abdou walked in and, approaching my father, said there was someone on the telephone asking for him. "Tell them we are praying," said my father. "But sir—" He seemed troubled and began to speak softly. "So?" "She said she wanted to apologize." No one said anything. "Tell her not now." "Very well."

We heard the hurried patter of Abdou's steps up the corridor, heard him pick up the receiver and mumble something. Then, with relief, we heard him hang up and go back into the kitchen. It meant she had not insisted or argued. It meant he would be with us tonight. "Shall we eat, then?" said my mother. "Good idea," I repeated. "Yes, I'm starving," said Aunt Elsa. "An angel you married," murmured my grandmother to my father.

After dinner, everyone moved into the smaller living room, and, as was her habit on special gatherings, Aunt Elsa asked my father to play the record she loved so much. It was a very old recording by the Busch Quartet, and Aunt Elsa always kept it in her room, fearing someone might ruin it. I had noticed it earlier in the day lying next to the radio. It meant she had been planning the music all along. "Here," she said, gingerly removing the warped record from its blanched dust jacket with her arthritic fingers. It was Beethoven's "Song of Thanksgiving." Everyone sat down, and the adagio started.

The old 78 hissed, the static louder than the music, though no one seemed to notice, for my grandmother began humming, softly, with a plangent, faraway whine in her voice, and my father shut his eyes, and Aunt Elsa began shaking her head in rapt wonder, as she did sometimes when tasting Swiss chocolate purchased on the black market, as if to say, "How could anyone have created such beauty?"

And there, I thought, was my entire world: the two old ones writhing in a silent stupor, my father probably wishing he was elsewhere, and my mother, whose thoughts, as she leafed through a French fashion magazine, were everywhere and nowhere, but mostly on her husband, who knew that she would say nothing that evening and would probably let the matter pass quietly and never speak of it again.

I motioned to my mother that I was going out for a walk. She nodded. Without saying anything, my father put his hand in his pocket and slipped me a few bills.

Outside, Rue Delta was brimming with people. It was the first night of Ramadan and the guns marking the end of the fast had gone off three hours earlier. There was unusual bustle and clamor, with people gathered in groups, standing in the way of traffic, making things noisier and livelier still, the scent of holiday pastries and fried treats filling the air. I looked up at our building: on our floor, all the lights were out except for Abdou's and those in the living room. Such weak lights, and so scant in comparison to the gaudy, colored bulbs that hung from all the lampposts and trees—as if the electricity in our home were being sapped and might die out at any moment. It was an Old World, old-people's light.

As I neared the seafront, the night air grew cooler, saltier, freed from the din of lights and the milling crowd. Traffic became sparse, and whenever cars stopped for the traffic signal, everything grew still: then, only the waves could be heard, thudding in the dark, spraying the air along the darkened Corniche with a thin mist that hung upon the night, dousing the streetlights and the signposts and the distant floodlights by the guns of Petrou, spreading a light clammy film upon the pebbled stone wall overlooking the city's coastline. Quietly, an empty bus splashed along the road, trailing murky stains of light on the gleaming pavement. From somewhere, in scattered snatches, came the faint lilt of music, perhaps from one of those dance halls where students used to flock at night. Or maybe just a muted radio somewhere on the beach nearby, where abandoned nets gave off a pungent smell of seaweed and fish.

At the corner of the street, from a sidewalk stall, came the smell of fresh dough and of angel-hair being fried on top of a large copper stand—a common sight throughout the city every Ramadan. People would fold the pancakes and stuff them with almonds, syrup, and raisins. The vendor caught me eyeing the cakes that were neatly spread on a black tray. He smiled and said, "*Etfaddal*, help yourself."

I thought of Aunt Elsa's chiding eyes. "But it's Pesah," I imagined her saying. My grandmother would disapprove too—eating food fried by Arabs on the street, unconscionable. The Egyptian didn't want any money. "It's for you," he said, handing me the delicacy on a torn sheet of newspaper.

I wished him a good evening and took the soggy pancake out onto the seafront. There, heaving myself up on the stone wall, I sat with my back to the city, facing the sea, holding the delicacy I was about to devour. Abdou would have called this a real *mazag*, accompanying the word, as all Egyptians do, with a gesture of the hand—a flattened palm brought to the side of the head—signifying blissful plenitude and the prolonged, cultivated consumption of everyday pleasures.

Facing the night, I looked out at the stars and thought to myself, over there is Spain, then France, to the right Italy, and, straight ahead, the land of Solon and Pericles. The world is timeless and boundless, and I thought of all the shipwrecked, homeless mariners who had strayed to this very land and for years had tinkered away at their damaged boats, praying for a wind, only to grow soft and reluctant when their time came.

I stared at the flicker of little fishing boats far out in the offing, always there at night, and watched a group of children scampering about on the beach below, waving little Ramadan lanterns, the girls wearing loud pink-and-fuchsia dresses, locking hands as they wove themselves into the dark again, followed by another group of child revelers who were flocking along the jetty past the sand dunes, some even waving up to me from below. I waved back with a familiar gesture of street fellowship and wiped the light spray that had moistened my face.

And suddenly I knew, as I touched the damp, grainy surface of the seawall, that I would always remember this night, that in years to come I would remember sitting here, swept with confused longing as I listened to the water lapping the giant boulders beneath the promenade and watched the children head toward the shore in a winding, lambent procession. I wanted to come back tomorrow night, and the night after, and the one after that as well, sensing that what made leaving so fiercely painful was the knowledge that there would never be another night like this, that I would never eat soggy cakes along the coast road in the evening, not this year or any other year, nor feel the baffling, sudden beauty of that moment when, if only for an instant, I had caught myself longing for a city I never knew I loved.

Exactly a year from now, I vowed, I would sit outside at night wherever I was, somewhere in Europe, or in America, and turn my face to Egypt, as Moslems do when they pray and face Mecca, and remember this very night, and how I had thought these things and made this vow. You're beginning to sound like Elsa and her silly seders, I said to myself, mimicking my father's humor.

The Last Seder

On my way home I thought of what the others were doing. I wanted to walk in, find the smaller living room still lit, the Beethoven still playing, with Abdou still clearing the dining room, and, on closing the front door, suddenly hear someone say, "We were just waiting for you, we're thinking of going to the Royal." "But we've already seen that film," I would say. "What difference does it make. We'll see it again."

And before we had time to argue, we would all rush downstairs, where my father would be waiting in a car that was no longer really ours, and, feeling the slight chill of a late April night, would huddle together with the windows shut, bicker as usual about who got to sit where, rub our hands, turn the radio to a French broadcast, and then speed to the Corniche, thinking that all this was as it always was, that nothing ever really changed, that the people enjoying their first stroll on the Corniche after fasting, or the woman selling tickets at the Royal, or the man who would watch our car in the side alley outside the theater, or our neighbors across the hall, or the drizzle that was sure to greet us after the movie at midnight would never, ever know, nor ever guess, that this was our last night in Alexandria.